TO SHIR

TRUST YOU ENJOY

SINCERELY

THE SACRED GEM WITHIN

MICHAEL PARLEE

authorHOUSE®

AuthorHouse™
1663 Liberty Drive
Bloomington, IN 47403
www.authorhouse.com
Phone: 1 (800) 839-8640

Cover By Juanita Parlee

Published by AuthorHouse 04/04/2019

ISBN: 978-1-7283-0560-8 (sc)
ISBN: 978-1-7283-0559-2 (e)

Library of Congress Control Number: 2019903578

Print information available on the last page.

This book is printed on acid-free paper.

DEDICATION

THIS BOOK IS dedicated to those who are suffering from the heavy hand that life has dealt them. There is much relief when we realize that God has given us great inner strength to help us deal with the disappointments that life has brought our way. In the depths of despair there is hope. By reaching out to others for guidance and with God's help, we can access that power.

That Power Is: The Sacred Gem Within.

ACKNOWLEDGMENTS

A S WITH MY other novels, Tanya, Son of Sister Maria and We Must Forgive to Live, I would like to acknowledge and thank my editor, Barb Baer and my wife Pauline for their advice, support and encouragement. The Sacred Gem Within has evolved for the better because of their help.

CHAPTER 1

I N THE EARLY summer of 1883, the building of Canada's
new transcontinental railroad was well under way. The
railroad bosses were bound and determined that come hell
or high water, they'd get the railroad built past Calgary and
into the Rockies before winter set in. Safety was the last thing
on their minds.

The railroad construction crew was working on a partially
built trestle across a ravine a few miles from what eventually
would become the Saskatchewan-Alberta border. At daybreak,
a strong wind was blasting in from the northwest, driving in
low clouds. As the crew left the cook car and headed to the
job site, a few drops of rain were starting to fall.

William Burke was on the crew that was working on the
railroad trestle. William was a big, powerful, outspoken lad
from southern Ontario. Because of the gale winds, he and his
co-workers, Neil and Ted were very apprehensive when they
reported to Ben, their shift boss, at the start of their shift.

"I don't like that strong wind," William began. "It's blowing
even harder now than it was last night and it looks like it
could rain. The trestle was doing a lot of groaning and it felt
like it was swaying a bit when we shut things down for the
night. I wonder if we should hold off until it's a bit calmer.

It's scarier than hell working 80 feet above the ground when your footing starts shifting with the wind."

"I know what you're talking about," Ben replied. "I was up on the trestle with you guys last night. Unless it really starts to rain in earnest, we have no choice but to keep at it. I talked to Murray, our foreman, a few minutes ago and asked him whether we should hold off until the strong wind lets up a little. He's getting a lot of pressure from management to make up for lost time. He told me it's crucial that we keep working on the trestle as long as we're able. He said he was sure it will be safe enough and just to be extra careful. So, I'm afraid we'd better get at it. You, Neil and Ted get out on the trestle. The rest of the crew, I and the steam crane will catch up to you in a few minutes. Murray said we just got to finish building this damn trestle by the end of the week. Some of the company's head honchos from out East are going to be inspecting the railroad next week. Murray's boss said we have to have the trestle completed by the time the inspection is made."

As William, Ted and Neil headed to their worksite on the trestle, the wind hadn't lost any of its strength. They had just started out on the trestle when a strong gust blew William's hat off. He watched it sail down into the coulee.

"What idiots!" William shouted above the roar of the wind. "It really bugs me when management won't listen to reason and asks us to do something that's so totally unsafe."

"You're right," Neil replied. "I don't like it one little bit either. I had this horrible nightmare last night that the trestle collapsed while we were working on it. I awoke with a start and for the life of me couldn't get back to sleep again."

"If I didn't need the money to help support my folks back East, I'd quit right now," Ted added.

"We'll just have to watch carefully," William continued. "If the damn trestle starts to sway and creak again, we'd better head for firm ground."

The wind had picked up intensity as William, Neil and Ted got to the worksite at the end of the partially constructed trestle. As they were preparing the spot for the steam operated crane to continue to lay down the trestle timbers, an extra strong blast of wind caused the partially constructed trestle to groan and sway.

"Let's run for it," William shouted above the roar of the wind. "We got to get off this damn trestle before it collapses!"

As they ran for safety, another strong gust hit the trestle. With a shudder and a resounding roar, the structure collapsed, tossing the three into the ravine below. Neil and Ted fell the 80 odd feet into the rock-strewn ravine. By God's grace, in the mayhem of the collapsing timbers and steel rails, William was catapulted off the trestle and landed on top of a large poplar tree that was adjacent to the trestle. The impact of his fall was cushioned as he fell through the branches. He landed on the ground, bruised and scratched up, but with no significant injuries.

William slowly climbed to his feet. He tried to clear the cobwebs from his head as he limped over to his fallen buddies. Ted was laying on a large rock.

There was a huge timber across his chest and blood was oozing from his mouth and nose. By the death glaze in his unblinking eyes, William knew he was beyond help. He flicked a fly off Ted's forehead and slowly limped over to Neil, a short distance away. Neil's face was covered in blood. He was groaning and his legs were twitching.

Reaching down, William grasped Neil's hand.

"Hang in there, Buddy, we'll get you help as soon as we can."

Slowly, Neil turned his head and tried to focus his eyes on William. Struggling for breath he gasped, "I guess this is the end of the trail for me, Bud. It looks like my dream was right on."

Suddenly, Neil took his hand from William's grasp and reached upward.

"There's a bright light up there," he said, pointing with his finger.

A smile crossed his face and his whole body shuddered. As his eyelids closed, he whispered, "Bye, Willie."

"Bye Neil," William replied in anguish.

"Dear Lord, they're both gone." he muttered, laying Neil's limp arm across his chest.

Ben and the rest of the crew had been getting the steam crane ready when they heard the roar of the trestle collapsing.

"Oh, my God," Ben cried out as he got to the edge of the ravine. "I should have listened to the boys. There's nothing left of the trestle."

Climbing over the maze of fallen timbers and twisted rails, Ben made his way down into the ravine as quickly as he could.

"Over here," William called out. "Ted and Neil are dead and if I hadn't been thrown onto that big poplar tree, I'd be dead too. We told you it was too windy to work on the trestle, but oh no, production is more important than saving lives. I lost my two buddies because this damn company couldn't give a rip about safety!"

"Son of a bitch," Ben cried out in anguish as he looked at the two dead workers. He peeled off his hat and flung it as far as he could. "I told Murray that it would be too dangerous to work on the trestle if the wind picked up, but he said we were behind schedule and had to keep at it. I have to take some responsibility though. I told you guys to get out on the trestle. How will I ever live with myself with Neil and Ted dead? Damn it all! Damn it! Damn it! This is my worst nightmare. If only we had waited until the wind died down."

"Ted was dead when I got to him," William added. "I was holding Neil's hand when he died."

"How are you doing?" Ben continued. "Your face is a little cut up and your shoulder is bleeding a bit."

"Yeah, I'm cut up some. The fall made me a little sick to the stomach, but I'll manage. Let's get the hell out of here."

Ben helped steady William as they started to climb out of the ravine.

"Why on earth did I ever leave Ontario?" William kept asking himself.

Half way out of the ravine, William became nauseated. He went to the edge of the trail and threw up.

Ben and William met Murray, the foreman, running to meet them.

"Problems?" he called out. "I heard word that the trestle just collapsed."

"You're damn right we got problems," Ben hollered. "We just started working on the trestle a short time ago when it blew over. Two of my boys are dead. Like I told you last night, we shouldn't have been working on it in these high winds. The only thing that saved William's life was that as the trestle was collapsing, he was thrown onto a big poplar tree that cushioned his fall."

"God Almighty," Murray cried out, beating his hand against his thigh. "I know I'm responsible for their deaths seeing I told you to keep working on the trestle. Oh, dear God! Why, oh why didn't I go by my gut instinct and tell you guys to hold off until the wind died down? I know it's not the time to make excuses, but you have no idea the pressure I'm under from the higher ups to keep production up. Come hell or high water, they insist that we make up for lost time. They want us to make it to the Rockies before winter sets in."

"I've learned my lesson now, though," Murray continued. "From here on out, I'll let you and the other shift bosses call the safety thing. This is my wake-up call. I don't know about you, Ben, but if those in charge insist that I make the guys work when it's unsafe, they can find someone new to take my place."

"My condolences to you, son," Murray said, placing a hand on William's shoulder. "Losing your two workmates is heavy stuff. It was my fault having you guys work when it was unsafe. Damn it all to hell," he added shaking his head. "I don't know what more I can say. Ben will take you to the safety station. The nurse will check you over and patch you up a bit. She'll see if you need further medical help. I just feel horrible over losing two good men."

"I feel horrible too," William replied. "I lost my two buddies because this rotten company could care less about safety."

Nurse Emily Stevenson was an older lady with many years of nursing experience. Ben briefed her on the accident. After checking William over for broken bones, she began cleaning and bandaging up his scrapes and cuts.

"There's a bad cut on your left shoulder that needs some attention," she said. "I'll swab the spot with something to deaden the pain and then I'll close up the cut with some stitches."

William took a deep breath and gritted his teeth as Emily began stitching up the laceration.

"I'm sorry to hear that your two buddies didn't make it," she said after she had finished patching William up. "Thank God you were thrown onto that big tree as the trestle was collapsing. I imagine you're pretty well shook up."

"That I am," William replied, shaking his head. "Here one moment, gone the next. I had breakfast with Neil and Ted just a few minutes before they were killed. As the three of us were walking to the trestle, Neil told me he had a dream last night that the trestle collapsed. Makes you wonder doesn't it?

For sure, this will be the last day I work for this damn outfit. They couldn't give a rip about us workers. They insist on us working when it's not safe. All they care about is keeping their quota up so they can show a profit. If it wasn't for what liquor has done to my old man, I'd tie one on right now."

"What will you do, then?"

"I don't really know," William replied, shaking his head. "I guess I could try to get on with some rancher around here or maybe on a ranch down in Montana. I was raised on a farm so I'd be familiar with that type of work. If I have to, I suppose I could go back to Ontario. Right now, all I know for sure is that I won't be working another minute on this bloody railroad."

"I think it would be wise for you to rest here for an hour or so, just in case you feel nauseous again," Emily said, pointing to a couch beside her desk. "You had quite a fall so it wouldn't hurt for you to take it easy for a while."

"I was talking to Charlie, the paymaster the other day," Emily continued. "He said a rancher friend of his from Montana was up here looking for land. When you see Charlie, you should ask him about his friend. Maybe he'd have work for you back on his ranch."

As William lay on the couch, he could hear that it was now raining in earnest. After resting for a couple of hours, he slowly headed towards the paymaster's car. The strong wind had subsided, the rain had stopped and there was a band of clear sky to the Northwest.

"Damn Neil's and Ted's luck," he muttered. "If it had been as calm as this when we were on the trestle, chances are they'd still be alive. Damn it all to hell!"

Charlie, the paymaster was a big portly man, well into his fifties. He sat in silence, slowly shaking his head as William unloaded his anger and grief.

"I don't blame you a bit for quitting, lad, not a bit," he replied after listening to William. "Ever since we started building this railroad, all it's been is production, production, production. That's the only thing that matters with management and to hell with the workers' safety. On all the crews, so far, well over a hundred men have died in work-related accidents. As you're probably aware, the billeting for the men is a total disaster. Scores of men have died in the filthy camps from dysentery. I hate to think of what it will be like when we get into the Rockies. It's dangerous enough for the workers here on the open prairies, but it's going to be ten times as dangerous trying to push a railroad through the mountains in the winter, what with the possibility of avalanches and rock slides. It seems they don't view life as having any value. What you just said is dead on. To them, only profits count."

"I was just talking to Murray about Neil and Ted," Charlie continued. "He said they are going to have their funeral tomorrow."

"I won't be looking forward to burying my two buddies," William replied shaking his head, "but that's the hand that fate dealt them, I guess."

"Now I've got to figure out what I'll do. The nurse said you knew a rancher from Montana who's up here looking for land by the Cypress Hills. I was wondering if he'd be looking for help. I grew up on a farm in Ontario. I've worked with horses since I was a kid."

"You're right. Michael Francis is up here looking for grazing land. I was talking to him a few days ago. A bigger ranch that abuts his land in Montana is looking to expand. He's interested in the Francis spread. Michael said he wasn't in a hurry to sell out yet, but if the price was right, he'd give it serious consideration."

"I'm originally from the States. A few years back, Michael and I rode together doing cattle drives. I would highly recommend Michael. He'd be a good one to see. If he drops in, I'll put in a good word for you."

"On Sunday, Michael's going to look in on me again. If you hang around for a day or two, I'll see that you get to meet him. I'm pretty sure he'll have work for you. He told me he was looking for some additional hands for his ranch back in Montana."

"When I get your time from Ben, I'll pay your wages in cash. Of late, I've heard word that a few of this company's checks have bounced. We won't settle up until you're ready to pull out. That way you'll be able to have your meals and a place to sleep."

That evening, William was having difficulty getting to sleep. Every time he closed his eyes, he heard the roar of the trestle collapsing and could feel himself being flung through the air.

When he finally got to sleep, he dreamt he was back on the farm in Ontario. As he was heading to the pasture to bring the milk cows in, he observed someone walking towards him. When they met, he was astounded to see it was Neil.

"Ted and I are happy and doing well," Neil stated. He smiled and instantly disappeared.

William awoke with a start. "Was that really Neil's spirit that came to comfort me or was it just a dream?" he pondered. "It was so real. He was even wearing that old tattered hat of his."

Saturday was a heavy day for the trestle construction crew. Murray had made arrangements with Don Neufeld, an Anglican minister, to conduct the funeral for Neil and Ted at a small native cemetery close by the railroad. A few of the railroad workers had dug the graves on Friday afternoon.

By the time the funeral service started on Saturday morning, the weather had cleared and a gentle breeze was blowing in from the Southwest. Although those that worked on the building of the trestle attended the funeral, the company insisted that the rest of the construction crew keep working. They were already hard at it, rebuilding the collapsed trestle.

It was just a simple graveside service with William and a number of Neil's and Ted's fellow workers present. Ben, Murray, Charlie and Emily also attended. After the minister gave a short sermon, Nurse Emily sang 'God Be with You Till We Meet Again.' Ben did his best to accompany Emily on the guitar. Murray gave a brief eulogy for the two men, based on the little information that he had.

"Before we close, is there anyone else who would like to say a few words about Neil or Ted?" the minister asked.

William ran his fingers through his hair, nervously cleared his throat and stepped forward.

"I was on the trestle with Ted and Neil when it collapsed. I'm only here because as it broke apart, I was flung onto the top of a big poplar tree that was growing by the trestle. As I fell, the branches of the tree cushioned my fall. I was just scratched, bruised and cut up a bit. I was at Neil's side, holding his hand when he passed away. Strangely, just before he breathed his last, he reached up his hand and it looked to me like he was pointing to something in the sky. Anyway, he smiled and whispered, 'There's a bright light up there.' Then he was gone. Last night I had trouble getting to sleep. When I finally dropped off, I had a wonderful dream that I'll never forget. In my dream, Neil came to me. He smiled and said he and Ted were doing well."

"Thank you, William," Don said as William stepped back. "We can take great comfort from these occurrences. What you said about Neil's vision at the moment of his death is much more common than one would think. I've heard the same thing many times before and experienced it myself once when I was at the death bed of a member of my congregation. Sometimes the dying person sees a light and at other times they see a departed loved one coming to get them. I firmly believe that as Neil was dying, he had a glimpse into the spirit world. I also believe that the departed one's spirit can visit us in dreams as Neil's spirit did with William. This helps to give us closure."

As soon as the simple caskets had been lowered, the co-workers backfilled the graves. Murray had two small temporary crosses made up with their respective names and date of death. He placed them at the head of the graves.

Once the funeral was over, with the exception of William, all the workers attending the funeral were summoned back to work.

"There's something that's really bothering me and I don't quite know how to figure it out," William said to the minister once everyone else had left. "I'm trying to figure out why God would allow Neil and Ted to die, but save my life? It just beats me."

"That's a question that I and many others have asked," Don replied. "When I was ten, my five-year-old sister died unexpectantly. For years I tried to figure out why God took her rather than me. Finally, when I was studying to become a minister, I found my answer from a retired missionary who had been working with native people."

"Years back, the missionary's wife was on her way from Scotland to Canada to be with him. The ship she was on sank in a storm. He said he suffered for many years trying to figure out why God would allow his wife to die so tragically. He finally realized that the soul of his beloved wife had either learned all of life's lessons here on earth or that God had need for her soul elsewhere. According to him, our body was just a shell for the soul to live in and that although the body would soon return to dust, the soul would live forever. The old missionary told me he was looking forward to the day his wife's soul and his soul would be re-united forever. His explanation certainly helped me."

Over the next few days William often thought of Don's words. They were of great help to him as he dealt with the grief of losing Neil and Ted.

CHAPTER 2

E ARLY SUNDAY MORNING, William dropped in on Charlie.

"Michael said he'd be here by nine," Charlie began. "As long as I've known him, he's always been on time. We'll have coffee when he gets here. Correct me if I'm wrong, but you look a little uptight."

"Yes, a little. I'm having a rough time over the loss of my two buddies. We were such good friends. Poor Neil was going to quit this fall, head back East and get married. As Ted and I were walking to the trestle that morning, he said if he didn't need the money, he'd quit."

"It's also worrisome for me not knowing if Michael will have work for me and if he does, how I'll fit in on his spread in the States."

"Well, Michael dropped in for a bit last night. I told him about the trestle collapsing and you losing your two buddies. I also mentioned that you were looking for work. I'm sure things will work out for you. Michael is a laidback guy. He's certainly a hard-working sort, but he's fair. He never asks his help to do anything he wouldn't do himself. I'm confident he'll offer you work. I'm sure you'll fit right in. Both Ben and Murray told me you were their most reliable hand."

"Losing Neil and Ted is a tough break for you. From my own experience, it's best to deal with your grieving rather than trying to cover it up. It will take a while to get over your loss, but time will heal."

"Just a word of caution if you go to work for Michael. I don't know if you do any drinking, but I should tell you that he hates alcohol with a passion and doesn't allow booze on his property. I won't go into it any farther than that. If you hire on with him, he'll certainly let you know about it."

Soon there was a knock at the door and Michael stepped in. He was a stocky, well-built man in his mid-fifties. Although he was pretty well bald, he sported a bushy black mustache. After introductions were made, Charlie poured everyone a cup of coffee.

"Last night Charlie told me about the trestle collapsing and you quitting your job," Michael said, turning to William. "I don't blame you a bit. I'm so sorry to hear of the deaths of your two friends. That's pretty heavy stuff. Both Charlie and I have been down that road before when we rode together. One night the cattle stampeded in a lightning storm and one of the boys riding nightshift was trampled to death when he was thrown from his horse. We lost another rider when he drowned when we were crossing a river. It takes a while to get the death of a workmate out of your system."

"I was wondering if you'd need an extra hand on your ranch," William interjected. "I was raised on a farm in Ontario. I've had a lot of experience in riding and driving horses."

"I'd be glad to have you come work for us. Charlie has already told me that you have a good work record here, building the railroad. You can come back to Montana with me.

It's positive that you're familiar with farm work. As Charlie probably told you, I'm up here scouting for some good grazing land. Things are on the change in Montana. The big outfits are trying to buy out the smaller ones. My neighbor is looking to expand. I've given him first option on our place when he's ready to buy more land. I've had a good look at the lay of the land up here. I wouldn't mind a piece of land that's available up against your Cypress Hills. We'll just have to see how it all works out."

"I'll tell you a bit about our operation," Michael began, when Charlie went for a bathroom break. "We own a spread down in northcentral Montana that's on the north side of the Missouri River. Our land abuts the river. It's our neighbor to the east of us, Eli Lopez, who talks about expanding. There's a big ravine running north and south to the east of his buildings that marks the east edge of his ranch property. On our ranch, there is a big ravine running north and south that marks the western edge of our property. In between the two ranches there's a small creek that meanders north and south dividing the two ranches. The Lopez spread covers something like 12,000 acres while our ranch covers about 7500 acres. We have about 200 head of cattle. The Lopez ranch has close to 350 head. We're both going to fence the north side of our properties to keep the free ranging cattle out. We brand all our livestock. In case the herds get mixed up it's easy to separate them. If our neighbor does buy us out and we were to relocate to the Cypress Hills area, we'd drive the cattle up here. As of yet there are no roads connecting Montana with this area. It's about 150 miles as the crow flies."

"You'll meet Maud when we get back home. She's my wife and our cook. As you'll find out, she's a damn good cook. Maud was my cousin's wife. He died of TB a few years after my wife died. Anyway, she came on board and we got hitched. She's been cooking for us for close to 20 years now. She has two sons in their late twenties. They grew up on our ranch, but a couple of years back, Carl and Paul decided to go on their own. Just this spring they bought into the Lopez ranch and became junior partners. As I just mentioned, he's the fellow who is talking about buying our ranch."

"If the Lopez ranch buys us out and we get land up here, we figure it will take about two weeks to drive the cattle here. Some of the drive will be through other ranchers' land, some along road allowances."

Michael took the last swig of his coffee and continued. "By the way, did Charlie mention my feelings on bringing booze on the ranch?"

"Yeah, he did. He said that you'd fill me in on the wherefores and whys of it all."

"Okay. You see, Kate, my first wife and I had been married a couple of years when our baby boy was born. The little guy's heart gave out and he died when he was only two months old. Kate had been suffering with what the doctor called post-partum depression ever since his birth. Anyway, this dumb broad from the Lopez ranch came to visit her one day when I was out. Of all things, she brought along a bottle of whisky to try to cheer Kate up. The two proceeded to tie one on. Up to this point, Kate had never even had a sip of liquor. When I got home, the other woman was gone, but Kate was completely wasted."

"After that, she couldn't get enough of the rotten stuff. She went completely to pot and turned to the bottle with a vengeance and I do mean a vengeance. Nothing I did seemed to help the poor girl come to her senses. The truth of the matter is, she simply drank herself to death. After I saw what booze did to Kate, I swore I'd never touch liquor again. There are some people who abide alcohol on their spreads, but I'm not one of them. What my hands do on their days off is none of my business, just as long as they come back to the ranch sober."

"I'm sorry to hear about your first wife's drinking problem," William said. "I know where you're coming from on the booze thing. My old man has become a real booze hound. Up till three or so years ago he hardly ever touched the stuff. Back then, he'd take the odd social drink, but none of us ever saw him take more than a couple of drinks. Anyway, one day he and I were putting up hay and he had a bad accident that injured his crotch. He was in the hospital for a bit and once he got home, he seemed to be doing alright for a spell. Then he went to see a specialist in the city. When he got back from seeing the specialist, he was drunk and has pretty well been drunk ever since. He just sits around and nurses a bottle of his homemade brew. Mom and I were left to do all the farm work. One night, when he was hammered, he got into an argument with Mom and backhanded her hard. He gave her a black eye and bloodied her nose. I grabbed the drunken old asshole, rammed him up against the wall and threatened him with a damn good beating if he ever touched Mom or my sisters again."

"At any rate, that night, the old fool continued drinking until he passed out. Mom and my sisters packed up some of their personnel stuff. We loaded their stuff into the buggy and I drove them over to stay with my aunt and uncle. I stayed on the farm to look after the livestock and keep an eye on the drunken old fool. Then one night, Dad was pretty well hammered again and started an argument with me. He said he was going to overhaul me and took a swing at me.

I just ducked his wild haymaker and threw him into his bedroom. I'd had enough. I grabbed a bit of my stuff and left on horseback to my aunt's and uncle's place."

"Of course, in his drunken state there was no way the arse could look after the livestock so Mom and I got in touch with our bachelor neighbor. We hired him to look after the livestock until it could be decided what they would do with the farm."

"So sad what that bloody alcohol did to both our families," Michael said.

"Yes, it's a shame. There was no way I'd have anything more to do with the farm with the old man still boozing so I pulled up stakes and got on the crew building the railroad. Other than family, I didn't really have any ties left in Ontario. My girlfriend, Tina, was a legal secretary for a lawyer and decided to run off with him. So that was that."

"You won't have to worry about me doing any boozing. After seeing what it's done to the old man, I don't touch the damn stuff and never will. It's ruined a lot of lives."

"You can say that again," Michael replied, shaking his head. "Sorry to hear about the tough luck you had with your girlfriend. There are those who can handle booze without a problem, but for those like my Kate and your old man, it's either their ruination or it kills them."

"I'll be pulling out tomorrow. I trailed another horse up here so you'll have your own mount."

The next morning, after a hearty breakfast, Charlie settled up with William. As he had some American currency, he paid him in American funds. Charlie made sure they were well supplied with a good batch of groceries for their return trip. Soon Michael and William were on their way.

"If you don't mind, I'd like to go over to that tract of land I have in mind that's up against the Cypress Hills," Michael said as they were heading out. "I'd like to have another look at it."

"Sure, that's fine with me. I wouldn't mind a gander at it myself."

The property had no fences, but on all four corners of the ranch there were single fence posts to mark the boundaries. Running south, part of the eastern boundary of the property cut 500 acres of forested land off the Cypress Hills. A cutline had been cleared by hand through the forested land. Other than the forested part, the land was all in grass. Up against the forested area was a large slough fed by water running down from the tree-covered hills. From the edge of the slough a creek meandered west through the property.

Once they had looked at the land, Michael and William turned south and headed towards the Montana border.

Just north of the Montana border they had to cross the steep-banked Milk River. On his way up North, Michael had scouted the river banks to find a hogsback that the horses could manage. As it was mid-summer, the river was low and they had no problem in fording it.

"If we do move up North, we'll have to use this spot to ford the river with the cattle," Michael said. "It's got a good solid rocky bottom to it. Hopefully, if we make the move, the river will be as low as it is now."

William marveled at the immensity of the land. Other than the Milk River and a creek or two, the land was gently rolling treeless prairie. It was interspersed with the odd high hill. Once they crested the hill, as far as the eye could see there was just grass and more grass.

"You have a mixed farm in Ontario?" Michael asked after they'd finished setting up camp for the night and were eating supper.

"Yes, we mostly were into beef cattle, but not like your big operations out here though. We had about 50 head of Black Angus cows and usually around 30 or so pigs. Our farm land has deep black soil that's very productive. We'd raise 100 acres of corn each year that we put up as silage for livestock feed and had another 80 acres of corn as a cash crop. Something like 60 acres of our land was in pasture. We were managing pretty well until the old man started to really booze it up. Shortly after I left home, Mom wrote me that he got into a scrap with the guy who was looking after the livestock and sold all of the cattle and pigs. What a dumb ass! Mom was pretty upset. So now Ross, the guy who was looking after the livestock, is renting the land and just growing grain. Because they owned the farm jointly, Mom at least got half the money from the sale of the livestock. She also gets half the rent. Mom told me that the whole family has spent enough time waiting for Dad to smarten up. The last time she wrote, she said she had started on divorce proceedings. What a shame. As I grew up, he was such a dependable sort, but now he's as useless as tits on a boar."

Michael looked off in the distance and shook his head. "That bloody alcohol is the ruination of your old man and killed my poor Kate. I give you credit for putting up with your dad as long as you did. There's no question that we both could write a book about the pain of living with an alcoholic."

"We plant something like 150 to 200 acres of green feed oats each year. A lot of the ranchers don't believe in putting up hay or green feed, but all it takes is a harsh winter and they're in deep shit. There have been past winters where the ranchers lost a lot of animals when the snow was too deep to graze and they had nothing to feed the poor critters. If we ever get more stashed up than we need, we sell the surplus."

Three days after leaving, they were on a knoll, looking down on the Francis ranch. They arrived just as the crew was coming in for supper. Michael introduced William to Sam, Dave and Tom, the single fellows and Wilfred and Rex, the married hands. While the married fellows went to their houses in the compound, Michael and William followed the single guys into the cookhouse. Michael introduced William to Maud.

"Well, we saw a lot of country," Michael said as they were eating supper. "Before I get into that, though, I should tell you guys a little about William, our new hand. He was working on the railroad that they're pushing from eastern Canada to the West Coast."

Michael summarized the collapse of the trestle, the deaths of William's workmates and William's escape from death without serious injury.

"My, that must have been a horrible experience for you," Maud interjected. "My heart goes out to you over the loss of your friends."

"Yes, it was pretty hard to deal with, especially when we had told our shift boss before we started work that morning that with the high wind, it wasn't safe to work on the trestle. There wasn't anything I could do for my two friends. Anyway, as soon as I got patched up, I quit my job. The contractor we were working for was only interested in production and they could have cared less about the workers' safety. I guess Charlie, our paymaster and Michael used to ride together, years back. Charlie introduced me to Michael and here I am."

"William grew up on a farm in eastern Canada," Michael continued. "He's had lots of experience riding and driving horses and by the size of him, I imagine he'll swing a pretty mean post maul when it comes to building fences. William will be a welcome addition to our ranch."

"Now, I did see a nice piece of grazing land that's less than 100 miles north of the Canadian border. It's up against a ridge of hills called the Cypress Hills. The hills are forested in spruce, pine and poplar so there would be lots of logs for fencing, buildings and corrals and an abundance of firewood. We'll just have to wait and see if Lopez really wants to buy our spread like he says he does. According to the real estate people, the land has been on the market for a couple of years now without any interest in it. The question is whether the land will still be available in the future. Time will tell, I guess."

A week into his new job, William was fitting right in. Michael was pleasantly impressed with his overall ability. Not only was he adept at riding and driving horses, his strength made him hard to beat when it came to pounding in fence posts with a 10-pound post maul.

As their regular work permitted, Michael delegated William, Dave and Tom to build the fences on the north boundary of their ranch. Michael and many of the neighboring ranchers had heard via the grapevine that the government was making moves to bring the days of open grazing to an end. Many ranchers were now fencing their property or planning on doing so. Since the Lopez ranch was planning on buying out the Francis ranch in the future, they agreed that no fence would be built between the two properties. By freeze-up, they were close to finishing the fencing.

At Christmas, William took off a couple of weeks to go back to Ontario to visit family. He had good visits with his mom, his sisters and all the kinfolk. Mildred, his mom, had gotten a job as a clerk at a hardware store and she and the girls had moved to town. Sisters Beth and Becky were in high school. William also phoned Neil's and Ted's families and filled them in on the horrific accident that took the boys' lives. He also told their folks of the dream he had of Neil the night after his death.

As William expected, his sisters and mom did their best to convince him to move back to Ontario.

"I miss you guys a lot, but now my heart is out West," William stated. "There's something about those windswept prairies and wide-open spaces that gets into your blood."

When William dropped in to visit his dad, it was the same old heavy go. The inside of the house was a pigsty and smelled to high heaven. Eric was far from sober and in a most disconsolate frame of mind.

"I guess you heard I sold all the livestock," Eric slurred. "I should have been looking after the cattle and pigs myself, but then, seeing I can't get a handle on my drinking, I wouldn't have been able to manage. Anyway, I didn't cotton to having that asshole of a Ross always over here, so I sold the livestock. Was your mom ever torn up with me for doing that! I guess you and the rest of the family must really hate me. I certainly hate myself. As you probably know, the last time she visited me, Mom said she was going for a divorce and I can't blame her, seeing I'm such a loser."

"As you can see, things are kind of a wreck here in the house," he continued. That old saying, 'life's a bitch and then you die, sure applies to me. If I had the guts to pull it off, I'd do myself in and end this damn misery I'm in, but again, I'm just a gutless wonder. I don't blame everyone for leaving me. I got reasons for the shape I'm in and why I drink so much. If I had the balls, I'd tell everyone my reasons, but I just can't get up the strength to do so."

"You know why Mom, the girls and I left?" William replied acidly. "It was because you'd become a drunk and were impossible to live with. Remember, you attacked Mom and then you attacked me. Maybe I should have stayed on and beaten the ever-living crap out of you, but really, what good would that have done?"

"I can't say I can remember attacking you, but if you said I attacked you, I guess I did. I really feel bad being such a loser to everyone. Hopefully, someday I'll kick the bucket and you'll be rid of me. Life's not worth living right now."

"Mom, the girls and I have done everything we can for you, Dad. God only knows how much we wish you could come to your senses. It's sad because before you hit the bottle you were a dependable, hard-working, decent sort. All we can do now is wish that somehow, someday you'll smarten the hell up."

William felt numb as he headed back to his mom's place. With the promise of seeing his mom and sisters again next Christmas, William soon was on his way back to the Montana ranch.

CHAPTER 3

A S TIME PASSED, work was going well for William and he was fast becoming Michael's most trusted hand. Not only was he excellent on horseback, he was Michael's best hand when it came to driving a team or a four-up.

There were roundups for spring branding and roundups again in the fall when the young stock was sent to market. With the building of the fences, the two ranches did not have much sorting of the two herds. Still, there was always the chance that some of the livestock could get lost on the drive to market and mixed into some other rancher's herd. Without a brand, it would be hard to lay claim to your cattle. The Francis hands would help the Lopez ranch with their branding. Once their branding was completed, they would all come back to the Francis ranch for their branding. Work aside, it was a social time for the two ranches.

In spite of the comradery of the hands on the two ranches, there was the odd problem with the two crews working so closely together. Andrew, the foreman for the Lopez spread, was a good straw boss and physically, a big man. He was the type, however, who would hold a grudge and could be a bully. At six foot-three and 235 pounds, none of the crew at either ranch could come close to matching William for strength. Andrew had heard stories of William's remarkable strength and this irked him as he thought himself as strong as they made them. After supper, one evening, while branding at the Lopez spread, Andrew had been into the tequila and challenged William to an arm-wrestling contest. William obliged and soundly beat him. After the match, William extended his hand for a friendly handshake. Andrew, however, thought he could overpower his opponent by forcing him to his knees. They locked hands. It was Andrew who ended up on his knees. In anger and with the tequila really kicking in, Andrew threw a wild haymaker at William. William ducked low and the shot sailed harmlessly over his head. William came back with a powerful right overhand blow to Andrew's jaw. Andrew was knocked flat on his butt. The fight was over. When Andrew regained consciousness, a few minutes later, there was no more fight left in him. He climbed to his feet, subdued and nursing a very sore jaw. He claimed his poor showing was a result of the tequila, but he swallowed his pride and called it a day.

For the rest of the branding season, Andrew kept a low profile with William and was wise enough not to re-challenge him as he was still suffering from a sore face. It was really irking him, however, that he'd lost face in front of both crews and he was waiting for the opportunity, sometime in the future, of having a return match. He was of the mindset that if he was sober, he could give William a damn good licking.

Carl witnessed the fight between Andrew and William. Because of his former ties to the Francis ranch, some of the hands had told him of William's strength and boxing skills.

"I'd advise you to give William a wide berth," he said to Andrew. "Not only is he as strong as a bull, but from what I've been told, when he lived back in Ontario, he learned to box from his uncle who was a professional boxer. One of the Francis hands saw him pick up a 500-pound flywheel off a steam engine and carry it fifty feet. In dealing with the big bruiser, you'll find that wisdom is the better part of valour."

Andrew paid no heed to Carl's warning. His nose was out of joint. Now that his face felt back to normal, he made it known to one and all that he was just waiting for his chance to even accounts with William. The evening of accounts did come. Strangely, though, it was not exactly how Andrew had envisaged it.

Once the fall cattle drives were over for the year, the ranch hands were enjoying a bit of a breather before winter really set in. A number of the Lopez and Francis cowboys were taking a few days off the regular grind. Some were heading to town for a booze up while some were hunting in the river valleys.

It was a cold morning in mid-December. There still was no snow on the ground, but the wind was blasting in from the north. The temperature was a few degrees below freezing and falling. Andrew had headed out on foot three-quarters of a mile to the river valley to hunt for deer or elk. Seeing the weather was so inclement, none of the other hands offered to accompany him. In the afternoon, they would do some dehorning on a few cows, but Carl had advised him that they could manage without him.

As Andrew was nearing the bottom of the riverbank, he came to a very steep part of the grade. Suddenly, he lost his footing and went cartwheeling through the air. His rifle went flying and when he came to a sudden stop, his right foot was wedged between two trees that were growing only a few inches apart. His ankle was badly broken with his toes facing sideways. When he extracted his foot, the pain was excruciating.

He gritted his teeth and tried to straighten out his foot. The pain was too much to bear and he had to stop. After gaining his composure, a sobering thought occurred to him.

"God help me. I'm in a real bind. Like a fool, I didn't tell anyone where I was going to hunt and there is no snow to track me. To make matters worse, the crew isn't expecting me back until late."

His rifle lay thirty feet from him. He tried to crawl to his gun and fire three shots to signal for help, but the pain was so excruciating that he had to give up.

"Damn it. The wind's roaring and I'm in the bottom of the river valley," he muttered. "Even if I could get to my gun, I'm sure that the sound of the gun won't carry far. With the wind coming from the north, the sound of my rifle shots would be carried away from the ranch buildings, not to them."

He lay in agony, hoping that someone would find him before he froze to death. His plan of evening accounts with William now seemed so far away, so foolish and childish.

Finally, he muttered, "Dear God, if you get me out of this alive, I'll bury the hatchet with William."

And then, to add insult to injury, it started to snow.

"I just must get to my rifle to signal for help," he said. He steeled himself and in agony, again began crawling to where his gun was. The pain was so intense that after getting to his rifle he collapsed and nearly blacked out.

At the Francis ranch, just before the snow started falling, William saddled up his horse and rode the mile and a half south to the riverbank. He dismounted and tied his horse to a tree out of the wind. He, like Andrew, planned on doing a little hunting. He knew that game off-times would be on the move during a storm. He descended down the river bank, not knowing that Andrew lay in agony less than a mile from him.

It was William's plan to walk along the bank of the river heading upstream. He had just taken a few steps upriver when he got a strange, but strong urge to go downstream. William stopped and headed in the other direction. By now it was snowing heavily, but the wind had eased up a little. William had walked a couple of hundred yards when he stopped to adjust his backpack.

To add to Andrew's excruciating pain, he was now shivering uncontrollably. As he was going to be doing a lot of walking, he had not worn his heavy winter coat. Recognizing that he was in desperate straits with nothing to lose, Andrew fired three quick shots, the method they used in the bush to signal for help.

"What was that?" William said aloud. The sound was faint, but he was sure he heard three shots, evenly spaced, fired in rapid succession. "Is someone else out here hunting? Yes, probably there's another hunter out here."

But then, that same feeling that made him change directions and head down river was there again. "I wonder if someone is signaling for help. Could someone be in trouble?"

William fired two quick shots in return, the signal used to tell the party in distress that their signal for help had been heard.

William kept heading down the river flats in the direction of the three shots he'd heard. Then he heard a faint shrill whistle coming from further down the river valley. William took his bearings and whistled back.

The whistlers kept whistling back and forth to each other as William kept walking. Then, William saw Andrew curled up on the ground, covered with a skiff of snow. Despite being nearly froze, when Andrew saw that it was William, he broke out in a cold sweat.

"God Almighty, am I ever glad to see you," Andrew finally began weakly. "I fell and broke my damn ankle about an hour ago. The ankle hurts like the devil. As you can see, it's badly broke and I'm damn nearly froze."

"Don't worry. We'll get you out of here. First, we'll have to try to make you a splint and then I'll carry you piggyback style up the way I came down. The slope is much more gradual there. I left my horse up on top. Once we climb out of the river valley, we can get you on the horse and head to our ranch."

"I know this is going to hurt like hell," William continued. "I'm going to have to straighten out your broken ankle before I can splint it. Go ahead and scream if you have to."

Andrew clenched his teeth and groaned as William straightened his mangled ankle.

From his backpack, William retrieved his hatchet and a coil of heavy cord. In jig time, he fashioned a rough splint made from a few ash saplings. The splint was crude, but would keep Andrew's foot straight and protect it from further injury should he snub it on something.

"Just how the hell are you going to carry me out of here?" Andrew moaned. "I weigh over two hundred twenty pounds."

"You let me worry about that," William replied. "Our only choice is for me to piggyback you. Once you're up on my back, you can lock your arms around my neck and I'll support your legs. We'll have to leave our guns here. I'll put them up in a tree and we can get the boys to pick them up later."

Once the guns were looked after, William helped Andrew stand up on his good leg. He took off his coat and helped Andrew put it on over his light coat. William then bent over and with some difficulty, Andrew positioned himself on William's back. Once William had Andrew's legs under his arms and Andrew had his arms locked around William's neck, they set off. It was a primitive way of transporting an injured person, but it was the only method they had.

It was uncomfortable for William and very painful for Andrew, but slowly they made their way along the river flats.

"What a fool I've been," Andrew thought as they struggled along. "I was dead set on evening accounts with William and here he is, saving my life."

Andrew was amazed at William's strength and stamina. When William needed a rest, he'd get Andrew to stand on his good leg. William would then bend over, brace his hands on his knees and take a breather. Andrew would lean on William to keep his balance. Finally, they were at the spot where William had come down into the valley. Climbing the slope took quite some time as William had to watch his footing and stop more often to catch his breath. As William wove his way through the dense growth of trees, he also had to be careful not to bang Andrew's injured ankle against a tree.

Both William and Andrew breathed a sigh of relief when they crested the river valley. Soon they were in the bluff where

William had left his horse. Both of them were completely exhausted and it took a bit of ingenuity on William's part to get Andrew up on the horse without causing him too much extra pain.

Once Andrew was aboard, William began leading his horse and injured rider back to the ranch buildings.

It was still snowing heavily and then the wind started to pick up again. Soon they were in a near white out. William was well acquainted with the lay of the land though and soon they were back at the ranch cookhouse, in out of the cold.

Despite being in physical agony, Andrew was constantly thanking William for saving his life. William had never in his life been so played out and cold.

Although in a great deal of pain, Andrew only groaned the odd time, when the pain became unbearable.

Late in the afternoon, the Francis hands loaded Andrew up in a buggy, covered him with lots of blankets and transported him back to the Lopez ranch as gingerly as possible. Until the doctor arrived, the only pain killer they had at the Lopez ranch was tequila and rum. And yes, a sip or two or more of the spirits, did help deaden the pain. Because of the inclement weather, it wasn't until the next day that Andrew got medical attention.

Dr. Richard Drummond arrived in the morning. He had served as a doctor in the Civil War and though up in years, had handled similar cases before. Seeing the injury to Andrew's ankle was so severe though, he opted to take Andrew to the nearest hospital to deal with his injury. After giving Andrew another stiff shot of tequila plus an injection of morphine to handle the pain, the doctor took Andrew by team and buggy and finally by the newly constructed Great Northern Railroad to the nearest hospital and set the broken ankle.

Andrew was forced to lay low for a couple of months. Although he did recover, he would walk with a limp for the rest of his life.

A close bond was now developing between William and Andrew. It became very apparent to one and all that Andrew's comportment evolved for the better because of his mishap. His bullying days and his vindictive mindset seemed to be a thing of the past. When he got into the tequila, which he occasionally did, he never tired of telling the tale of how he escaped death and about the giant of a man who carried him for over a mile up out of the river valley without a problem. He always remembered to give credit to William for saving his life. In the past, he had an axe to grind with William. Now, he fondly referred to William as his friend who was "strong as two men."

CHAPTER 4

THE BUILDING OF the Great Northern Railroad in the northwestern states in 1885 was a godsend for the Francis and Lopez ranches, not to mention the other ranches in the areas. They no longer had to use long cattle drives to get their cattle to market. Not only had the cattle drives been time consuming, the animals lost a lot of weight on their long trek to market.

The strategy of putting up feed in case they had a bad winter paid off for the Francis and Lopez ranches the winter of 1886-1887. It was a brutal winter with heavy snow that made grazing poor to nonexistent. The warm chinook winds that would usually melt the snow did not come. The blizzards kept piling up the snow making it nearly impossible for the poor critters to get to the grass. Those ranchers who didn't have feed put up were in dire straits. The poor starving animals died by the thousands. Some ranchers lost up to a half of their herds. The Francis and Lopez ranches fared well as they had an abundance of feed put up. They did share some their surplus green feed with neighboring ranches that had none, but because of such a strong demand for feed they had to carefully ration it out. It was a horrific sight when spring finally came. The range lands were strewn with the carcasses of thousands of cattle that didn't make it through the winter. The poor animals gnawed on anything they could find, even trees and fence posts. In the spring, they found undigested wood slivers in the dead cattle's stomachs.

Although William had a number of male friends, because he was still smarting from the betrayal of his old girlfriend, Tina, he shied away from making friends with any of the eligible females. On his days off, he tended to be a loner. Seeing he was a teetotaller, unlike the other hands, he wasn't into partying or the bar scene.

Rosemary, a single lass from the Lopez ranch, had eyes for William. At the Lopez Christmas party, a lot of the Francis people came over to join in the celebration. After a few drinks, Rosemary was feeling no pain and tried to shine up to William. He was flattered by her interest, but kindly made it known to her that he was single and intended to keep it that way.

William tried to get back home every year for a visit. He always enjoyed visiting his mom and sisters, but dreaded visiting his dad. It was the same old, same old. Shortly after William's last visit to Ontario, his mother got a divorce. She still felt duty bound to drop in on her ex-husband though for the odd visit. Seeing he had assaulted her in the past, she would always make sure she was accompanied by a friend. She had now started seeing Ken, an old family friend whose wife had passed away a few years past.

Finally, in the early spring of 1889 came the day Michael, Maud and William had been long waiting for. The Lopez ranch bought them out. A year before, through a real estate firm in Medicine Hat, Michael made a deal, subject to financing, on the Mulby holdings on the northwest side of the Cypress Hills. Ernest Mulby was a British absentee land owner who had never set foot in Canada. He had a contractor fence the east side of the property that ran through the forested part and erect a fairly large shed. Having lost interest in ranching and immigrating to Canada, he listed the property for sale.

As soon as the snow was gone, Michael, William and a few hands went by horseback and a couple of wagon teams up North to what would be their future ranch. A recent forest fire had burned through a lot of the Cypress Hills. Fortunately, the fire missed most of the treed part of their ranch. They mapped out where the cattle drive would go and transacted the purchase of the Mulby ranch. They also did a detailed inspection of the Mulby holdings before Michael headed back to Montana. William and the rest of the crew stayed on. They found a tamarack swamp in the forested area that supplied them with plenty of fence posts. They were grateful for the large shed. It would take a bit of renovating and although somewhat crude, would provide them accommodation until they could erect their own living quarters.

The boys were able to get fencing supplies in Irvine, a small town, some twenty miles north of the ranch. They were soon building fences. In early June, William and the boys headed back into Montana to help with the cattle drive.

Since Michael had come up to the Cypress Hills looking for land, many more roads had been built in both Montana and what would become southern Alberta. In anticipation of the cattle drive, Michael had made arrangements with all the ranches they might have to cross.

Once back in Montana, they were hard at it getting ready for the big move. All their equipment and household effects were transported east on the newly built Great Northern Railroad to where the spur line intersected with the Canadian Transcontinental Railroad and from there back west to

The Sacred Gem Within

Medicine Hat. Michael lamented that there was no direct road from Montana up across the Milk River into the Cypress Hills area.

The Lopez's and surrounding neighbors had a going away party for Michael, Maud, William and the hands. As the party was winding down, Andrew approached William.

"I wonder if you could drop over to our place tomorrow morning. If you'd like, maybe you could bring Michael with you. I have a little something I'd like to give you before you head up to Canada."

At 10 am, William and Michael were sitting with Andrew having coffee. Andrew's wife was gone for a few days visiting family. After chatting for a few minutes, Andrew got up, retrieved a box and set it down in front of William.

"I'd like you to have this as a thank you gift for saving my life," Andrew said as he lifted the lid.

Inside the wooden box was an old single action 44-Colt revolver in a holster and a box of ammunition.

"This here revolver has quite a history to it as it probably saved my dad's life," Andrew continued. "You see, one day before any of us kids were born, this idiot comes barging into our house. He had a revolver in his hand and was shouting that he was going to shoot the old man for something that my dad was supposed to have done to this guy's brother during the Civil War. I guess he was pretty well hammered. At any rate, this arse is holding the gun on the old man and wasn't paying any attention to my mother. So, Mom, bless her heart, slips up behind this character and cold cocks him by hitting him over the head with the butt end of this Colt. When the guy comes to and sobers up some, the dumb ass discovers that he'd somehow mistaken the old man for the guy he wanted to even accounts with. The stupid bastard apologizes and takes off. Dad was thinking of tying a damn good licking on the fool for holding him at gunpoint. But then, I guess he thought the large lump on the idiot's head was payment enough."

"Anyway, William, you showed me what life was all about. You see, before you rescued me, I was waiting for the chance to even accounts with you over the fight we had. I know that you knew this. Like a dummy, I wasn't into this kindness, forgiveness thing, but you were. I really didn't deserve good treatment from you, but you gave it to me just the same. I'll always be in debt to you for saving my life. You showed me that there is more to being a man than being a 'Bull of the Pampas.' Thank you for showing me what being a real man was all about."

"Oh, just one more thing. If you can, please keep all of this just between the two of you and Maud."

William was touched by Andrew's gift. He thanked him for his kindness and said he and Michael would keep it to themselves. After finishing their second cup of coffee, William and Michael headed back to their ranch.

Finally, they began the cattle drive. Carl, Paul, Andrew and three extra hands from the Lopez ranch were there to help with the move. On the Montana stretch they had stockpiled hay at the spots that would be at the end of each day's drive. As all the cows still had their calves at side, they only traveled 10 to 15 miles a day. By the luck of the draw, it had been a dry spring and the Milk River was low. They crossed the river without a problem. Following the route Michael had previously made, it was easier for the cattle to handle the steep grades of the river valley. Maud and Michael came in the chuckwagon with the groceries, stove and bed rolls. Another team pulled a rack full of hay that was used as needed. Both wagons had a good breaking mechanism that they used when descending the steep grade getting into the Milk River valley. Going up the north slope they hooked another two teams to each wagon.

The drive went like clockwork and two weeks later the herd was grazing in their new home by the Cypress Hills. As a safeguard for a bad winter, Michael bought hay locally from a rancher.

Their work was cut out for them with the constructing of barns and corrals. They also continued with the fencing. They had a good supply of logs from the forested part of their property and brought in a contractor with his steam-powered sawmill to cut dimensional lumber for their buildings and corrals. Some of the ranch hands felled and limbed the trees while other hands skidded the logs out to the sawmill with teams of horses.

While the logging and the sawing was going on, William, Dave and Tom helped fell the trees. In addition, they were still cutting fence posts and fencing the west and north boundary of the ranch. The building crew built two barns and some corrals. They also built a small one-room building that they hoped would serve as the school. The original shed was fixed up for their temporary winter living quarters. It may not have looked like the Taj Mahal, but it would do for now.

While logging, William and the crew ate their lunch in a small cleared-off site adjacent to the spot they were logging. One day when they were eating dinner, a large raven swooped down and perched on a stump, some fifty feet from them.

William took a meat sandwich from his lunch and laid it on top of a stump quite a distance from the raven. In due course, the raven hopped off his perch, retrieved the sandwich and flew back to its own stump. The raven stood on its lunch with one foot and tore away at the sandwich until it had devoured its meal. Having finished its dinner, the huge raven leapt into the air and winged its way back into the timber.

The next day the raven was back looking for another sandwich. By the end of the month, the raven was so trusting and tame that it would land on William's outstretched arm and retrieve its dinner from his hand. Strangely, when William was not there, the raven would only circle around and then head back into the bush. As much as the other hands tried to get the big bird to come to them, the raven only had eyes for William and would only land on his wrist. Everyone wondered what the cheeky bird did for dinner when William wasn't there and once the crew finished logging. William often thought of the mysterious raven.

CHAPTER 5

A S SUMMER TURNED to fall, William took a break from the fencing and began plowing up 60 acres of their more productive land. While he was breaking the prairie with a four-horse outfit and a sulky plow, Wilfred was working the plowed land down with a team of horses and a disk. They would grow green feed on the newly cultivated land the following year.

The school teacher who taught on the ranch in Montana decided to stay in the States. In midsummer, the wives of the married ranch hands met with Michael and Maud to see about finding another teacher. The married families had nine kids of school age. Despite making numerous inquiries, by late August, Michael and Maud still had no leads on finding a qualified teacher willing to teach at the ranch.

William wrote his mom in Ontario and told her about their problem in locating a teacher. She wrote back that Myrna, the twenty-year-old daughter of her best friend, had finished her normal school in the spring and was thinking of heading out West to look for a teaching position.

"I had a bit to do with Myrna's brothers, Harry and Stuart," William said to Michael and Maud after getting his mom's letter. "They were about my age. They lived in a town about twenty miles from our farm. Of course, we went to different schools. Our school ball team would play their school team at sports days and the like. I knew Myrna just to see her. She'd be something like five or six years younger than me. Near as I know they were good people. If you'd like, I could write her a letter offering her the job."

"We'd sure appreciate that," Maud responded. "Knowing the family, you should have an inside track with her."

William wrote Myrna outlining the grades and the number of the kids that she would be teaching should she accept the position. He advised her on the salary that they were able to pay. He also told her that they had already started building a teacherage abutting the school.

Myrna telegraphed back:

Re. Michael's and Maud's offer: Finished normal school last year: If position still open, will accept: Be available the first week in October.

William telegraphed back that Michael and Maud were looked forward to her arrival.

A week before Myrna arrived, they finished adding a one-room teacherage addition to the school with an adjoining door. By the end of September, everyone was waiting expectantly for the arrival of the new teacher.

The first week in October, Myrna was on her way. William drove to the railroad station at Irvine, just east of Medicine Hat, with Michael's best team and buggy to pick her up.

The last time he saw Myrna, she was just a cute blond girl who tagged along to the ball games with her brothers. Myrna sent a recent picture of herself in her last letter. William was more than pleasantly surprised. The slip of a girl had grown into a beautiful young woman. William wanted to look his best. He spruced himself up and was decked out in his Sunday best clothes when he went to meet the train.

When Myrna stepped off the train in Irvine, it was her turn to be pleasantly surprised. She remembered how handsome William was, but she couldn't remember him being so husky and tall. He had fine features, longish black hair and deep blue eyes.

Michael and Maud had sent Myrna money to buy school supplies. She brought two large trunks of school supplies in addition to her own personal belongings. William loaded the trunks and Myrna's luggage into the buggy and they were on their way.

Myrna was a chatterbox and on the long trip back to the ranch she was bringing William up to speed on all the comings and goings of their old neighborhood.

"I don't know if you knew this, but the day before I left, I was talking to your mother. She told me your dad had what appeared to be a slight heart attack and was hospitalized for a few days. She wondered if all his drinking could have been a contributing factor."

"Yeah, Mom sent me a telegram about that. It's a shame that he can't get off the bottle. Up to the time I was sixteen or seventeen he was a social drinker, but his drinking never was a problem. The sad part is there doesn't seem to be anything anyone can do for the old goat. Hopefully, now he'll smarten up. I won't hold my breath though. I'll tell you one thing. Seeing what booze has done to the old man, I don't touch the stuff and never will. His boozing has pretty well wrecked our family."

"Yes, it's a shame he can't break the cycle. It must be especially hard on your family considering that he was so responsible before he started drinking. Mom and Dad are teetotallers. I've had the odd glass of wine, but I really don't like the taste of the stuff."

Maud prepared a welcoming supper for Myrna. One of the boys had shot a couple of Canada geese so they had roast goose with all the trimmings. For dessert, they had saskatoon pie with cream. Myrna raved about the pie. It was the first time she had tasted saskatoons.

Over the weekend, William helped Myrna set up the small schoolroom. They had been able to find a blackboard and ten old school desks. Monday morning, school began with nine kids in attendance.

Myrna always maintained that her relationship with William began the moment they met at the railway station. If not love at first sight, it certainly was a strong attraction at first sight. The more William and Myrna hung out together, the stronger the feelings between them grew.

Myrna ate dinners and suppers in the cookhouse with Michael, Maud, William and the other single hands. Most evenings, after Myrna helped Maud with the supper dishes, she and William would be together. They'd go for walks, horseback rides or hang out at the teacherage.

Myrna was enthralled with the ballplayer that she used to stare at when she was a young girl. In her view, without question, he was the handsomest man in western Canada.

William was as enthralled with his blond lady friend as she was with him. Myrna was a full foot shorter than William and had a figure that would turn any man's head.

They had a short courtship, often going for jaunts on the weekends in the buggy or on horseback. What they did when they were by themselves made for some interesting speculation and gossip by the single hands, especially when William would tip-toe into their makeshift bunkhouse in the wee hours of the morning after being out with Myrna. Recognizing what a big bruiser William was, the hired hands realized that wisdom was the better part of valour and never discussed their speculations with the man in question.

Although initially the single hands tried to shine up to this new single lady, it didn't take long for Myrna to make known to them that she was in William's camp. By his comments and actions, William too made it known that they were a twosome. His unspoken message to the single guys was for them to butt out.

Shortly after Myrna arrived, she and William went to the local fall supper and dance. There were plenty of young lads wanting to dance with this pretty, young blond teacher. William let a few of the fellows dance with his lady friend, but after allowing them one dance with Myrna, he'd be in there like a dirty shirt to reclaim his girl. It made Myrna feel so safe and special that her big boyfriend was so protective of her.

Myrna was in love, but missed her kinfolk and her old stomping grounds back in Ontario. As for William, he had spent many years on the windswept plains and was completely sold on the West. Although it was a constant struggle for Myrna to put up with the isolation, she made up her mind to try to live with it. William loved hearing the coyotes howling on the still nights. To Myrna, the howling of the coyotes was a reminder that she was in a wild, pioneer country.

Just before the Christmas school break, William went into Medicine Hat and bought Myrna an engagement ring. He wanted to give it to her in the ranch cabin back in the Cypress Hills. The next Saturday morning, he and Myrna saddled up and headed back to the cabin. It was a crisp bright day with the temperature just below freezing. When they reached the cabin, William started a fire in the heater and soon it was getting warm. Myrna had packed a lunch. After they had finished eating, William reached into his pocket, retrieved Myrna's engagement ring and put it on her finger. She was elated! Tears of joy slipped down her cheeks.

Whether it was the heat of the moment or the heat of the cabin's airtight heater, soon the newly engaged pair began removing each other's clothes. William led Myrna to the small cabin cot. There they lay, discovering and sharing each other's bodies.

On the way back to the ranch, they talked of their wedding plans. They agreed on getting married during the Easter school break. It was a happy time for the young couple. After supper, Myrna proudly showed off her ring to one and sundry.

During the Christmas break, William took Myrna down to the Lopez ranch to show her off to his Montana friends. Andrew and his wife Lyla had them over for the evening. Lyla was an artist and she and Andrew presented Myrna and William with a painting for an early wedding present.

William gasped when he looked at the painting. Lyla had painted a picture of him packing Andrew, piggyback, up out of the river valley. Under the painting was printed:

THANK YOU FOR SAVING MY LIFE

CHAPTER 6

T HROUGHOUT THE WINTER, Myrna and William were inseparable. William would sometimes creep into the bunkhouse in the wee hours of the morning. Occasionally he wouldn't make an appearance until breakfast.

By and large, the local dances were enjoyable occasions, but with liquor flowing liberally, the occasional fight between the males did occur. William and Myrna had just arrived at the dance when a fight broke out between Cam and Jim, two local gentlemen. Cam Niles was a fifty-year-old single hand from a neighboring ranch, while Jim was a new hand from the Francis ranch. Cam was a descent sort, but when he got a few drinks under his belt, he became quite a belligerent ass. Both cowboys were fairly well lubricated.

It didn't take long for William to break up the fight. Jim took things in his stride and walked off, but Cam promised William that he was going to give him a good licking for interfering in their squabble.

"Bring it on," William responded, with a broad grin. "Whenever you're ready, I'm ready."

William rolled up his sleeves and stopped a few inches from Cam.

After glancing up at his six-foot three, 235-pound foe, Cam had a change of mind.

"Well, I could a handled yer in my prime," he slurred.

"Oh, come on, let's call it a day, Cam," William replied with a smile, putting his hand on Cam's shoulder. "Scrapping never got anyone anywhere."

"Thank you so much for not flattening that character, dear," Myrna said once William was back with her. "I know you easily could have knocked him senseless. I'm so relieved that my man would rather make peace than war."

"Well, for the most part I'd rather make peace than fight," William replied with a chuckle. "I only get physical when diplomacy fails."

Myrna and William headed back onto the dance floor.

During the Easter school break, William and Myrna were on the train heading to Ontario. It had been Myrna's dream to be married back at home. William would have preferred it if they'd married out West, but acquiesced to his fair lady's wish.

As Myrna and William didn't arrive in Ontario until two days before the wedding, Myrna's folks, Maria and Ed, made a lot of the wedding preparations. It was just a simple wedding, with Julie, Myrna's best friend as bridesmaid and Bruce, Myrna's brother as William's groomsman. Mildred and Ken, her new boyfriend, also attended the wedding. Mildred was overjoyed that her son had found such a beautiful, responsible mate.

The night of their wedding was a bit challenging. Myrna and William were taking the train for a short honeymoon to Niagara Falls in the morning and Myrna's folks insisted they spend the night at their place. All went well until everyone was in bed. As it turned out, the bedframe in William's and his bride's bed proved to be none too stout. Their intimate endeavors caused their old bed to collapse with a horrendous bang. They scrambled off the bed, but before they could get any attire on, Myrna's folks rushed in to see what the loud bang was all about. The conversation was limited. What could the naked pair say, especially when all they had to cover themselves was their pillows?

Without repairing the collapsed bedframe, the newly-weds put the mattress on the floor. After regaining their composure, the newly-weds resumed what they had been doing before that made the bed collapse.

At breakfast the next morning, Ed, Myrna's dad said, "We'll have to get a better bedframe. I hope you had a good sleep."

Both Myrna and William responded with red faces. Before either one could get a word out, Ed burst out laughing.

"I imagine that you did," he added once he regained control.

William and Myrna spent a few enjoyable days at Niagara Falls and several more days visiting family.

When William and Myrna dropped in on William's dad, it certainly was not the highlight of their honeymoon. Eric was anything but sober. For the most part, his drunken rambling made little sense. The house looked like a pigsty and stunk to high heaven. The fact that the drunk had just peed his pants didn't help the aroma in the room any. William was disgusted and embarrassed with his dad's behavior.

"There's nothing anyone can do for the old drunken sot," he said to Myrna as they pulled out of the driveway with the team and buggy. "It's sort of a lost cause visiting him, but then, for better or worse I guess he still is my dad."

William had forewarned Myrna of what to expect when visiting his dad so she took it in her stride.

All too soon for Myrna's likening, they were on the train heading back to the ranch.

Throughout the spring, Myrna continued to make a concerted effort to accept rural living. She vowed to stay as positive as possible, living on the bald prairie.

Once the fencing and building had been completed, Michael and William brokered a deal in which William and Myrna started their own small herd of cattle. The small herd would be integrated with Michael's much larger herd. William's and Myrna's brand was WM. William would continue to draw wages while working at the ranch until their herd grew larger.

A year and a few months after the wedding, Myrna was expecting. The due date would be in mid-July. With her due date fast approaching, Myrna was in a quandary about who she could get to help her out once the baby was born.

"I would like to keep teaching," she commented to William. "If I do, we'll need a live-in baby sitter. Another thing that might be a bit of a problem is that I definitely want to nurse the baby."

"There's no question you're going to need help," William replied. "I've been wondering about my mom's younger sister, Edith. You met her at our wedding. She's really had a hard time of it. Her husband, Ben, was as lazy as a cut cat. Poor Edith broke her butt trying to provide for them. A year or so ago, the idiot ran off with some hooch. It was a blessing that they had no kids. She was working in a café the last I heard. I can vouch she's a good sort. When I talked to her on our honeymoon, she mentioned that she hoped that eventually she could get a better job than the café thing. If you'd like, I can contact her and see if she'd be interested in coming out here to give us a hand, before and after the baby is born. I'm pretty sure we could convince her to stay on, so you to go back teaching in the fall."

"That sounds good to me. You have my blessing. Go ahead and contact her. I remember talking to her at our wedding. She seemed like a very nice lady to me."

William wrote his aunt a letter offering her the live-in job of helping out when the baby was born. He also asked her if she'd be interested in staying on so Myrna could keep teaching. He advised Edith what they could afford to pay her and the type of living accommodations she would have.

When Edith received the offer, she dropped in on Mildred and showed her William's letter.

"I can't think of a better person to care for Myrna's baby and my grandchild than you," Mildred responded. "You've also been a midwife to a number of births around here. They're quite a distance from a hospital so your experience would be invaluable."

"Their offer is very tempting," Edith replied. "I know William is solid and dependable. Without having to worry about rent and my living costs, I'd also do a lot better financially. I got good vibes from Myrna when we met at their wedding. I've got so many bad memories from my marriage to that loser of a Ben that I've been thinking that I'd like to move away and begin a new chapter in my life. I'm still young enough to make another start."

With Mildred's blessing, Edith wrote back accepting their offer. William and Myrna sent Edith a money order to cover the cost of her train ticket. When Edith arrived at the end of June, William was at the train station to pick her up.

That spring, they added two more rooms to the teacherage. This gave Edith her own bedroom, with one small room for the baby.

With Myrna's due date fast approaching, it helped so much to have both Edith and Maud for support. Maud had also assisted in many births, both locally and while she lived in Montana.

When Myrna went into labour, both Edith and Maud were there as midwives. Maud was of the firm conviction that the birthing room was no place for husbands. To that end, while the two ladies catered to Myrna's needs, her anxious husband was outside pacing, waiting for the news of the birth of his daughter or son.

After three hours of pacing, in the early morning hours, the cry of a newborn brought William racing for the door. Both Myrna and William were overjoyed with the birth of their son. All and sundry marveled that in looks and huskiness, the wee boy was a carbon copy of his dad. They named their son Rob, in honour of William's baby brother who had only lived for a few days.

Both Edith and Maud were elated that Myrna was fast bonding with her baby. When she was not breast-feeding the hungry youngster, Myrna spent countless hours holding and playing with her son.

Once school started in September, Myrna and Edith engineered a unique breast- feeding plan. While Myrna was teaching, Edith would bring young Rob into the classroom for Myrna to nurse. Edith would maintain order with the kids, allowing Myrna to sit at the back of the classroom and nurse Rob. The kids soon learned that with their substitute teacher, no tomfoolery was allowed. When Edith was at the helm, although kind and fair, she adhered to a much stricter discipline regime than Myrna did.

Things were going well for William, Edith and baby Rob. Not only was he bonding with his mother, the older he got, the stronger the bond grew between the young fellow and his dad.

Myrna loved her husband and son dearly and was most grateful for Edith's help. As time passed, she continued to do her level best to fall in love with the wind-blown prairies as William had. Despite her efforts, her heart was still back in Ontario. Having always lived in an urban setting, the rural pioneer life style grated on her. She talked longingly of her life back East to William, Edith and Maud.

"Is there any chance you could see us moving back to Ontario some time in the future, dear?" Myrna asked William one day after getting a letter from her mother. "I know you like it out here, but I get so lonely for home."

"Both of us have good jobs and we have a small, but growing herd of cattle," William responded quietly. "Besides, the ranch is a good place to raise our son. Like Edith, I have many bad memories from Ontario. Aside from our individual preferences, let's get back to Rob's needs. Edith, Michael and Maud have all said that Rob will flourish here in a rural setting. Maybe you should try to make friends with a few of the ladies here on the ranch or in the surrounding area. That might help you out some."

"Well, Edith is really close to me and I get along well with Maud, but the other women here on the ranch don't seem to have the same interests that I have. Remember, before Rob was born, I did visit the wives here on the ranch and went to a couple of the local ladies' meetings. It seemed all they could talk about was crocheting, knitting, gardening, their favorite horses, how insensitive their husbands were to their needs, how isolated they felt and how they longed for indoor bathrooms."

William smiled, shook his head, but did not reply.

It took Myrna some time, but eventually she accepted William's position on making the West their home. Accepting his view didn't dissuade her personal longings though. She didn't bring it up anymore, but still felt sure that they'd be better off out of the wild West and back in what she considered to be the civilized part of the country.

It didn't help any that in their letters, both of their mothers were constantly lobbying Myrna and William to give serious thought to moving back East.

Back in Ontario, in a quiet ceremony, Mildred and Ken were married. As Ken was a successful businessman and financially secure, there was no need for Mildred to keep working. She left her job and got into volunteer work.

Since Michael's and Maud's grandchildren were all back in Montana, they cheerfully took on the role of surrogate grandparents to young Rob. Whenever William, Myrna or Edith were indisposed, Grandpa and Grandma Francis were there to look after the young gaffer.

For Rob's first birthday, Myrna's folks came out West to help celebrate the occasion. Although the accommodations were a bit more primitive than what they were accustomed to in Ontario, the couple had an enjoyable time visiting with Myrna and William and bonding with the youngster.

With the passage of time, William, Myrna and wee Rob were doing well and Myrna was becoming more and more aware that the rural setting was the place to raise Rob. By the time he was three, William would occasionally have Rob ride the range with him checking on the cattle.

On the ranch, they had a couple of milk cows. When Rob would accompany his dad for the evening milking, the young gaffer would get on his haunches close to the cow. William would squirt a fairly well-aimed stream of milk from the cow's teat into Rob's mouth. Mom and Aunty had Rob wear a large bib when he accompanied his dad for the evening milking. This saved a lot on shirt laundering when William's aim was a little off.

The young cowpoke was also bonding well with Edith. Although in her discipline of Rob, Edith was no pushover, in his view, Aunty could do no wrong. Edith loved the young rascal. To her, Rob was the son she never had.

The summer Rob was three, his grandpa Eric had a slight stroke. He was confined to bed for a short period, but suffered no paralysis and his speech was unaffected. All the family was keeping their fingers crossed that after the stroke, Eric would stop boozing or at least slow down some. Sadly, as with his heart attack, no sooner was he discharged from the hospital than he was back on the sauce again with a renewed vengeance.

On the ranch, young Rob was having the time of his life playing with the ranch kids. By the time he reached four, he was also doing more riding the range with his dad and now, occasionally with Michael.

Years before, a very stout cowboy well in excess of 300 pounds had hired on with Michael. Although the big cowboy was a dependable hand, Michael had to have a custom-built saddle made for him. The large cow puncher had moved on, but the saddle now came in handy. It was big enough for an adult and a child. Rob and his dad or Rob and Michael could quite comfortably ride the range together in the big saddle.

One day, while riding the range, Rob and his dad came upon a wild strawberry patch at the edge of the forested area. William tied up their horse and father and son began feasting on the berries.

As they were finishing their strawberry lunch, William found an agate in the grass. He showed Rob how to see its translucence by holding it up to the sun. It would be Rob's treasure and he put it on a shelf in his bedroom.

One of Rob's sidekicks was Ralph. Both young guys were full of vim and vinegar. Their caregivers didn't let them wander too far afield. Despite being relegated to an area within shouting distance of the buildings, the two were still capable of getting into plenty of mischief. In the summertime, for the most part, the boys went barefoot. As Myrna was to find out, foot-washing at the end of the day could be a bit challenging.

One day, Ralph decided it would be fun for the two of them to step in cow pies with their bare feet. Over the next hour or so he found about twenty semi-fresh cow pies to step in. Rob tried a couple, but the feeling of the cold cow manure squishing up between his toes was not to his liking. Myrna and Ralph's mother were not exactly tickled pink when it came time to clean the two rascals' feet that evening.

On another occasion, the two musketeers wandered a fair distance from the ranch buildings and ended up at the creek that ran down from the Cypress Hills. Soon they were scouring the creek bank looking for frogs. Ralph got a bit too close to the edge of the creek and fell in. The water was less than three feet deep, but in his attempt to pull his buddy out, Rob also fell in. Once they were out on terra firma, they thought it prudent not to go back to the buildings looking like two drowned rats. They lay on the creek bank drying themselves off in the afternoon sun. It was their hope that by the time they got back to the buildings, their care givers could not tell that they had been immersed.

Mildred took the train out West to help William and Myrna celebrate their sixth wedding anniversary. Mildred thoroughly enjoyed her visit with her sister, Edith, son William, daughter-in-law Myrna and grandson Rob. Even in the short time she had with Rob, they too were fast becoming buddies. She talked longingly of having Myrna, Rob, William and Edith move back to Ontario.

Back home, Mildred was thought to be a clairvoyant by some of the locals. She had premonitions of the deaths of several in the community. While staying at the ranch she had a very strange dream. She was flying like a bird above what looked like the body of a man and the body of a large bear on the ground. As at the time it seemed inconsequential, she thought of it as just a strange dream and kept it to herself.

Mildred thoroughly enjoyed her visit, but left for home before the school year started.

CHAPTER 7

B ACK AT THE ranch, the fall roundup had been completed
and the young stock destined to be marketed were shipped
out. With the rail head only twenty miles from the ranch, it
didn't take long to herd the young stock to the stockyards.

Fall had now turned to early winter. As they were eating
supper on Friday evening, William turned to Myrna. "I'm
riding over to the northeast end of our range in the morning
to see if I can find some stragglers back in the bush. When we
tallied up all of the cattle, there were twenty or so cows and
their calves that we couldn't account for. Chances are they
were back in the bush and we missed them when we did the
roundup. It snowed a couple of inches this morning so if the
critters are out there, I should be able to track them."

"Can I come with you, Daddy?" Rob asked.

"Not this time, son. It's okay for you to ride with me on the
open range, but it's too dangerous back in the bush."

There were a couple of rituals that were followed in the
Burke household. After helping Myrna and Edith with the
supper dishes, William would take out his pipe and light up.
He was very disciplined with his smoking and would only
smoke one pipe full. It was a quiet time for the small family
and both Myrna and Rob grew to love the aroma of the pipe

smoke. Edith abided it. Before Rob went to sleep, the second ritual came into play. Myrna, William and Aunty Edith each had to read him a bedtime story.

This evening, after the customary three bedtime stories were read, they all turned in.

William had a troubled sleep. In the early morning hours, he dreamt that he was at the edge of the timber. Suddenly, he found himself flying like an eagle. As he soared higher and higher, he could see the ranch buildings some distance to the southwest.

When he looked down, he saw what looked like a man and a large bear sprawled on the ground. William awoke with a start to a strange feeling of foreboding.

William, Myrna and Edith were up early. While they were eating breakfast, William told the ladies of his odd dream.

"The dream gives me an uneasy feeling. I guess I have to remember though that it's just a dream."

Myrna wrote it off as just an interesting dream. Still, the dream gave her pause. Although Edith did not make any comment, like William and Myrna, she too had an uneasy feeling. She remembered some of her sister Mildred's dreams that foretold of deaths back in Ontario. She also recalled a recent letter from Mildred. While visiting the ranch in the summer, Mildred mentioned the strange dream she had about flying high and seeing a man and a bear laying on the ground.

William had been gone for several hours when Rob got up. As Myrna was in the school marking papers, Edith made the young lad breakfast.

"I had a funny dream," he began as he was eating. "I saw Daddy flying like a big bird, only he didn't flap his arms like birds do. Anyway, he just flew up so high that I couldn't see him anymore."

Edith sucked in her breath. The uneasy feeling she had over William's dream was returning. While Rob was playing with his toys, Edith went into the school to talk to Myrna.

"It's unreal, but Rob had basically the same kind of dream that William had," Edith said. "Back home in the native culture when two people close to each other have the same frightening dream at the same time, it's an omen of trouble. Maybe I shouldn't be so superstitious, but I just have this heavy feeling."

"I'm sure everything will be alright," Myrna replied, fighting panic. "Who knows, maybe it's something that William read to Rob that they both dreamt about." She tried to laugh it off, but her laugh was forced.

William decided to take a new horse to look for the stragglers rather than his regular mount. He made sure he had his rifle with him in a scabbard. A strong wind had been blowing from the west all night and now with daylight coming, it was howling. As the sun was coming up, he was on his way. When he neared the forested area, he picked up fresh cattle tracks in the snow. By the number of tracks, he was sure he'd found the stragglers. Sometimes the tracks were in the bush, sometimes out on the range. At last, he followed the tracks deep into the bush. As the tracks headed back to the open range, it looked like the cattle were running. Just as he got to the edge of the prairie, he noticed a strange track. With his rifle in hand he dismounted and led his horse.

"Damn it," he muttered. "That's a bear track. It's big enough to be a grizzly. That's probably why the cattle are running."

As he looked towards the buildings, he saw the cattle some half mile ahead, running towards the building site.

Had William not been so intent on looking at the bear tracks, he'd have seen the freshly killed calf off to the left, a short distance from the edge of the bush. He would also have noticed a large raven slowly circling above him. With the strong wind blowing, he didn't hear the sound of something approaching him from the rear.

Suddenly, William heard a sound from behind him.

"God Almighty!" he blurted out as he turned around. A horrifying sight met his eyes. A huge grizzly had been stalking William and his horse and was only 15 feet away. With a terrifying roar, the bear stood up and swatted the back of the horse. The horse screamed in pain, yanked the reigns from William's hand and bolted.

The bear was still standing on its hind legs as William dropped to one knee and furiously pumped six shots from his lever-action 30-30 rifle into the bear's huge chest. The last shot was right into the heart. As the bear was reeling in its death throws, it hovered over William and delivered a vicious blow to his head, breaking his neck.

The bear fell backwards, collapsing dead in a pool of its own blood. The powerful blow knocked William for several feet. He lay there, motionless, sprawled in the snow.

"Please, God, look after Myrna, Rob and Edith," William whispered as his soul left his shattered body.

Instantly, William was hovering over the death scene. Glancing down, he saw the dead bear and his body sprawled on the ground.

"Oh, dear God, so this is what my dream was about," his spirit mused.

Looking far to the southwest he saw the ranch's buildings, the cattle running for the corrals and his horse hobbling home behind them.

"I must try to get in touch with Myrna, Rob and Edith."

Instantly, William was in Myrna's classroom, trying desperately to communicate with her. As she was concentrating on her school work, William failed to make his presence known.

Edith was sitting watching Rob play, her thoughts centered on William's dream. Suddenly, she saw an apparition of William come in through the unopened door. The spirit hovered over Rob, but was unable to communicate with him either as he was concentrating on playing with his toys.

William moved toward Edith. He smiled, hovered for a moment and slowly passed through the wall. He rose up in the air again. Glancing upwards, he saw a bright light opening up in the cloudy sky. As he whispered, "I love you, Myrna and Rob," his soul sped towards the light and into the next dimension.

Edith again dropped in on Myrna and told her about William's spirit visiting her.

"Oh, my God," Myrna gasped. "I wonder what it all means. I guess there's no sense panicking though. Despite your vision, all we can do is hope that all is well."

"When William told us about his strange dream this morning, it brought to mind something pretty scary that Mildred wrote about in her last letter," Edith replied "I didn't mention this to you before because it seemed so inconsequential and I didn't want to frighten you. She wrote that while she was here in the summer, she had a strange dream about flying high and looking down on a big bear and a man lying on the ground. Her dream is getting too close to William's and Rob's dreams for comfort."

"God help us all," Myrna said. "Oh, dear God, please help us all."

"A bunch of cattle are coming," Tom called out. "Probably they're the stragglers William was looking for." Tom was glancing out the cookhouse window as the crew was having their morning coffee break.

"There's a saddled horse hobbling home behind the cattle, but I don't see William."

Michael and the hands went out to open the corral gate. Once the stragglers saw the other cattle in the corral, they headed in the gate. Finally, William's horse hobbled in.

"I'm afraid we got problems, boys," Michael called out after checking over the injured horse. "Wilfred, could you put the horse in the barn? See what you can do for the poor critter. I'm positive those deep slashes to its rump are from a grizzly bear attack. Although some people think otherwise, I believe there are still grizzlies up in the hills. Dear God, I hope William's okay. Let's saddle up and see if we can find him."

The men all hustled to the barn and mounted up. Michael led the way as they followed the cattle and horse tracks back towards the bush. A short distance from the edge of the bush, Michael spotted the dead grizzly bear. As they rushed up, they saw William sprawled in the snow beside the bear. He was still holding his rifle in his right hand. Although there was very little blood on his face, by the horrible angle of William's head they knew the bear had broken his neck. Michael got off his horse and went over to William to check him for vital signs. He found none. The death stare from his open eyes told all.

"My son, my son," Michael whispered. As he stroked William's forehead, tears were slipping down his old weather-worn cheeks. "God Almighty, I should have gone with you. I should have gone with you. Why, oh why didn't I go with you?"

Regaining his composure, Michael continued. "I wonder if a couple of you fellows could go back to the ranch and get a team and democrat. We'll have to bring the body back to the building site. I'll go and break the news to Myrna, Edith and little Rob. God only knows how I wish I'd have gone with William this morning."

"In the next few days we must bury this damn grizzly bear. The last thing we need is for Myrna, Rob or Edith to see the horrible creature."

As Michael headed to the buildings, he was constantly chastising himself for not going with William. Finally, he rode up to the school.

Maud had gone over to the school to tell them about the injured, rider-less horse returning to the buildings and Michael and the hands heading out on horseback looking for William. Once Maud had gone back to the cookshack, Edith returned to the teacherage to look after Rob.

Myrna sat at her desk, writhing in anguish, so terrified of what it all meant. She was hoping against hope that it would not be the news of her beloved's death that Michael and the boys would bring her.

"Please dear God, don't let the news be bad," she constantly prayed.

When Myrna saw Michael ride up, she opened the school door. The look on Michael's face told her that her worst suspicions had come true.

"There's bad news about William?" she blurted out.

"I'm afraid so," Michael replied, striding over and wrapping his arms around her. "William and his horse were attacked by a grizzly bear on the edge of the timber. The horse escaped with bad lacerations to its rump, but William didn't make it. He managed to kill the bear, but it looks like the bear broke William's neck before it died. The boys will bring his body in with the team and the democrat. God, how I wish I'd gone with William this morning."

Michael held Myrna close as she cried uncontrollably. Between sobs she told Michael of William's, Rob's and Mildred's dreams and William's spirit visiting Edith. Gaining some control, Myrna opened the door to their living quarters and she and Michael stepped inside.

"Bad news," Michael blurted out to Edith and Rob. "I'm afraid a grizzly bear attacked William and his horse. The horse escaped, but has bad cuts to its rump. As near as we can piece it together, though William shot the bear, before the bear died, it killed him. It looks like the bear swatted him, breaking his neck."

Myrna hugged Rob and Edith. They all cried.

Growing up on a ranch Rob had seen a lot of animals die, but the news of his dad's death was a horrible blow to the lad. He and his dad were very close.

"I should have gone with my daddy to help him fight the bear," Rob cried out between sobs. "I'm glad Daddy killed that bad bear."

Just before noon, the democrat carrying William's body arrived at the buildings.

"What are your wishes about viewing William's body?" Michael asked Myrna when they were alone. "I've looked the body over and it appears to me that the only injury was a broken neck. Tom is on his way to town to report William's death to the police. They may have to make out a report and might want to do an investigation."

"Edith and I would like to see William one more time," Myrna replied, fighting for composure. "Rob says he wants to see his daddy too, but I don't know if that would be wise. Edith thinks it might help to give him closure. Edith and I will have to talk it over."

They lay William's body on a low table in one of their sheds. When the men discovered William's body, Tom had closed his eyes and placed a couple of coins on his eyelids to keep them closed. Michael and Maud cleaned off the little blood there was on William's head and neck to make the body appear as normal as possible.

By mid-afternoon, Tom was back with the police. After extending his condolences to the family, the officer took statements from Michael, the other hands and briefly examined the body. Michael and the officer then rode out to the site where the bear had killed William. They found the empty cartridge shells from William's rifle beside the dead bear. After looking things over, they returned to the buildings.

Edith and Myrna discussed Rob's request to see his daddy's body. They decided to let Rob see his dad one more time. It was now late afternoon. With Maud and Michael leading, the sobbing trio of Myrna, Edith and Rob stepped inside the shed.

"My daddy, my daddy," Rob cried out as he went over to his dad's body and placed his little hand on his dad's forehead. "Why did that bad bear kill you, Daddy? Why is Daddy's skin so cold?" Finally, he turned to his mom and Edith. "Will I ever see my daddy again?" he sobbed.

"You will Rob," Edith replied. "Your daddy's soul is as alive as you are. Remember, your daddy came to me today. I'm sure he will come to visit you. You'll just have to be patient."

Rob, Edith, Michael and Maud left to allow Myrna a few minutes alone with William.

"If only you had listened to me and we'd moved back to Ontario," she sobbed. "I hate this wild savage country, hate it, hate it, hate it! Why were you such a risk-taker?"

No one was that hungry, but the single hands, the North West Mounted Police officer and the rest of the family sat down for supper. After talking things over with Michael and the hands, the officer made out his report. He advised them that though William died tragically, as no foul play was involved, no further investigation would be needed.

Michael and Myrna contacted the Anglican minister who conducted the funeral for Neil and Ted many years before. Pastor Neufeld agreed to do the service. Rather than moving the body the long distance to the church by horse and buggy, then back again for the interment, he agreed to come to the ranch to hold the interment service at the graveside. The funeral would be held Monday afternoon.

Sunday morning, the hands rode out to where the grizzly lay. They dragged the body a quarter of a mile away and buried it in a shallow grave. They then went back to the place where William had died and erected a small cross. Before they left, they placed a block of wood at the base of the cross in case a person wished to come and sit for a spell.

When they had finished, the hands returned to a small knoll overlooking the ranch buildings and dug William's grave. Although there was a fair amount of cursing that accompanied the burying of the grizzly, quite a few tears were shed by the hands as they dug their friend's grave. While the grave was being dug, some of the other hands built a simple box that would be used as a coffin.

Word spread fast about William's death and by Monday afternoon, 50 plus neighbors had gathered for the service. At the close of the service, Eleanor, one of the neighbor ladies, sang 'It is Well with My Soul', accompanied by her husband on the violin. With a chinook breeze blowing from the west, the whispering of the prairie wool (grass) added to the beauty of the song. The rendering of the hymn brought many a tear to the family, work hands and neighbors.

In the morning, there had been a private viewing of the body. On Myrna's request, there was no public viewing at the funeral. Myrna and Edith thought it would be less traumatic for Rob if the casket wasn't lowered at the close of the service. They draped a blanket over the casket. At sunset, after all the funeral guests had left, the hands lowered the casket and back-filled the grave. Michael and the hands placed another wooden cross at the head of the grave. When summer came, they would replace the cross with a headstone.

The day following the funeral, Myrna, Rob, Edith, Michael, Maud and all the ranch families made a pilgrimage to the spot where William had died. Pastor Neufeld accompanied them on his own mount. The women and children rode in horse drawn buggies. All the adult men were on horseback. Michael used his big saddle so Rob could ride with him. Michael and Rob trailed William's regular horse. The horse was saddled up with a pair of William's cowboy boots placed backwards in the stirrups to indicate that its rider had passed away. Although the men tried to hold a stiff upper lip, the women and children for the most part were in tears. Despite their resolve not to break down, Michael and some of the hands were in tears too. Michael tacked William's cowboy hat to the centre piece of the cross and slipped his cowboy boots, one over each end of the cross arm. After a few words of comfort from the minister, he and Eleanor, accompanied by her husband on the violin, sang 'God Be with You Till We Meet Again.' After Pastor Neufeld offered a humble prayer, the entourage headed back to the ranch. Back to a life without William.

CHAPTER 8

THE NEXT DAYS and weeks were hard on the family, especially for Rob. Every night he cried himself to sleep, needing so badly to have his daddy read him his bedtime story.

Although it was difficult for her, Myrna returned to the classroom a week after the funeral. Keeping busy with her pupils was good therapy. When she broke down in class, she would send one of the students to fetch Edith. Rob would tag along and Edith would maintain order with the students until Myrna was able to gain control of herself again.

Finally, Edith devised a plan she thought would help Rob with his grief and give him some closure.

"When I was a young girl my grandma lived with us," she said to Rob one evening. "She told me that as a young girl, she lived in a native village. Their Medicine Man told them that if someone we like dies, sometimes their spirit will come to us if we call for them every day."

It was all the encouragement that Rob needed. Late in the afternoon, while there was still daylight, he'd walk to the gate where he could see his dad's grave and in his strongest voice call out, "Daddy, Daddy, Daddy." Edith advised him that he should only call for his daddy three times. In the weeks to come, it became a heart-rending ritual listening to the wee lad calling out for his daddy.

It was now winter and Rob was still having a difficult time as his calling had brought no results. His nightly, "Daddy, Daddy, Daddy," was also getting heavy for Myrna and Edith and everyone else at the ranch. Several weeks after William's death, Edith talked with Myrna on Rob's lack of closure over his dad's death.

"I'm wondering if I should have promised young Rob that someday his dad's spirit would visit him," Edith began, shaking her head. "Rob was telling me today that maybe his daddy has forgotten him."

"What to do, what to do?" Myrna replied. "We're all trying so hard to help him, but nothing seems to work. I was talking to Maud today. She said that Rob might have to work out the loss of his dad on his own."

A few nights later, Rob awoke at two am from a vivid dream. He and his dad were riding the range. They stopped near a clump of trees and climbed off the horse. The ground was covered with wild strawberries. After getting his fill of the sweet berries, Rob turned around to see where his dad was. His dad was nowhere in sight.

Rob was in a panic. When he awoke, he realized to his sorrow that it was only a dream and that his beloved daddy was no more. His loneliness was so acute that he devised a plan so he could be close to his dad. He decided to take his feather tick sleeping bag and go sleep by his dad's grave.

Because Rob's bedroom was a bit drafty, Edith had taken a feather tick and made it into a sleeping bag for him. He quietly dressed, hoping that he wouldn't wake his mom or Edith. He had watched Edith roll up the sleeping bag and slip it into its sack. He found the storage bag under his bed. He tried hard to stuff the sleeping bag into it's carrying case, but finally had to give up.

Pulling on his winter boots, he quietly stepped outside without waking anyone and headed out to his dad's grave. It was a warm evening at the end of a chinook with the temperature still above freezing. Being it was so warm, he didn't bother with his winter coat. He had problems with handling the awkward sleeping bag and ended up half carrying, half dragging it.

The chinook winds had melted almost all of the snow, but now the chinook arch in the southwest had shifted to the northwest, a sign that winter was on the verge of returning. Michael and the hands had built a small wooden shelter around the grave to keep the cattle from knocking the cross over. Reaching his dad's grave, Rob took his winter boots off, put his sleeping bag beside the cross and wiggled into it. He pulled it up over his head and soon was fast asleep.

By four am, winter returned with a vengeance and the temperature was dropping. Snow was falling and being driven by a strong northwest wind. Soon the ground was blanketed with the white stuff. Being inside the grave shelter and in his warm sleeping bag, Rob had protection from the falling temperature and the driving snow. The young guy, oblivious to the change of weather, lay snug as a bug in his own cocoon.

At five am, Myrna awoke to the hissing sound of snow being driven against her bedroom window.

"It`s good being in a warm house with a winter storm blowing in," she thought, "I`d better put some more wood in the heater."

She lit the coal oil lamp and filled the heater. She was about to climb into bed again when her mothering instinct kicked in. "I'd better check on Rob and see if he needs another blanket," she thought.

Carrying the lamp, she headed into Rob's room. "Oh my God, oh my God!" she cried out. "Rob's not here!"

She checked under the bed, but there was nothing there. "I can't find Rob, he's not in his bed," she called out to Edith.

Both Edith and Myrna checked the house and school, but Rob was nowhere to be found. Myrna and Edith were in a dead panic as they pulled on their winter clothes and hurried to Michael's and Maud's house.

"Bad news," Myrna blurted out when Michael came to the door. "Rob's missing. With this storm coming on, I checked his bedroom to see if he needed another blanket and he was gone. We have no idea how long it's been since he left the house."

Soon Michael had the whole crew up and they were checking every building and haystack in the yard-site.

"A short time ago, Rob told me that he wanted to go to the spot where his dad was killed by the bear." Edith said to Michael. "Could he have headed out that way?"

Michael sent two of the hands, on horseback, to see if Rob had headed out to that spot. The boys had to turn back a quarter of a mile from the buildings as it had become a complete white out.

At six am everyone was back in the cookhouse feeling very disconsolate. They were all silent. Finally, Edith spoke. "When Myrna and I checked out our house we were in a dead panic. I know we checked his room for his clothes and the porch for his winter boots, but I don't think we checked to see if his sleeping bag was still there."

"You're right," Myrna replied. "We were in such a dither, I'm sure we didn't check on his sleeping bag. I'll go check it out now." Myrna jumped to her feet and headed out the door. In a few minutes, she was back. "The sleeping bag is gone, so at least he has some protection from this storm, but where on earth could he be?"

"While you were gone, Myrna, another thought occurred to me," Edith replied. "I don't know why I didn't think of this up until now, but many times since William's death, Rob had me take him for a walk up to his dad's grave. Is there a possibility he went up to the grave to be close to his dad?"

"Oh God, I hope so," Myrna blurted out, again jumping to her feet.

In a few minutes, the whole entourage was heading up to William's grave. One of the hands was pulling a toboggan. By the light of a lantern, they saw a lump under the snow near the cross. There was Rob. Although his sleeping bag was completely covered with snow, he was warm as toast and not all that happy to be wakened from his winter slumber.

Still in his sleeping bag, Rob was loaded onto the toboggan and they headed back to the kitchen. Soon Michael and the hands were drinking coffee. Everyone was relieved that the lost boy had been found.

"Whatever possessed you to go to your dad's grave in the middle of the night in a snow storm?" Myrna asked Rob while Maud and Edith were making breakfast.

"Well, I had a bad dream. I was with my daddy. We were out on the range picking strawberries. When I turned around, he was gone. I looked and looked for him and called and called for him, but I couldn't find him. When I woke up, I was crying and really sad. I was so lonely for Daddy that I thought I'd take my sleeping bag and go up to his grave to sleep beside him. I didn't want to wake you or Aunty up. It was warm and wasn't snowing then."

"You must promise Aunty and me that you'll never do this again. If you get really sad, you must come to us even though it's the middle of the night. We were all worried sick."

"Okay, I won't do it again. I was just so lonely for my daddy."

"What do you think of the idea of taking Rob to the place where his dad died?" Myrna asked Edith later that day. "He told you that he wanted to go there again. Do you think that would help him some?"

"It well could help," Edith replied. "It's certainly worth a try. I'm beginning to wonder if my suggestion of him calling for his dad every day was such a good idea. I think we're both at the point where we should be willing to try anything that might help him. Maybe we should talk to Michael and see if he could take him out there on horseback."

On Friday, after school was out for the day, Myrna went over to the cookhouse. While the crew was having their afternoon coffee break, she talked to Michael about their plan.

"I'll come right over," Michael replied. "I'll ask Rob to come out with me tomorrow to check on the cattle."

Before Rob could do his calling for his dad, Michael dropped in. "Say Rob, I'm going riding out on the range tomorrow. Would you like to come with me and give me a hand?"

"I'd like that. I'll ask Mom."

Mom gave her blessing. Rob was very excited with the invite to go riding with his big buddy and even forgot to go out to call for his dad.

After breakfast, Michael was at the door to pick up his small hand. As Michael was using the large custom-made saddle, he and Rob were able to ride together comfortably. It was a pleasant day with a strong southwest wind blowing. The snow from the recent storm was melting and the cattle were again grazing on the range. After riding for three hours, checking fences close to the forested area, Michael and Rob rode to the small log cabin they had back in the bush. Maud had provided them with a big lunch. Michael lit a fire in the airtight heater and soon the cabin was starting to warm up. Both cowboys ate heartily.

"If you'd like, maybe we could go again to the spot where your dad shot that grizzly," Michael said when they'd finished eating.

"I'd like that," Rob replied. "Maybe we'll see another bear we can shoot."

"Yes, we just might see one. We'll have to keep our eyes peeled."

In a few minutes, they were at the cross that marked the spot where William and the grizzly had died. The block of wood was still there.

"I have an idea," Michael said. "Every night you call for your daddy. If you wouldn't be too scared, maybe you could sit on that block for a bit and call your daddy again. You can't be disappointed if he doesn't come though. Your daddy came to your aunty the day he died, but as she said, you have to be patient. I could just ride away some. You'll still be able to see me and if you get scared all you have to do is call me."

"Okay, but don't go too far away. I'll be a little bit scared sitting here all by myself."

After helping the small cowboy off the horse, Michael rode off a short distance and then turned so he could see Rob. Rob looked at the cross for a spell and then sat down on the block. Michael had just dismounted to adjust the saddle when he saw a large raven slowly circling high over the cross.

While he was looking up at the bird, he heard the plaintive call of, "Daddy, Daddy, Daddy!" Michael glanced back at Rob. The young lad suddenly leapt off the block and ran a few feet to the west, all the while calling, "Daddy, Daddy!"

Michael could hardly believe his eyes. A short distance from Rob, he saw a bright, shining cloud that had descended from the sky. Light was radiating from it. As he watched, spellbound, the young lad ran towards the bright cloud. As the cloud started to thin out, Michael observed what looked like a human figure inside it.

"My God, that's William!" Michael exclaimed. William seemed to float rather than walk.

In a moment, the cloud started to thicken. It completely encompassed Rob, cutting off Michael's view. For some time, the bright cloud hovered around Rob. Then, as the cloud grew brighter, it started to lift up. Michael lost sight of the cloud as it shot skyward.

"Grandpa Francis, Grandpa Francis, Grandpa Francis!"

Young Rob was racing towards Michael. "Grandpa Francis, Daddy came to visit me and he was bright. He said he was happy. He said to look after Mom and that he'd watch over us. Then he hugged me and he was warm, really warm just like he used to be and then he went straight up into the sky!"

"Yes, I could hardly believe my eyes, but I saw your daddy too," Michael replied. "I saw you going to the cloud and then the bright cloud and your daddy shot up into the sky."

As Michael hugged his little cowboy, Rob was shaking with excitement.

"Should we go back to the ranch and tell Mom, Edith and Maud what happened?"

"Yes, let's go, let's go!" Rob cried out as he jumped up and down.

Just then, something caught the young lad's eye. Close to where his dad's spirit visited him, Rob saw something shining on the path. He went over and picked it up.

"Look Grandpa, it's an agate, just like the one my daddy found this summer! See how shiny it is!"

Michael took the agate, held it to his eye and glanced up at the sky.

"It's an agate alright, Rob. They're very rare. Over all the years we've been down here we've only found three or four of them."

Rob held the agate up to the sky so he could see its translucence.

"Do you think Daddy brought it?"

"That's possible, son, but we'll never know."

Rob put the agate in his pocket and they headed out.

Soon they were back at the building site. Michael rode up to Myrna's house. He dismounted and helped Rob down. Rob raced to find his mom and Edith. They had seen Michael and Rob riding up and were already at the door.

"I saw Daddy. I saw Daddy, I really saw him," Rob cried as he ran to his mom. After telling of his dad's visit, he added, "and you know what Mom? When Daddy hugged me, he was warm, Mom, he was really, really warm, just like he used to be. And he said I didn't have to call for him anymore and then he went shooting up into the sky really fast. And then I found this agate right beside the cross." Rob showed the ladies his precious rock. "I wonder if Daddy left it there for me?"

"I've never seen anything like this in my life," Michael added, shaking his head. "To give Rob some privacy, I was about a hundred feet away." Michael told Myrna and Edith about Rob's and his remarkable experience. "There's no question in my mind that William came to Rob to give him closure."

When Michael described the incident to the crew at supper, no one made light of it. They all shook their heads in amazement.

With the visitation of William's spirit, a new chapter had opened up for all of them. Although they still pined for him, everyone knew that though William was dead, they had assurance that his soul lived on.

The agate was very special to Rob. He kept it on the shelf in his room by the other agate and spent many an hour of his leisure time thinking of his dad and playing with the translucent gems.

Michael did his best to take Rob under his wing and provide him some adult male influence. There was no question that the young lad loved and admired his surrogate granddad. In the weeks after William's death, Michael would take Rob with him, riding the range, visiting the neighbors or even for the long trip to Irvine or Medicine Hat with his trotting team and buggy.

Although Rob was basically a good, kind lad, he now lacked the influence of his dad. William was never harsh with Rob, but didn't allow him to get away with any tomfoolery. Like William, Michael expected and insisted that Rob comport himself properly when he was with him. Considering his great loss, Myrna didn't have the heart or the will to be too strident in her disciplining of Rob when he misbehaved. Edith confided to Maud and Michael that Myrna's lack of discipline with Rob was no gift to the young guy. They both agreed.

Christmas was a heavy time for Myrna, Rob and Edith. It was a tradition for William, Myrna, Edith and Rob to head back into the forested part of the ranch for Christmas trees. They used a team of horses and a sleigh if there was snow on the ground and a wagon if the ground was bare. This year, Michael offered to take them out for the trees, but the three were feeling too down to accept his offer. Michael and some of the hands did the Christmas tree run. They dropped off Myrna's tree and Maud came over to help Edith decorate it. It was a very subdued Christmas. Maud and Michael had Myrna, Rob and Edith over for Christmas Day. Many tears were shed as they played Christmas carols on their gramophone and talked of past Christmases with William.

CHAPTER 9

AFTER MUCH AGONIZING over her new lot in life, Myrna felt very strongly that they should leave the ranch. While William was alive, Myrna depended on him for support, but with him gone, her dislike of the West started to manifest itself again. She had already started looking for greener pastures. Even though Rob missed his dad a great deal, he still loved the ranch with a passion. He was lobbying long and hard for them to stay where they were. The ranch was the only life he knew. In discussing the matter with Myrna, Edith tried to remain neutral though she thought that rural life was better for youngsters than living in town.

Although Edith was always there for Myrna, throughout the long winter months, she struggled with loneliness. Towards spring, depression was setting in. Edith, Maud and Michael did their level best to help her through the rough times, but the depression still lingered. When she felt that she was nearing the end of her rope, she sent a letter to her mom, Maria, asking her if she could come out West to visit her.

Maria arrived by train for the Easter break. Having her mom for support helped Myrna a great deal. Myrna spent many hours with her mom talking of the good times she had with William and then recounting the happy life she'd had before coming out West.

"Losing William is almost more than I can bear," Myrna said to her mom one day when they were alone. "God knows, I've done my best to fit into this wild, barren land. While William was still alive, I sort of leaned on him, but now, with him gone, living in this rural, forsaken country is grating more and more on my nerves. As I see it, this frontier land is a man's country."

"I can see where you're coming from," Maria replied. "I find the West more than a little primitive myself. With William gone, what have you got keeping you out here? Why not come back to Ontario? You've mentioned that Rob wants to stay here on the ranch, but you must remember, he's still a child. If you were to come back home, I'm sure that in no time at all, he'd fit right in."

Her mom's strong support and advice helped reinforce Myrna's mindset that she must make a change for Rob and herself. Moving off the ranch now seemed their only option. After much thought, Myrna decided that it would be easier on Rob if they could spend one more year close to the ranch before moving back to Ontario. A week after her mom went back East, she made an application for a teaching position in Medicine Hat for the next year.

Within two weeks of making the application, Myrna was notified that she was awarded the position for grade three in Medicine Hat for the next school year. As Myrna expected, Rob emphatically made known that he wanted them to stay on the ranch. Over time, his lobbying only intensified. He was concerned that he'd be losing Michael, his big buddy. He also didn't want to lose the ranch's younger kids that he played with. Both Michael and Maud in their quiet way did their own lobbying to try to keep Myrna, Edith and Rob on the ranch. Even though they had recently built Myrna,

Rob and Edith better living quarters and were planning on building a new schoolhouse, Myrna refused to change her mind. Edith, Maud and Michael finally threw in the towel and reluctantly began supporting her with her plan of moving off the ranch.

Myrna had always been somewhat jealous of the strong bond that had grown between William and Michael and now that William was gone, the closeness that was evolving between Michael and Rob. With each passing day, she grew more resentful of the ranch. In some convoluted way, she blamed the ranch for William's death. To add to her concern, although Maud and Edith had become very close over the years, Myrna and Maud's relationship, though pleasant, still remained a bit distant.

Myrna was now openly talking to Edith about the three of them moving back to Ontario in the near future to be closer to family.

Because William had worked faithfully for them for many years, Michael and Maude bought a fairly new house for Myrna and Rob in Medicine Hat. In addition, with Myrna's blessing, they bought William's and her small herd of cattle. Myrna deposited the money from the sale of their herd in the local bank. Seeing they would need accommodations when she and Rob moved back to Ontario, she thought it prudent not to touch the money until she and Rob moved back East.

At the end of June, Myrna and Rob were on their way back East to visit her folks and Mildred and Ken. Both Mildred and Maria thought the West to be a primitive country and were doing their best to convince Myrna to move back to Ontario as soon as possible.

By mid-July, having just returned from Ontario, Myrna, Edith and Rob were on the move into Medicine Hat. Michael and the crew loaded all of Myrna's and Rob's earthly possessions in a couple of wagons and delivered them to their new house in Medicine Hat. Michael and Maud insisted that Myrna, Edith and Rob stay in close contact with them. They encouraged Myrna to let Rob return to the ranch for visits and on holidays. Although they were aware of Myrna's intent to move back to Ontario, they were still holding the faint hope that she'd have a change of mind and stay in western Canada.

It was a difficult adjustment for Rob to move off the ranch into Medicine Hat. Not only did he lose his playmates and Michael, his big buddy, he pined for the wide-open spaces and the windblown prairies. The occasional visit back to the ranch helped, but living in town made him feel like a fish out of water. Starting school in an urban centre was traumatic for him as few of his classmates had his interests. Rob found himself on the outside looking in. Every opportunity that arose, he kept after his mom to move back to the ranch. Myrna in turn was lobbying long and hard on the advantages of living in town. Edith observed that a stalemate had been reached as neither one was being swayed by the other's arguments.

With Myrna, Edith and Rob gone, Michael and Maud had to find another teacher. They were also short-handed with William gone. Michael was now getting up in years and needed to start slowing down. Their answer came from Maud's sons Paul and Carl and their respective families.

Down on the Lopez ranch, Eli had retired and both Carl and Paul were having real difficulty working with Leroy, Eli's son. Leroy was only motivated by the dollar. He had made a big cut to his number of hands and was not above working the rumps off those that were left. Leroy made it known that he was aiming for complete ownership of the ranch. When he offered to buy out Carl's and Paul's interest in the ranch at a fair price, the brothers sold out to him.

Once the buy-out was made, Carl, his wife Wilma, along with Paul and his wife Sue traveled up to Michael's and Maud's ranch to talk things over with them. Wilma was a teacher and agreed to take over the teaching position. Paul and Carl would buy into the ranch. Before school started in the fall, Paul, Carl and their families left Montana and moved to the Francis ranch.

Michael and Maud were overjoyed to have Carl, Wilma, Paul, Sue and their families back in the fold again. Sue would give Maud a much-needed hand in the kitchen.

It became obvious to Edith that it was an increasing struggle for Myrna to keep a close bond with the ranch. She, Edith and Rob spent Thanksgiving at the ranch, but Edith observed that Myrna was having a hard time. "I'm happy for Michael and Maud," Myrna commented to Edith when they were alone, "but I can't help but feel uncomfortable and sad when I realize that Carl, Wilma, Paul and Sue are sort of replacing William and me."

Maud had invited the three of them to come back to the ranch to spend Christmas with Michael and her, but Myrna had her own ideas. She was making plans for Rob, her and possibly Edith to go back to Ontario to be with family for the holiday.

When the Christmas holidays came, Myrna and Rob were on the train for Ontario, while Edith had decided to spend Christmas with Michael and Maud. Rob was not a happy camper and made it known to his mom in no uncertain terms that he would have much preferred to spend the holidays at the ranch with Michael, Maud and the ranch kids.

After arriving back in Ontario, Myrna and Rob dropped in on Mildred and Ken. Mildred advised Myrna that nothing would make her happier than to have her, Rob and Edith move back to Ontario. Before heading back out West, Myrna made an inquiry of the local school superintendent about teaching opportunities in the immediate area. Although there were currently no positions available, he said he'd contact her if any opening were to come up in the near future. With each passing day, Myrna was becoming more determined to move back East.

All too soon for her liking, Myrna and Rob were on the train heading back to Medicine Hat.

"I really don't like going to school here," Rob said once they were home again. "I wish I could go to school at the ranch. Before Christmas, one of the grade two boys made fun of me when I told him that my daddy was killed by a bear. He laughed at me and said that I was just making the story up. He said everyone knows that bears never kill people."

"That sure was unkind of him. Why didn't you tell me about it? Did you at least tell your teacher?"

"No, I just punched him real hard in the face and he cried, but no one told the teacher so we didn't get in trouble."

After school, each Friday, the local churches in Medicine Hat, in conjunction with the elementary school, held a Bible club for an hour. Attendance was optional. The Protestant clergy and the Catholic priest held their classes in separate classrooms. Initially, Myrna observed that Rob really enjoyed the church classes.

"I've noticed that you no longer go to the church clubs," Myrna said to Rob one Friday after school. "You told me before that you liked going to the Catholic Bible Class. Did something happen that made you change your mind about the clubs?"

"I don't want to talk about it," was Rob's terse reply.

As it seemed inconsequential to Myrna, she didn't pursue the issue any further.

In late March, Myrna got notification from the school superintendent that they would have a vacancy in Benville, next fall as two of the older teachers were retiring. Myrna was elated with the news. Benville was her old hometown. Rob's reaction to moving back to Ontario was hardly what she'd hoped for though.

"You can go if you want to, but I want to go back to the ranch. That's where my daddy is. I don't like it here in Medicine Hat and I know I won't like it in Ontario."

Myrna shook her head, but could not think of a comeback. As time passed, the more she tried to convince Rob on the merits of moving back East, the more opposed he was becoming to the idea.

Edith kept mum over the arguments between Myrna and Rob. She was happy out West. She had such bad memories of her failed marriage that she had decided that she would never go back to Ontario to live.

Although Edith still did a lot of the housework, in early January, with Rob in school, she got a part time job in the Old Folks' Home. Not only did this give her the outing she had longed for, it helped Myrna out as she was only paying Edith at a half time rate.

"Honestly, Rob," Myrna said one day after another unsuccessful attempt at trying to get the lad enthused about moving to Ontario. "You really make Mummy upset. You're every bit as stubborn as your dad was."

"Don't talk mean things about my daddy," Rob shot back. "My daddy was my really good friend."

"I'm concerned that I can't get Rob even a little bit interested about moving back East," Myrna began one day when she and Edith were by themselves. "He's just so stubborn and determined. What are your thoughts about going back to Ontario?"

"I'm afraid I'd prefer to stay here," Edith replied quietly. "I hope that doesn't upset you too much. You feel it would be best for you and Rob to go back East to be near family and you're probably right. Certainly, it will be right for your own peace of mind. I feel that staying here will be best for my peace of mind. I was glad to help you out while Rob was not in school, but now, I must make some different plans. With William's death, you have bad memories about the ranch. With my failed marriage, I have bad memories about Ontario."

"I'm still not that old and the people at the Old Folks Home would like me to work more hours. I told them that come July, I could start working full-time. Once you and Rob have left, I guess I'll be looking for another place to stay."

"Oh my," Myrna replied. "I sort of had this feeling that you might want to stay here, but I was hoping I would be wrong. I do thank you for all the help you have given me over the last seven years. I should have realized that you had your own personal reasons for not wanting to go back East. Please try to accept that with William gone, my heart is back in Ontario."

"I understand. We'll have to try to work out all the details without getting uptight with each other. You'll just have to try to be patient with Rob. We have to remember that up until we relocated in Medicine Hat, the ranch had been the only life he knew. I'm sure in time, he'll come around. I'd suggest instead of trying to get him to abandon the ranch and ramming the advantages of moving back to Ontario down his throat, you should drop discussing your move altogether."

"What plans do you have for the house?" Edith asked.

"I was thinking of selling it, but that would put you out in the cold and I certainly won't go that route."

"You don't have to worry about that. Remember, for the last seven years almost all my wages you and William paid me have been put in the bank. Also, Mildred, my other sister Sybil and I got some inheritance money when our wealthy aunt passed on. If you're in agreement, I'd certainly want to buy the house from you. I 'm sure I should have enough funds for that."

"That would be fine with me. I'd be willing to sell it to you for what Michael and Maud paid for it if that would be alright with you. I guess we won't worry about it until the school year is over."

Michael came with the team and buggy and picked up Myrna, Rob and Edith for the Easter long weekend. Rob had a wonderful time riding the range with Michael and playing with his old playmates. Although Myrna enjoyed Maud's company, the nights were hard for her. She tried to think positively of all the good times she'd shared with William, but invariably she cried herself to sleep.

Once back from the ranch, she spent many hours talking her feelings out with Edith.

"The visit to the ranch just reinforced in my mind that to safeguard my mental health, I have to move back to Ontario. I know there will be things about the ranch and this area that I'll miss, like the closeness I've had with you and my friendships with Maud, Michael, and my school kids, but with William gone, this area is starting to feel like a foreign country to me."

"I understand where you're coming from," Edith responded. "You've said that you only chose the ranch style of living because of William. It may take a little time, but I'm sure Rob will eventually enjoy living in Ontario too. Kids are quite adaptable."

"As I've touched on before, you have been bending over backwards trying to make Rob feel positive about your move. He's a fine little man and I love him dearly, but he is still a child. Remember that old saying, 'don't let the tail wag the dog.' You're doing your very best for him, but don't forget, you're the adult and you are in charge. In a kind way, you have to show him that."

"Thanks so much," Myrna said after a long pause. "I really needed that. In fact, both Rob and I need that advice. I'll just have to lay off trying to convince him to like the idea of moving and also keep in mind that I'm his parent. It will save both of us an awful lot of energy."

The end of the school year brought mixed feeling for Myrna. Although she was looking forward to returning to her birthplace and her kinfolk, part of her felt guilty for leaving Edith, Maud and Michael. At times she thought she was betraying the memory of her beloved by leaving his remains behind. She felt at peace though when she recognized that William would always be near her and Rob wherever they went.

Rob had finished school for the year and was home with Edith while Myrna was still at the school making out her year-end reports.

"How are you feeling about going with your mom to Ontario?" Edith asked. "I imagine that there's a lot to think about."

"I'm kind of sad about it and a little scared," Rob replied, putting his toy soldiers aside. "I'd still like to stay at the ranch, but Mom doesn't want to. I don't know if I'll have any friends when we move and then my daddy is at the ranch."

"Do you remember what your daddy told you when you and Michael saw him at the cross?"

"Yes, he said he was happy."

"And did he say anything more?"

"Yes, he said for me to look after Mom and then he hugged me and he was warm."

"Your mom gets sad when you tell her you don't want leave the ranch and go to Ontario, doesn't she?"

"I guess so," Rob replied quietly.

"That's not looking after your mom like your dad asked you to do, is it?"

"I guess not."

"I know it's a big scary move for you, but if you look out for your mom it will make it easier for her. Remember your dad visited you, Edith, Michael and me and he could even come to you after you move."

"I hope he will," Rob replied, nodding. Soon he was back playing with his toy soldiers.

In the days leading up to their move, Edith noticed a change in both Myrna and Rob. Myrna was no longer trying to get Rob to be happy with the move and he was no longer whining that he didn't want to go.

Maud talked to Michael regarding Myrna's upcoming move to Ontario. She told him of her recent conversation with Edith regarding Myrna's and Rob's plans and suggested it would be better for them to speak encouragingly of their move rather than focusing on Rob's attachment to the ranch.

"You're right," Michael replied after some thought. "I guess we've been trying too hard to keep them here, close by."

"Yes, we tried hard to keep them on the ranch," Maud continued. "That didn't work, and now we've been trying to keep them in the area. That puts a lot of pressure on both of them."

Michael nodded and then sat there slowly shaking his head.

"Yes, I guess we have to accept that an era has come to an end," he finally added. "God knows how hard we've tried to make Myrna welcome here on the ranch, but it's just not working. About all we have left are memories. After they've moved, we must try to stay in close contact."

A few days before Myrna and Rob were to catch the train to head back to Ontario, Myrna borrowed a team and buggy. Early in the morning, Rob, Edith and she were off to the ranch to say their goodbyes. As the miles slipped by, Rob and Edith were very upbeat. Rob was looking forward with great anticipation to being back with Michael and his playmates. Edith was happy to visit what had been her home for six years. As the miles slipped by, Myrna was deep in thought. Although she was looking forward to visiting Maud and Michael, she still had feelings of guilt over the upcoming move.

They arrived late in the afternoon. At supper, Michael and Maud tried to encourage Rob about moving back to Ontario and to Rob's credit, he didn't do any yowling about wanting to stay at the ranch. As soon as they'd finished eating, Rob was out playing with his young friends.

Myrna planned on spending Saturday and Sunday at the ranch, returning to Medicine Hat on Monday. For some time, she felt strongly that before heading back to Ontario, she must again visit the spot where her beloved William breathed his last breath. In her mind, it was a pilgrimage she had to make. At breakfast, she mentioned this to Michael.

"I'd be happy to take you out to the cross with a team and buggy," Michael responded.

"Thanks for the offer, but I feel it's something I have to do by myself. If you have a gentle horse, I'd appreciate the use of it so I could ride out to the cross."

While Rob was busy playing with his friends, Michael saddled up his gentlest horse and Myrna was on her way. It was a pleasant warm morning, but Myrna felt raw inside. As tears slipped down her cheeks, she was reliving all the wonderful times she'd had on the ranch with her beloved William. Before they were married, she recalled going with William on horseback to the little cabin back in the bush on a brisk November afternoon. William had lit a fire in the airtight heater and soon the cabin was warm.

"It was there in the little cabin that William and I were intimate for the first time," she mused. "God, how I loved that man."

Soon she arrived at the spot where her beloved had died. She tied her horse to a tree, then slowly walked back to the cross. She sat on the block of wood that was close by the cross, the same block that Rob was sitting on when his dad's spirit visited him.

"My darling William," she sobbed. "Please, couldn't you visit me like you did with Rob, Edith and Michael? Why, oh why, did you have to die and leave Rob and me so alone? Please tell me if going back to Ontario is the right move for Rob and me."

Myrna sat on the block, with one hand on the horizontal arm of the cross, her eyes closed, reliving the day of her beloved's death. Suddenly, she felt a warm puff of air and then heard a loud fluttering sound. She glanced up to an astounding sight. A large raven swooped down and landed on the top of the cross, less than a couple of feet from Myrna's hand. The big bird cocked its head, looked directly into Myrna's eyes and croaked a couple of times. The raven then hopped into the air and winged its way back to the forest.

"Thanks so much, darling," Myrna whispered, smiling. "Thank you for coming and letting me know that moving back to Ontario is the right thing for Rob and me to do."

Soon Myrna was back at the barn. When she told Michael of the raven sitting on the cross and croaking at her, he shook his head. "There's no question in my mind that William visited you," he said quietly.

"There is something so miraculous about the bird landing right on the cross and croaking at me," Myrna added.

Before they sat down for dinner, Myrna told Rob about the big raven visiting her.

"That's a magic spot," Rob said. "My daddy visited me and Grandpa Francis there. Grandpa said he saw a raven flying around the cross. Now Daddy came to visit you in that bird."

As they were eating dinner, Michael turned to Myrna. "I don't know if anyone ever told you, Edith or Rob the story about the raven incident that happened the year we moved up here."

Both Myrna and Edith shook their heads.

"Well, we were logging in the forested area, straight east of the cross. William always had a special way with animals.

While we were logging, he tamed a raven. The bird was so tame that it would land on William's wrist and eat from his hand. The raven wouldn't make friends with anyone else. Makes you wonder, doesn't it?"

Edith nodded her head. Finally, she spoke. "Yes, I know from my own experience that there's something magical about ravens."

Myrna took great comfort from William's visit. It would always be indelibly imprinted in her mind. Before leaving Monday morning, they all went up to William's grave. Maud had cut a large bouquet of flowers and put them by William's headstone. Everyone stood in silence. Finally, Rob slowly walked to his dad's headstone and dropped to his knees.

"Bye, Daddy, Bye," he sobbed. "I'm so lonesome for you."

Everyone wept.

As Myrna, Edith and Rob were driving past the grave with the team and buggy on their way back to Medicine Hat, Rob looked over at the grave, tears in his eyes and whispered, "Bye Daddy. Please come to see me again."

All of Myrna's and Rob's belongings that they were taking with them had already been sent ahead to Ontario by rail. The parting at the train station was hard for everyone. Michael and Maud drove in to Medicine Hat to bid Myrna and Rob goodbye. The parting was especially hard for Edith, Myrna and Rob. Although Edith was quite a bit older than Myrna, they had become as close as sisters. Rob looked on his Aunt Edith as a second mother while Edith loved Rob deeply and thought of him as the son she'd never had.

As the train pulled out of the station, Rob face was pressed against the coach window, gazing back in the direction of the ranch. "Bye Daddy," he whispered. "Come visit me again."

Rob tried his best to be brave, but as the miles slipped by, he felt he was abandoning everything he had known and other than his mom, the many friends he had loved in his short life.

Although Myrna knew she was doing what she had to do, in her mind's eye she could see a young boy falling to his knees by his dad's grave and could hear him sobbing "Bye Daddy. I'm so lonesome for you."

"I desperately hope there will be good days ahead for Rob and me," she mused as she held her sleeping little man close. "God only knows how much we need them."

CHAPTER 10

WHEN THE TRAIN arrived in Benville, Myrna's and Rob's kinfolk were there to greet them. The first couple of weeks were a whirlwind of visiting friends, relatives and sightseeing.

From Rob's view, it wasn't exactly an exciting time. There were no young kids at any of the relatives' places that were his age. Myrna did her best to keep his spirits up. It didn't help the situation any that Rob had gone back to telling his mom that he wished they had never left the ranch. He was constantly harping that he had no one to play with.

Myrna had sold her house to Edith. With the funds from the sale of her house plus the savings from the sale of William's and her small herd of cattle, she had more than enough money to buy a nice medium-sized house and fully furnish it.

Myrna was now spending long hours at the school preparing for the upcoming schoolyear. While Myrna was working in the school, Rob would play in the school playground. He was always anxious to find someone his age to make friends with. One morning, when he got to the school playground, another young boy was playing on the monkey bars.

“Hello, there,” Rob began, walking up to the other lad. “My name’s Rob. What’s your name? I’m seven.”

“My mom calls me Jacob, but everyone else calls me Jake. I’m seven too. You just move here?”

“Yeah, my mom and I moved here a while ago from out West.”

“What does your daddy do?” Jacob asked

“I don’t have a Daddy,” Rob quietly answered, looking down and scraping the dirt with his toe. “My daddy died two years ago when a grizzly bear killed him, but he shot the bear dead before he died. What about your daddy?”

“I have a daddy, but he’s in jail,” Jacob replied looking most despondent. “Mom says he’s waiting for a trial. Daddy’s a carpenter and builds houses. My mom’s name is Eva. She told me and my sister that the police said that some woman told them that my dad did something not very nice to her. But Mom, my sister Ada and I don’t believe that. Daddy told us that he never did anything bad to that woman. My daddy’s boss got a lawyer who’s trying to get him out of jail.”

“Your skin is kind of dark,” Rob continued as they began swinging.

“That’s because I’m a Negro. All of us Negros have black skin. Have you never seen a Negro before?”

“No, you’re the first one I ever saw. I think it would be kind of fun to have skin your color.”

“It’s sure wasn’t fun for me and everyone else in our family. We came from Tennessee. That’s down south in United States.

Mean people there made fun of us because we were black. It's better up here, but some people still make fun of us."

"That's not nice. I'd never be mean to you, your mom, or your sister. Last year one of the kids at school made fun of me. He said I was just making up the story that a bear killed my dad."

"Yeah, it hurts when people say mean things. Some of the white kids in Tennessee called my sister and me niggers. That's a bad word for Negro. It makes us feel really horrible when people call us names."

"That's sad alright that people are mean to you guys. What does your mom do?"

"My mom works at cooking in the hotel. She had to start doing that when my dad went to jail because we didn't have much money. My sister Ada is my twin. She's better at doing stuff in the house than I am. She tries to cook a little when Mom's not home. Sometimes she even cooks supper for us. She's not as good at cooking as Mom is, but she's sure a lot better than I am. I help Ada by sweeping the floor and cleaning up the house a bit and washing the dishes. What does your mom do?"

"My mom is a teacher. She's in the school right now getting ready for when school starts."

"What grade will you be in this year?" Rob added. "I'll be in grade two."

"Me too. What grade does your mom teach?"

"Three and four. I guess next year she'll be teaching both of us if we don't fail."

Soon the two new pals were busying themselves on the monkey bars, maypole, teeter-totter and swings.

"You could come over to my house if you'd like," Jake said when they were taking a breather. "Ada is home."

"I'll ask my mom when she comes out for dinner. When she's working in the school, I stay in the playground. Mom can see me by looking out her classroom window. She doesn't want me to bother her when she's in the school unless I really need to see her. Her room is over there in the corner. If I have to get her, I just knock on the window. It's just about dinner time now. Maybe if we wait for a bit, she'll come out to get me and then I can ask her."

In a few minutes, Myrna left the school and came over to where the boys were standing.

"This here is Jacob," Rob began. "He's in the same grade as I am. Jacob's mom works at cooking at the hotel. He wants me to come to his house."

"That's nice," Myrna replied. "Is your mom home after supper?"

"Yeah, she's usually home around seven. Most of the time, Ada, my sister, makes us something to eat for dinner and then she starts to make supper for us if Mom asks her to. My mom's name is Eva Lewis."

"Yes, I've met your mom. A week or so ago we had a meeting here in the school for parents to meet the teachers. If you'd like, Rob and I could come over to your house after supper."

Myrna told Jacob that she'd phone his mom and see if it would be all right for Rob and her to visit them after supper. As Myrna recalled, Eva had mentioned that they only lived three blocks from each other.

Once Rob finished dinner, he went back to the school playground. In a few minutes, Jacob and his sister Ada arrived.

"This is my sister Ada," Jacob began. "She's my twin. Dad always says that because I was born first, I'm bigger. But Dad also says that Ada is better looking than I am, because she was born last."

Although he didn't reply, after glancing at the two, Rob concurred that their dad's assessment was right on both counts.

After supper, Myrna and Rob walked over to the Lewis place. Rob, Ada and Jacob spent an enjoyable evening. The two ladies shed a few tears as they shared the trials they were going through. Eva said her lawyer was working hard on digging into the credibility of the woman who claimed Jed had assaulted her. Their lawyer was confident that information he'd dug up on the woman would result in Jed being freed. The lawyer discovered that she had attempted the same scheme with another man down in the States a few years back. The judge had thrown that claim out of court when it was proven she had lied under oath. Her scheme was to blackmail men, threatening to lay charges against them for sexually assaulting her unless they paid her a handsome price.

"I'm so glad that Rob has found some friends," Myrna commented. "Ever since we moved here, he's been very sad that he has no one his age to hang out with. Rob's had such a hard time the last couple of years what with his dad's death and our moving."

"It's been difficult for Jacob and Ada too, especially when their classmates found out their dad was in jail. It's hard to understand how cruel some kids and even the odd parent can be."

While Myrna and Eva were visiting, Ada and the boys were having the time of their lives, playing snakes and ladders.

When school started, Myrna and Rob left in the morning together. They usually took their lunch with them as the school was a fair distance from their house. After school, Rob would either stay at the school until his mom was through her school work or go home with Jacob and Ada. It helped Jacob and Ada to have Rob as a friend. Rob was a fair amount bigger than kids his age and he made a good bodyguard. If any of the school kids tried to pick on them, Rob would give Ada's and Jacob's tormentors a good tongue-lashing for their misdeeds. If he deemed it necessary, the males who picked on Jacob or Ada would get a good punch or two.

Although they couldn't publicly acknowledge it, the teachers were relieved that Ada and Jacob now had a protector. As a rule, they looked the other way if Rob got a bit physical with those giving his dark-skinned friends a hard time.

Rob was elated that he had Jacob and Ada for friends. The threesome spent many a happy hour together after school and on weekends. Although not as rambunctious as the boys, Ada did play a modified tomboy role. Being female and more controlled, she acted as their governor, or junior mother. She always did her best to keep Jacob and Rob from getting too out of hand in their playing.

In late October, the happy day finally arrived for the Lewis household. Based on the evidence Eva's lawyer had unearthed, Jed did not have to stand for trial as the judge dismissed the charges brought against him. He was a free man. The crown in turn laid charges against the woman who had attempted to blackmail him.

Myrna and Rob spent Christmas with Myrna's folks and Boxing Day at Jed's and Eva's place. Myrna was amazed that Jed was not bitter over his incarceration.

"What will be, will be," he said. "Fate will deal with the lady who falsely accused me. The way I got it figured, it will be punishment enough for her having to live with herself. From what my lawyer said, the judge was very upset with her. This is the second time she's tried to blackmail a man. Our lawyer said that when her case is heard, she may be spending some time in jail. I'm just so thankful to be out of jail and back with my family and friends."

Jed had been the Light Heavyweight Boxing Champ in the northeastern states, a few years back. Prior to him being held in jail, with the blessing of the school's physical education teacher, he had started a boxing club for the grade seven and eight boys at the school in the evenings. Once out of jail, he carried on with his boxing club. Jacob and Rob wanted to join the club, but being so young, that was a no-go. Jed did, however, privately coach the two underage would-be pugilists. Jed was very impressed with Rob's skill, strength and tenacity.

While in Medicine Hat, Myrna fantasized on how full and rewarding her life would be once she was back in Ontario. Now, although back in a lifestyle she was more accustomed to, she was still overwhelmed with loneliness. Many of her old friends had moved. Because she'd been gone so long, some acted quite distant. Over the years, she had developed a strong bond with Edith, but now 2000 miles separated them. She was becoming close to Eva and though happy that Jed was out of jail, she thought of them as a twosome and felt that she was by herself again.

William and Myrna had enjoyed a very close relationship, but William had been gone now for over two years. Although very lonely, she couldn't help but feel guilty thinking of anyone else of the opposite sex. Nonetheless, she found herself again longing for close male contact. It was a no-win game for Myrna. The more she longed for male companionship, the guiltier she felt.

Morris Conrad, one of the male teachers at her school, showed a keen interest in her. Like Myrna, this was his first-year teaching in Ontario. Previously, he had taught in New Brunswick. Although Myrna found him quite attractive, she had turned down his requests for her to go out with him, still feeling loyal to William's memory.

During the Easter break, Myrna and Rob dropped in at the Lewis place. While Rob, Ada and Jacob were outside playing, Myrna bared her soul to Eva.

"I met Morris briefly before Christmas at a school function," Eva replied. "He is quite attractive. Really Myrna, do you think that William would want you to stay lonely for the rest of your life?"

"No, I guess not." After a long pause Myrna added, "No, I know he wouldn't want me to spend the rest of my life alone."

"You see, Myrna, you're still a young woman. Besides, if at all possible, Rob, like every boy, needs a father's guidance. All boys crave and need a strong male influence in their lives."

"Yes, I think you're right. Morris has asked me out a couple of times. Although I'm attracted to him, I always had some excuse for turning him down. I was letting the feelings I had for William override my need for male companionship and also Rob's needs. The more I think on it, the more I'm persuaded that you're right. They're having a Sadie Hawkins dance for the teachers in a couple of weeks. Maybe I should ask him to go with me."

Morris was tickled pink when Myrna invited him to the dance.

CHAPTER 11

MYRNA MADE ARRANGEMENTS with Eva for Rob to stay overnight with them the evening of the dance. She really enjoyed herself at the dance. It felt good to be able to go to a function as a couple again.

"I should tell you a bit about myself," Morris began when they were having coffee at Myrna's place after the dance.

"I was born and raised in New Brunswick. I taught there for four years. Three years ago, I married Florence. She was also a teacher. Unfortunately, or maybe fortunately, our marriage didn't last. I thought our marriage was going fairly well, but then, about a year and a half ago I discovered she was having an affair. So, I'm divorced. I fail to understand her logic, but in her view, I was responsible for the marriage failure. Maybe blaming me was her attempt to get rid of the guilt she felt. That's what my mother thought, anyway."

"Another problem for me was that she didn't have a strong religious background. My family and I are strong Catholics and I always attend Mass. For the first month or so of our marriage, she attended Mass with me, but then she refused to go to church anymore. I'm still smarting over my failed marriage."

"What about you? I was told that your husband died tragically. How was your marriage?"

"I had an excellent marriage. Physically, William was a big strong man. Emotionally, he was also strong. Nothing seemed to sway him. He could at times be a very stubborn sort, but he was kind, fair and compassionate to a fault."

"I came out West to teach school at the ranch where William worked. I had just finished my Normal School training. William was originally from Ontario. Anyway, we fell in love and a few months later were married. When Rob was born, Edith, William's aunt from here in Ontario, came out West and helped me with Rob's birth. Then she stayed on looking after Rob so I could continue teaching."

"It was horrible. The fall that Rob was five, William was attacked and killed by a grizzly bear while out riding the range. With William gone, I just couldn't bear the thought of staying out at the ranch anymore. I managed to teach there until the school year was completed. We then moved into Medicine Hat, a town a short distance from the ranch and I taught there one year. When there was an opening here in Ontario, I sold my house and came back East. Edith lived in and looked after Rob until he started school. When I got the job here, she decided to stay out West."

"It's been pretty heavy for me. Rob is every bit as stubborn as his dad was and wanted to stay on the ranch. I finally gave up on trying to convince him on the merits of moving back here and that helped both of us. He's doing much better now that he's made some friends here."

"Yes, it must have been hard for you and Rob, seeing the young guy had just lost his dad and you, your husband. You were wise though, in not letting young Rob rule the roost. I strongly believe that with children, we must remember that we are in charge of their welfare. Children must follow, not lead."

"I had a very strict upbringing. Although Dad provided well for our family, he was a firm believer that sparing the rod ruined the child. At the time, I thought his strict, corporal discipline was a bit excessive, but now that I'm an adult, I think his ideas on childrearing have merit. I'm not too impressed by this new parenting style of never getting physical with children. There are those who figure that physical punishment is cruel, but I think, at times, it's necessary to be firm with kids."

Over the next couple of months Myrna and Morris were seeing a lot of each other. Myrna was initially relieved when Morris advised her that because of his religious convictions, he believed that premarital sex was wrong. When she recalled how hot-to-trot William was when they were courting, at times, she did wonder about his sex drive.

"I had one good Dad and that's enough for me," Rob stated emphatically one evening to his mom. Morris was over for supper and had just left. "Morris never even talks to me and I really don't want him to. Why do you have to get someone to take Dad's place?"

Myrna couldn't think of how to answer Rob's question so quickly changed the subject.

Morris was very eager to get married. Although Myrna was also looking forward to being married again, at times she felt a bit uneasy as she really didn't know Morris all that well. His views on the use of corporal punishment were also troubling for her.

At Myrna's urging, Morris tried to reach out to Rob. Although his attempts were awkward, he was doing his best to befriend him. Now, when Morris dropped over for a visit, Rob was at least tolerating him. Although Myrna had been confident that Morris was the man she wanted in her and Rob's life, the odd hug, good-night kiss and handholding was the only physical contact Morris seemed capable of or willing to show. She constantly told herself that the lack of physical contact would change once they were married.

When Myrna told Rob of her plans to marry Morris, he sat for a long time in stunned silence. "I just want my daddy so bad," he finally blurted out, tears running down his cheeks. "Why did my daddy have to die?" He just sat there, looking most dejected, slowly shaking his head. All Myrna could do was to go over and hug her distraught son.

During the school summer break, recognizing that Rob was having a hard time accepting Morris into his life, Eva and Jed graciously invited Rob to accompany them on a trip back to Tennessee for a few weeks.

They stayed at Jacob's and Ada's grandparents farm. The kids had a blast playing with Jacob's and Ada's many cousins. They also spent a few days at a lake close to the farm. With Jed's assistance, Rob caught his first fish. All too soon for Rob's liking, it was time for them to head back home.

While they were gone, Myrna and Morris set their wedding date for the 22nd of December, during the Christmas break. They had been seeing each other for several months. As Myrna had no close church affiliation, she agreed to have the wedding in the Catholic Church. Morris advised her that to be married in a Catholic Church she would have to become a Catholic. Myrna talked to Father Parent and began the process of becoming a Catholic. She also started attending Mass with Morris.

Morris was happy with Myrna becoming a Catholic. While he and Myrna were attending Mass, Rob accompanied the Lewis family to the Methodist church. Morris advised Myrna that once they were married, he wanted Rob to start attending Mass with them.

When Rob returned from his holiday in Tennessee, he was shocked over the news that his mom would soon be getting married. With Morris in the picture, Rob was spending as much time as possible at the Lewis place.

When Myrna formally introduced Morris to the Lewis family, he didn't exactly hit a home run with either Jed or Eva. He started to wax eloquent on his ideas on child discipline, stressing the need for corporal correction. Like Rob, neither Jed or Eva were overly impressed with Myrna's choice for a life partner.

The days up to the wedding were difficult for Rob. He was so lonely for his dad. The day before the wedding, he stopped in at the Lewis place. He was very distraught and tried in vain to hold back the tears. He felt his mom was betraying his dad's memory. Eva did her best to comfort him. That evening, he cried himself to sleep.

It was a small wedding with only a few relatives and friends in attendance. Mildred and Ken couldn't attend as they were on holidays. At the wedding ceremony, at his mom's request, Rob reluctantly sat with his Grandma Maria and

Grandpa Ed. He felt horrible as his mom and Morris were exchanging their vows. The wedding ceremony was almost more that Rob could bear. He had his eyes closed tight and was shaking. The sight of the priest in his garb made Rob panic. He had lost his dad and now he felt he was losing his mom. He just wanted the day to end.

At the reception, Rob was again asked by his mom to sit at the family table between his grandparents. He was torn between going along with his mom's wishes and feeling the need to be faithful to his dad's memory. For a long time, he stood by the reception table, looking off into space. He was no longer at the wedding, but back at the ranch riding the range with his dad. Finally, he reluctantly went and sat between his grandparents.

As the reception began, he was in emotional agony. He sat between Ed and Maria as long as he could bear it. When Father Parent stood to ask the blessing, Rob couldn't stand the pressure anymore. Once Father Parent sat down, Rob leapt to his feet, went over to the Lewis table and sat with them.

When Myrna noticed that Rob had moved to the Lewis' table, she decided not to make an issue of it. She recognized that Rob was very distraught. She knew it was a very hard day for her son. However, Morris' temper flared when he noticed that Rob had left the wedding table. Paying no heed to Myrna's plea to 'Cool it,' he leapt to his feet and rushed over to the Lewis' table.

"What are you trying to pull off?" he snapped at Rob. "Your mom told you to sit at our table. You're coming with me, young man!" Morris reached down, grabbed Rob by his jacket and hoisted him to his feet.

"Not so fast," Jed said, getting to his feet and putting his big hand on Morris' shoulder. "As you can imagine, Rob is having a hard time. Just leave him with me. I'll talk to him and try to persuade him to sit at your table."

"Why don't you mind your own business?" Morris snarled, glaring at Jed.

"I am, Morris, I am," Jed quietly replied, smiling. He was squeezing Morris' shoulder hard. "Now unhand the young fellow and I'll talk to him."

His face flushed in anger, Morris let go of Rob, turned and stomped back to the family table.

"I was going to bring Rob back to our table, but this Jed guy had to stick his nose in," Morris whispered to Myrna. "Just because he's an ex-boxer doesn't give him licence to get physical. He squeezed my shoulder so hard that it still hurts. I wish the big brute would mind his own business."

"He is, Morris," Myrna replied calmly, "and he's not a big brute. Unless you press his button, he's a very gentle sort. You've got to remember that Jed knows Rob very well. They're very close. Jed has been a surrogate dad for Rob. He recognizes that this is a heavy day for him. You'll have to try to slack off on Rob. Just before the ceremony, he was in tears. He told me that he was having a hard time. Please, for my sake, cut the pressure tactics and try to be a little more patient with him."

Morris did not reply, but by the color of his face, Myrna knew that he was very angry.

"My God," Myrna thought, fighting panic. "I haven't seen this side of Morris before. Maybe I should have clued in when he was always harping about child discipline. Hopefully, it's just the pressure of the wedding that precipitated it. Yes, it's probably just the pressure of the wedding." Saying it to herself was one thing, truly believing that all was well was quite another matter.

Jed led Rob to the back of the hall where they had a bit of privacy. "I know this is a rough day for you, but it would make your mom very happy if you'd sit with them. Just remember Rob, I'll always be here for you if you ever have trouble with Morris."

Jed led Rob back to the family table and he dutifully sat between his grandma and grandpa.

It burned Morris' butt that Jed interfered in his first attempt to discipline his stepson. He observed what he considered Myrna's rather laissez-faire discipline of Rob and had determined that he'd do his best to bring that to an end.

Myrna had wanted to spend Christmas at home with Rob, before going on a short honeymoon. Seeing Morris' parents couldn't make it to the wedding, Morris wanted to take the train to New Brunswick to visit his family and spend Christmas with them. After Christmas, they would go on their short honeymoon. Morris reluctantly agreed to take Rob along with them. When Myrna suggested to Rob that he accompany them, he told his mom that he preferred to stay with the Lewis'. Myrna talked things over with Eva and Jed. They said that he would be welcome to stay with them.

After the reception, Myrna and Morris caught the train to Toronto. They would leave the next morning for New

Brunswick. Once on their way, Morris again zeroed in on Rob's behavior at the reception and Jed's interference.

"I believe that we, as parents, must demand respect from our children. That's the way I was raised. I have noticed that Rob isn't quite as respectful to you as he could be."

"The way I see it, the only way that we can expect respect from our children is to earn it, not demand it," Myrna responded. "Listen, dear, we're on our honeymoon now, so let's change the subject."

Their first night together was not exactly the joyful occasion Myrna had envisaged it would be. William had been a skilled, compassionate lover. His mission in their lovemaking was to give both Myrna and himself satisfaction. Myrna felt that Morris's lovemaking skills, when compared to William's, were more than a little wanting.

Morris' hostile reaction over the problem of Rob not wanting to sit with them at the reception and now his lack of finesse in their lovemaking, were making Myrna uneasy. After some thought, she again wrote both issues off to the pressure of just getting married.

Although Myrna found Morris' folks somewhat rigid in their thinking, the rest of their honeymoon was much less stressful than their wedding day. When Morris would turn the discussion to Rob's comportment at their wedding, Myrna would quickly steer the conversation away to a different topic. She recognized that her new husband was fixated on child discipline and the need for the parent to mould the child into what they wanted the child to be.

Another thorny issue arose on their train ride back to Ontario. As of yet, they had not discussed birth control or their thoughts on having their own family.

"I only believe in the rhythm method," Morris stated dogmatically. "It's the only birth control method the Catholic Church believes in. From the Catholic's point of view, this allows God to bring children into a marriage without any artificial method of preventing conception, yet it allows the couple the control over planning their family."

"But aren't you aware that the rhythm method is classified by most medical professionals as not being a foolproof method of birth control?"

"Well, the couple can plan for children and the Church encourages that. The rhythm method is the only method I could conscientiously agree to."

Myrna decided not to press the issue anymore, but was relieved that on her doctor's advice, before their marriage, she'd taken the intra-uterine device route.

"My God," she mused silently as the miles slipped by. "I wish I'd have been bright enough to have had this conversation with Morris before we got married. Oh well, it's too late now, but I guess what Morris doesn't know won't hurt him. The last thing I need now is to get pregnant again."

Once back from their honeymoon, things got back to the regular grind. As Myrna owned her house, Morris moved in with her and Rob. Although not becoming close, Morris and Rob were making some progress in abiding each other.

When Morris and his mother were by themselves, he told her of Rob's antics at the reception and the need for Rob to have better discipline. Morris' mother advised him to allow some time to become better acquainted with Rob before he attempted better discipline. Myrna had also done her part in coaching Rob. She advised him to take guidance from his stepdad and not be obstinate with him. Without question, it vexed Morris that he couldn't be more assertive in disciplining Rob, but he decided to take his mother's advice and bide his time.

Myrna had only been married for a few months when she got a bombshell of a letter from Morris's ex-wife, Florence Brown. Florence had mailed the letter to Myrna in care of her fellow teacher, Alice Bouke. Florence didn't want her ex-husband getting his hands on the letter.

Dear Myrna.

My name is Florence Brown, I'm Morris's ex-wife. I am aware that Alice works with you so I've addressed this letter to her in care of the school. Alice and I have been friends for years.

Alice told me that you have a young son and that you and Morris had married. It is certainly not my intention to stick my nose in where it isn't wanted, but I feel obligated to caution you for both your son's and your welfare.

I have a seven-year old daughter from a previous marriage. My first husband died suddenly when Jill was one year old. Jill was three when I married Morris.

Months after we married, I found out that a year before we met, they terminated his job because he was using the strap liberally and very harshly on both the girls and the boys in grade three and four for minor misdemeanors.

One evening, I had to go to a teacher's meeting and left Jill with him. I was just coming into the house after the meeting when I heard Jill crying hysterically. I rushed to her room. That monster of a Morris was whaling away on Jill's poor little bare legs with a belt. He said he was correcting her for wetting herself. The poor little tyke had big red welts on her legs all the way down to her ankles.

I grabbed her away from him and told him if he ever touched her again, I'd not only leave him, but report him to the police. He stormed out of the house.

I took a photo of the welts on Jill's legs.

I slept with Jill that night. It was heavy going between Morris and me for the next while.

As I no longer trusted Jill with Morris, I took her with me when I had to go out in the evenings. One morning, I told Morris we might be late getting home. After school was out, I picked up Jill from the babysitter and went to visit a friend. We didn't get back home till midnight. Morris was livid with me for not making him supper and for getting back so late.

The fight was on. When I asked what was wrong with him making his own supper, he hit me hard across the face with the back of his hand. I fell down. My nose was bleeding and my face was a bloody mess.

When I finally gathered myself together, I took Jill and we went to my friend's place.

The next morning, I contacted the police and my school principal. When they saw Jill's legs and my bruised face, Morris was again in trouble and looking for a new job. In the hullabaloo that followed, I got a restraining order to protect Jill and me from him and started on divorce proceedings. Shortly thereafter, we were divorced. He spread a false rumor that I'd had an extramarital affair while we were married. Possibly he was trying to save face. In closing, I could only rest if I forewarned you on what happened between Jill, Morris and me.

Yours truly,
Florence Brown

CHAPTER 12

A S MYRNA READ the letter, she broke out in a cold sweat. The next evening, while visiting with Jed and Eva, she let them read Alice's letter.

"To be frank with you, I was never overly impressed with Morris right from the start," Jed responded. "I heard from another source that he'd been fired from his teaching position a few years ago for being abusive to the kids he was teaching. For both your and Rob's welfare, it's important to watch him carefully. Just remember, Myrna, if you ever need a bodyguard or an enforcer, I'm at your service. Any bastard that would beat on a small child or a woman needs a damn good licking. Promise me that if he's ever abusive, or starts to act in a threatening manner, you'll come to us for support. Rest assured, I'll be right there."

After promising that she'd reach out for help if Morris ever became threatening or physical with them, Myrna and Rob left.

Myrna was now very much on edge. She wanted desperately to keep peace and make the marriage work and was bending over backwards to keep things on track. Still, she was haunted by Florence Brown's letter and was reticent to leave Rob alone with Morris.

Although it bothered Rob, he gave in to pressure from both his mom and Morris and went to Mass with them Sunday mornings a few times. Seeing the priest in his robes struck terror in Rob's heart though so he kept his eyes firmly closed during Mass. The pressure was reaching the crisis point for the young lad. Finally, on the Sunday after Myrna received Florence Brown's letter, things came to a head for Rob. Unable to bear the pressure anymore, halfway through Mass, he jumped to his feet and rushed out of the church.

"I just can't stand seeing the priest," Rob blurted out when his mom caught up to him. "It makes me scared all over again."

"What are you scared of?" Myrna asked.

"I can't tell, but it was awful. I'll tell you about it some other time. It happened when we were living in Medicine Hat."

They were soon home. Myrna tried in vain to get Rob to tell her what frightened him so much when they lived in Medicine Hat, but he just shook his head and refused to talk any more about it.

Morris returned from Mass in a white-hot rage.

"Have you two no respect for the sanctity of the Catholic Church?" he hollered. "Why would you allow Rob to run out of church in the middle of Mass? I had to apologize to Father Parent for Rob's action."

"I was just so scared I couldn't help it," Rob cried out.

"You're lying," Morris roared as he whipped off his belt. "I'll teach you to revere God's Church." Morris grabbed Rob by the arm. "I should have worked you over at the reception."

126

Before Morris could hit Rob, Myrna jumped in and snatched the belt from his hand.

"One more flair up of your temper and you can pack your stuff and leave!" Myrna screamed. "Remember, this is my house."

Morris stormed out of the house without saying another word and spent the rest of the day and night at a friend's place. The following evening, Morris returned. While Rob was at the Lewis' place, Morris and Myrna talked.

"The reason Rob ran out of church stems from a bad memory he's had from when we were still living out West," Myrna began. "He won't tell me what happened, but I surmise it has something to do with the clergy in Medicine Hat. One day a week, the ministerial association, both Protestant and Catholic, used to have a church club after school. As we had no church affiliation, I gave Rob permission to go to either the Catholic club or the Protestant club. He was eager to go and soon was exclusively attending the Catholic club. One afternoon he came home from the club very upset and refused to go anymore. Something happened that turned him off. I should have tried to get to the bottom of it then, but I didn't."

"I don't understand. Why didn't you insist on him going?"

"Within reason, I think there's nothing wrong in encouraging people to go to church, or in this instance a church club, but in Rob's case, where something about church was very terrifying for him, I didn't think I should force the issue."

"How do you know he wasn't lying about his fright like he was lying about why he ran out of Mass? Maybe he just wanted to get out of going to the church club and now wants to get out of coming to Mass with us. It sounds to me that he's a bit of a rebel."

"Rob does not lie. I'm positive he wasn't lying about being frightened by something that happened at the church club in Medicine Hat. That no doubt is why he doesn't want to attend Mass here. His dad and I taught him to always tell the truth. To the best of my knowledge, he's never lied to me or his dad. Another thing you should recognize. Like his dad, Rob is a free spirit. I have found that trying to force something on him only makes him more stubborn."

"Always bringing up your former husband," Morris replied sarcastically. "Remember, you're married to me, now. We have no choice but to break that rebellious will of his. That's all there is to it. This is going to cause a huge problem if we don't insist that he attend Mass with us. I think he needs a lesson on obeying his parents."

"Let me handle it, Morris. Maybe I can get him to tell me why he's terrified of coming to Mass. Just don't put any more pressure on him or me for that matter. I'm sure I can get to the bottom of it."

Morris was upset with Myrna, but grudgingly agreed to let her handle it.

Myrna continued her attempts to get Rob to divulge what happened back in Medicine Hat that made him so frightened of the priest, but Rob refused to talk anymore about it. The more she tried to get Rob to talk, the more traumatized he became.

As much as it infuriated Morris, Myrna and Rob stayed home from Mass the next Sunday. Myrna had brokered a temporary deal with Rob. She'd stay home from Mass with him this Sunday, but he'd have to come to Mass with Morris and her the following Sunday. Myrna was still hoping to get to the bottom of Rob's old fear. While Morris was at Mass, Myrna again did her best to get Rob to enlarge on his fear, but he stubbornly refused to talk about it. Throughout the rest of the week, Rob remained tight-lipped over what had frightened him in Medicine Hat.

The following Sunday, Rob steeled himself and accompanied his mom and Morris to Mass. He was so upset that he started to shake uncontrollably. Even though he kept his eyes firmly shut, the fear continued to build. Unable to control his fright anymore, he whispered to his mom, "I'm so scared. I got to get out of here." Again, he hustled from the church and ran home as fast as he could. Morris was right behind him.

They only lived a few blocks from the church and Rob got home just seconds before Morris did. Myrna was moving as fast as she could in a dress and high- heeled shoes. When Myrna burst into the house, she could hear Morris shouting and Rob crying in pain.

Morris had ripped off Rob's pants and was beating his bare legs mercilessly with his heavy belt. Myrna screamed for Morris to stop and rushed in to rescue her son. In the mix-up that ensued, Morris again swung his belt at Rob, missed him and hit Myrna full force across her face. It left nasty cut just under Myrna's eye.

With blood running down her face, she clutched Rob close and screamed, "Get out of my house, you monster! I'm phoning the police and Jed. If you're not gone by the time Jed gets here, he'll beat you senseless!"

Rob's legs were a mass of welts and blood was oozing from some of the swollen cuts.

Still enraged, without offering any assistance to either Rob or Myrna, Morris stormed out of the house.

After contacting the police, Myrna phoned Jed, the school superintendent and her principal. Jed arrived first. With clenched teeth, he checked over the welts on Rob's legs and the cut on Myrna's face.

"Say the word, Myrna," he growled "and I'll put that son-of-a-bitch out of commission for a long time. Anyone who beats on a kid and a woman like this needs to have the crap beaten out of him and like I said before, I'm just the guy who can do it."

"Thanks for your support," Myrna responded, "but please hold off until the police arrive."

"Okay, I won't go after that bastard rat now, but believe you me, his day of reckoning will come."

The police, doctor, school superintendent and Myrna's school principal arrived shortly. They took statements from Myrna and photos of the bruises and lacerations that Morris had inflicted on them.

"Do you know where we can find your husband?" the constable asked Myrna. "This is a case of assault on you and your son."

Before Myrna could reply, the doctor interrupted.

"I'm very concerned for the young lad. One of the blows your husband struck the young lad was across his kidneys. He has a large welt there that's bleeding a bit. Rob just told me he has to take a leak and I want to check his urine for blood."

After Rob relieved himself in a glass jar, the doctor examined the sample and continued. "I'm afraid it's as I thought. There's some blood in his urine. I should treat both of you in the hospital. There are some lacerations that may need to be stitched up, Myrna, especially that cut under your eye."

After finishing his examination of Rob and Myrna, Dr. Evenson put his hand on Rob's shoulder. "I'm so sorry you and your mom had to go through this horrible ordeal."

Having made out his report and taken the necessary pictures, the constable was about to pick up Morris when he made an appearance.

"Sit," Jed bellowed, grabbing Morris by the shirt and thumping him down hard in a chair. "If I hadn't promised Myrna not to beat on you, at this very instant I'd be working the ever-living pee out of you. Anyone who beats on a woman or kid needs his knackers lopped off. But I promised not to work you over, so I'll let the law handle you."

Jed's action had Morris in a daze. Without paying any heed to his excuses or alibis, the constable arrested Morris, handcuffed him and advised him he'd be jailed until an inquiry took place.

The lacerations on Myrna's face and Rob's legs required a few stitches. Once Myrna and Rob were attended to in the hospital, they were released. The doctor advised Myrna to keep a close check on Rob and to bring him back to the hospital if he continued to have blood in his urine.

The school principal told Myrna to take a few days off work and to keep Rob home from school for a spell. Eva offered to give her a hand and insisted that they stay in close contact. As for Jed, his comportment was that of a caged bull. He was constantly lampooning himself for not being able to protect Myrna and Rob from Morris.

When the police ran a check on Morris, they unearthed his assault on his former wife and daughter and his dismissal for using unreasonable punishment on his former pupils.

When Morris appeared in court, the magistrate paid little heed to his ramblings about the need for children to be disciplined by corporal means. The doctor testified that Rob's beating had been very severe and that there had been blood in his urine because of the blow to his lower back. He had the photographs as proof of the viciousness of the attack. Morris was sentenced to six months in jail with an additional one-year probation. Myrna and Rob were both relieved when the judge put a restraining order on Morris. He was never again to have contact with either of them.

It took some time for Rob and his mother to heal from their physical abuse. Healing from the emotional abuse was an ongoing process that took much longer.

Some time after the incident, Myrna phoned Father Parent and then dropped over to see him while Rob was at the Lewis' place. Father Parent was shocked at the photos of the beating Morris had inflicted on Rob and her.

"I'm trying to get to the bottom of why Rob was so terrified of seeing you in your priest's garb," Myrna said. "I think it goes back a couple of years to when Rob and I lived out West." Myrna told Father Parent about Rob attending the Catholic Church club in Medicine Hat.

"You wouldn't remember the priest's name, would you?"

"Yes, I was teaching at the same school. His name was Father Dobbs."

"Oh my, Heaven preserve us," Father Parent responded, sucking in his breath and looking most ashen. "From the bottom of my heart, I must apologise to you and your son on behalf of the Catholic Church. I don't know what Father Dobbs did to your son, but it's on record that he sexually assaulted boys in that area. I can assure you that he's no longer a priest. Please believe that most of the clergy in the Catholic Church are devout Christians. We do our best to be good emissaries of God. Unfortunately, there is the odd priest, or minister for that matter, who do not live the Christian walk. Again, my apology to you on behalf of our church."

"Regarding the abuse you and Rob suffered at the hands of your husband: The Catholic Church does not usually support divorce, but in my view, you must separate yourself and your son from this awful person. He's a very dangerous man. If there's anything I can do to help you or your son, let me know."

After talking to Father Parent, Myrna stopped at the Lewis' house and picked Rob up.

"I just talked to Father Parent," Myrna said as soon as she and Rob were back home. "He told me that Father Dobbs, the priest in Medicine Hat, did a lot of bad things to kids and that he no longer is a priest. Was Father Dobbs the one who scared you? Could you tell me about it?"

For a long moment Rob sat in silence, staring at the floor. Finally, he nodded and began, his voice breaking.

"See, at first, Father Dobbs was very nice to me and the other boys. He used to give us kids chocolates after our church class. The last time I was at the club he said he'd walk me home, but first he wanted to show me something at his house. I was standing in his house, looking at a picture on the wall when he came up beside me. He said he had some more pictures he wanted to show me and handed me a book with photos in it. The pictures were awful. They were of Father Dobbs and some young boys without any clothes on. They were doing sex things with each other."

"I was awfully scared," Rob continued, tears slipping down his cheeks. "I didn't know what to do."

"While I was still looking at the pictures, he moved over behind me. He held me tight with one arm. He shoved his other arm down the front of my pants and started rubbing my penis. I told him to stop, but he wouldn't. Then he pulled my arm behind my back and put my hand against his penis. It was hard. He told me to take my pants down."

Rob couldn't go on and started to cry. Myrna went over and wrapped her arms around her distraught son. Finally, Rob gained control of himself.

"I started to shout and tried to get away, but he grabbed me and put his hand over my mouth and I couldn't breathe. I was trying hard to breathe and everything started to go black. Then someone knocked at the front door. He told me not to tell anyone or he'd really hurt me. I was just so scared. When he let me go, I ran to the back door and raced all the way home. I didn't want to tell you in case he'd find out and really hurt me. Now, when I see a priest, I get scared again and can hardly breathe."

Myrna held her distraught son until he calmed down.

Telling his mom about Father Dobb's attack did help Rob, but he still felt under a lot of pressure. It didn't help that he was still trying to deal with the beating he got from Morris.

The Lewis family was a godsend for Myrna and Rob. They spent many hours with the Lewis', talking out their pain. It still vexed Jed that he hadn't been able to repay Morris for his savage attack with a good drubbing before he was sentenced.

Myrna was racking her brain on how to help Rob get over his fear of the clergy. Finally, she came up with a plan. In conversation with Father Parent, she learned that he was raised on a ranch in Texas. She talked to Father Parent about setting up a meeting between him, Rob and herself. She thought it would be far less traumatic for Rob if Father Parent could meet them in street clothes. He felt bad for Rob and was enthused with Myrna's plan. They would meet at Myrna's and Rob's place so Rob would feel less threatened. It took some doing for Myrna to sell the idea to Rob, but finally he agreed to the visit with the proviso that Jed would also be present.

When they met at Myrna's place, Father Parent was in street clothes. With his mom and Jed there for support, Rob felt more comfortable.

Father Parent was a great story teller and the tales of him riding the range on their ranch in Texas and shooting rattlesnakes had Rob sitting on the edge of his chair. Now feeling at ease with his new cowboy friend, Rob was soon spinning his own tales of his time at the ranch. He told of riding with his dad and Michael and then his dad's horrible death. He also told how his dad's spirit had visited him and Michael.

"That must have been a great comfort to you," Father Parent responded.

After an hour of Father Parent, Rob and Jed swapping tales, Myrna made a lunch. As Father Parent was leaving, he presented Rob with a pair of his old cowboy boots that he wore as a young range rider. Rob was thrilled with the gift. They were a bit too big, but with a couple of pairs of heavy socks, they fit not too badly.

The visit went better than Myrna had imagined. She was very encouraged when the next Saturday evening, Rob asked his mom if they could go to Mass in the morning.

Soon the trauma of Morris's attack and the fear of priests were fading into the background for Rob. Father Parent went out of his way to befriend Rob, always stopping to chat with him once Mass was over. Father Parent practiced what he preached.

CHAPTER 13

R OB AND MYRNA continued to attend Mass until Father Parent was transferred to another parish. He, along with the Lewis', helped Myrna contact a lawyer to begin divorce proceedings from Morris.

After Father Parent left, Myrna and Rob began attending the Methodist church with the Lewis family.

With Jed's help, Jacob, Ada and Rob built a fort-playhouse in Lewis' backyard. Unless the weather was too inclement, their fort was the three musketeers' hideout. Jed had the boys and Ada working for him Saturday mornings at his worksite to earn a little spending money.

During the summer school break, after Rob had finished grade three, Michael and Maud sent Myrna a return train ticket for Rob so he could spend two weeks with them on the ranch.

When the train pulled into Medicine Hat, Edith was there to greet him. She was delighted that Rob had made friends with Ada and Jacob and was fitting into his new life in Ontario. Rob enjoyed his stay at the ranch, playing with the ranch kids and riding the range with Michael.

One morning, Michael and Rob rode out to the ranch cabin in the bush as they did on the day William's spirit visited Rob. Maud again packed a big lunch for them. Before returning to the ranch buildings, the two stopped at the cross for a few minutes.

"Do you think my dad's spirit hangs around the cross?" Rob asked.

"I really don't think so. As I understand it, your dad's spirit can kind of see what is happening here and can come when he's needed. He came to Edith right after he died and then to you and me a bit later. Before you guys went back to Ontario, he came to your mom when that raven landed on the cross right beside her."

"Maybe some day Dad will come and visit me again," Rob replied. "Anyway, I sure hope he does."

Rob enjoyed his time at the ranch, but with the close friendship that had developed between Jacob, Ada and him, he was eager to head back home to his new friends.

Although Myrna had a good relationship with Eva and Jed, she still was very lonely. After the debacle with Morris though, she was afraid to even look at another man.

Rob was always there for Ada and Jacob if any of the students attempted to give them a hard time. Although Rob had intervened on their behalf the odd time in the second grade, in grade three, other than the odd comment about their skin color, there had been no real racial problems for Jacob and Ada. All that changed when Ada and the boys started their fourth grade.

Darin Brown and his family had just moved to Ontario from South Carolina. Although they claimed to be devout Southern Baptists, they were firmly prejudiced against blacks. The Brown family was of the mindset that blacks were a subculture and they certainly treated them as a subclass. They even had their pet passages from the Old Testament to back up their beliefs. Back in South Carolina, the Browns and many of their white neighbors practiced what they preached. Both the schools and churches were segregated.

Darin had failed a grade, and with the exception of Rob, he was bigger than all of his classmates. Both his parents were firm believers that 'sparing the rod spoils the child.' Having been raised in this type of corporal environment, Darin was not above being physical with other smaller boys in his class at school if he got the chance.

During the morning recess, the second week of school, all hell broke loose.

"Well lookie here," Darin jeered as Jacob and Rob were headed to the monkey bars. "I didn't know that up here that they allowed niggers to go to school with us whites."

Jacob looked most uncomfortable as Rob stepped forward.

"Let me tell you something," Rob shouted, stopping a few inches from Darin's face. "In this country, we don't say nigger unless we want a damn good beating."

"Oh yeah?" Darin shot back, giving Rob a hard shove. "What are you going to do about it, nigger lover?"

A sharp left hook to Darin's nose, followed by a solid right to the side of his jaw was Rob's answer. Darin went reeling back and fell flat on his butt.

The fight was over. Darin was crying as he got to his feet.

One of the girls ran to tell the teacher and soon Rob, Darin and Jacob were standing in front of Myrna. Seeing Rob was her son, after listening to what had taken place, Myrna ushered the three boys to the principal's office.

Once he heard the boys' account of their altercation, Ian Dane, the principal, turned to Darin. "I'm sorry young man, but although I don't usually condone fist–a-cuffs, you got what you deserved. We don't allow any racial discrimination in this school. By pushing Rob, you were the first to get things physical."

"But where I came from, they have a separate school for niggers," Darin replied.

"Well, we don't in Canada. Here, all races of people are treated equally. If I ever hear of you using that word to describe black people again, you'll be in an awful lot of trouble. If you don't treat Jacob or his sister Ada with respect, you could be expelled from our school. That will be all, boys. I'll be speaking to your parents later today."

After school was out, Ian talked with Myrna about the incident. That evening, after contacting Jed and Eva, Ian dropped in at the Brown's.

Darin's father, Horace, was the area superintendent for the railroad. Once home from school, Darin told his dad about the thrashing Rob had given him. He neglected, however, to tell his father about pushing Rob and what he'd said to Jacob that precipitated the shellacking he got.

Ian's meeting with Horace did not go well. When Ian briefed him about the incident, Horace was quite rude and refused to acknowledge the seriousness of his son's racist remarks.

"I'm not swayed by your views on what took place," Horace stated emphatically. 'I'll be taking this up with the school superintendent. Darin may have had a slip of the tongue, but I won't tolerate my son being attacked and beaten up by some school bully. I've a good notion to see this bully's father and give him a piece of my mind."

"Rob doesn't have a dad," Ian interjected. "His father died tragically a few years ago. From what I've observed, he's a good kid. We've never had a problem with him. Now about the young fellow that Rob was defending. It would be wise to leave his dad well enough alone. Jed is the former Light Heavy-Weight Champion of the northeastern states. Although a fair man, he's certainly not to be trifled with. He has a boxing club for the grade seven and eight boys in the school on Tuesday evenings."

"I think it would be a great idea for you to talk with Larry King, the superintendent," Ian added, smiling. "This is Larry's first year with us. He just moved here from Nova Scotia. I'm sure the superintendent will be of great help to you. Have you met Mr. King yet?"

Horace shook his head.

"I'll contact Larry and tell him you'll be in to see him," Ian concluded. "I think you'll be impressed with him. He's a very fair guy."

Ian was chuckling as he headed home.

Ian got Larry on the phone, gave him a heads-up on the problem they had at school earlier that day and the contact he had made with the boys' parents.

"I tried to get through to this Horace Brown guy, but I'm afraid I didn't make much progress with him. He was belligerent and said he intended to take up the issue with the superintendent. The best of luck to you in dealing with the ignorant ass."

The next morning at nine am, sharp, Horace stormed into the School Division Office and approached the secretary.

"I need to speak to the superintendent," he shouted.

"Mr. Brown here to see you," the secretary said, ushering Horace into the superintendent's office.

Larry leapt to his feet and greeted Horace with a bone-crushing handshake. Larry stood 6 feet 4 inches and weighed 220 lb. Mr. Brown stood there dumbfounded and speechless.

Larry King was black.

For the rest of the year, the matter of discrimination against Jacob and Ada was muted. As usual, Rob was always there for Jacob and Ada. For the most part, Darin kept a low profile, recognizing that wisdom was the better part of valour.

The year after Rob's fight with Darin, Maud and Michael took the train to eastern Canada. It was the first time either of them had been off the prairies. The 25 pounds of home-grown beef jerky they brought with them made a hit with all those they shared the treat with. Myrna took Rob, Ada, Jacob, Maud and Michael to Niagara Falls and many of the local points of interest.

Michael was a great storyteller. In the evenings, Ada and Jacob would sit totally transfixed as Michael wove his tales of stampedes, cattle drives, swollen rivers, prairie fires, rattlesnakes and the natives, some very hostile, some very kind. Michael and Maud were a hit with Eva and Jed. The Westerners gave the Lewis family a standing invitation to come out West to visit them. All too soon for the kids' liking, Maud and Michael were on their way to the Maritimes and then back to the ranch. Eva and Maud began corresponding by letter on a regular basis.

In July of the year that Rob, Ada and Jacob were twelve, the threesome were on the train heading west to the ranch. Michael and Maud split the cost of the train tickets with Myrna, Jed and Eva. Ada and the boys were so looking forward to their ranch holiday.

Edith met the three junior cowboys at the train station. Seeing it was late in the day, the three spent the night with Edith. At noon the next day, Michael picked them up with his team and buggy.

They spent many enjoyable days riding the range, sometimes by themselves, sometimes with Michael or one of the hands. Michael supplied the three young wranglers with gentle horses. Knowing Rob was familiar with saddling up and bridling horses, Michael delegated that chore to him. He gave them a couple of hours of chores each day and paid them for their work. The boys would do outside chores, while Ada assisted Sue and Maud in the kitchen. Ada had become a good cook under Eva's tutelage and both Sue and Maud were very appreciative of her help.

One afternoon, Rob took Jacob and Ada to the place where his dad died.

"This cross marks the spot where the grizzly killed my dad," Rob said. "Michael figured the bear snuck up behind Dad and the horse he was riding. By looking at the tracks in the snow, Michael figured Dad was leading the horse. The wind was blowing hard that day so he probably couldn't hear the bear. Anyway, Michael figured the bear swatted the horse on the rump. The horse pulled the reins out of Dad's hand and ran for the ranch buildings. Dad emptied the 30-30 rifle into the bear's chest, but before it died the bear swatted Dad, breaking his neck. Michael found Dad and the bear right here. Both were dead. This is also the place I told you about where Dad's spirit visited me a short while after he died."

"Yes, I remember you talking about it," Ada replied. "Being here must make you kind of sad."

"You're right," Rob replied wistfully. "You see, I was having such a rough time after Dad died. Back then, Edith told me my dad might visit me if I called for him every night. I did, but nothing was happening. I thought that he might have forgotten about me, but then he visited me right here. Although I'd have given anything if I could have brought Dad back from the dead, seeing his spirit helped me an awful lot."

"I'm so sorry for you," Ada interjected, wrapping her arms around him. "Father Parent was right. When you were so in need, your dad came here to comfort you."

One day, early in their stay, the three were out riding the range. Rob and Jacob decided they should do some exploring, east of the ranch boundary, up into the forested hills. Michael had advised them to make sure they stayed on the ranch property. Ada lobbied them to do so, but the boys could not be dissuaded. It was two against one so she reluctantly went along. They found a gate in the northeast corner and were on their way. After an hour of exploring the forest, they decided it was time for them to go back. They frantically tried to get their bearings, but finally had to admit that they were lost.

Rob and Jacob were very concerned and Ada was crying. Finally, Rob remembered a trick Michael had told him about when he was out with him on horseback a few years back. "If you ever get lost on horseback, either in a snow storm or if you're out in the bush, let the reins go lose and tell the horse, 'Go Home.'" Rob did just that and his horse struck off to the west. The other horses followed Rob's mount. In a few minutes, they were back at the gate they had come in at. All three breathed a sigh of relief, but agreed that they would keep this tale to themselves.

The three young cow punchers so thoroughly enjoyed their ranch holiday that they talked wistfully of forgetting about going back to Ontario and making the ranch their new home.

Ada was well into puberty, while Jacob and Rob were just starting into their growth spurt. Michael was well aware of the male- female thing. He watched his single hands like a hawk to make sure none of them tried to sidle up to his young female guest.

With their hormones becoming active, Rob and Ada were now starting to have strange, different feelings for each other. In the past, Rob and Jacob just treated Ada as one of the boys. Now when they were by themselves, some primal feelings were stirring within Rob and Ada. When they were alone, they occasionally held hands.

One day, Jacob chose to go to town with Michael, leaving Rob and Ada to ride the range by themselves. Ada had made them a lunch. At dinnertime, they ended up back at the little cabin in the bush. After they found a patch of saskatoons at the edge of the forest. They tied their horses up and began feasting on the berries. Rob had taken a couple of small milk pails with them in case they found a saskatoon patch. Soon they had both pails full. For the next few days, to everyone's delight, there was saskatoon fruit or saskatoon pie for dessert.

Finally, it was time for Michael and Maud to take Rob, Ada and Jacob into Irvine to catch the train home to Ontario. As they were riding along, homeward bound, the three made a pact that some day they would return to the bald prairie to live.

CHAPTER 14

F OR SOME TIME, Myrna wanted to build a picket fence to keep the dogs out of her garden. Before the three children left for the ranch, Myrna, with the help of Rob and Jacob, placed the fence posts around the perimeter of the backyard. With the three gone to the ranch, Myrna contacted Emil Frum who ran the local lumberyard to get an idea of the lumber she'd need to finish the fence. Emil was a bachelor in his mid-thirties. He and his retired, widowed mother had moved to town and purchased the business a few years before Myrna and Rob arrived. Emil offered to come over to the house to measure things up for the materials she would need. Emil arrived after supper. In short order, they had a list of materials that were needed and Myrna invited Emil in for tea.

"I'll have the materials delivered tomorrow afternoon," Emil said. "Do you have anyone to give you a hand in building the fence?"

"Not really. I suppose I could wait till Rob gets back, but I'd really like to get it done before he returns. It would be a nice surprise for him."

"I'll tell you what," Emil replied. "I can give you a hand. I'd be able to help you for two or three hours each evening after work and all-day Saturday. We should be able to get it done in less than a week."

"You don't know how much I'd appreciate that. How much would you charge for labour?"

"Well, you're buying the materials from my store so throw in the suppers and there will be no charge for my help. Do we have a deal?"

"That's a most kind offer. When can we get started?"

"How about tomorrow?"

"Supper will be waiting for you."

The twosome started on the project Tuesday after supper. Myrna always said it was a strange way to start a courtship, but a good way to start one. As they worked together on the fence, they learned much about their respective lives.

"I've had no luck with relationships," Emil lamented one evening. "I guess part of the problem was the girls I chose. One girlfriend had two kids who were real brats. One was eight, the other one 10. The kids were spoiled rotten and had their mother completely under their control. When I tried to get the kids to treat their mother better, all three of them turned against me. Another girlfriend was single and had no kids. After we'd gone out for a few months I discovered she had a serious drinking problem. I guess my motto should read, 'you can't win for losing.' Mom was always sticking her nose in and critiquing the girls I dated. That didn't help."

"I had two relationships," Myrna responded. "I sort of had a crush on William when I was about 11. He was from a district a few miles from my home town. His school ball team sometimes played our school team. William had moved out West. When I finished normal school, William contacted me.

They needed a teacher at the ranch where he was working. I agreed to accept the position and headed out West to the ranch. It really clicked between William and me and in a few months, we got married."

"It was a good marriage. William was strong-willed, but he was a very compassionate, kind man. When he died, it was very hard on me. It was equally hard on Rob. They were such great buddies. After his death I came to realize that the ranch was a foreign country to me. I moved off the ranch some twenty-five miles to the town of Medicine Hat and taught there for a year. While teaching that year, I recognized that for my own mental welfare, Rob and I had to leave the West and return to Ontario to be with my kinfolk."

"I had this notion that once back here all would be well, but I was still very lonely. I got this brainwave that I should start dating Morris, one of my fellow teachers. He was good-looking, but sadly that was all that was good about him." Myrna told Emil of their marriage and troubled relationship.

"Without question, life throws us many curves," Emil responded. "With the loss of your first husband and the abusive relationship with this Morris creature, you and Rob have had more than your share of heartaches. My heart goes out to both of you."

Myrna was touched by Emil's words of compassion.

By four pm Saturday, the fence was finished.

Myrna and Emil had just started dating when Rob, Ada and Jacob returned from their western excursion.

Rob knew Emil to see him, but they'd never spoken to each other. Still being very loyal to his dad's memory and remembering his mom's failed marriage to Morris, Rob was not exactly elated with the news that his mom was inviting yet another man into their lives.

A few nights after Rob got back from the ranch, Myrna had Emil over for supper. Although Rob was polite and thanked Emil for his help with the fence, the conversation between the two gentlemen was strained to say the least.

"There's just too much difference between Dad and Emil," Rob said to his mom when Emil left. "I just remember my dad so clearly. Emil can't hold a candle to Dad. I guess it's your decision, but when Dad visited me at the cross, he told me to look after you and I'm just trying to do that. And then I remember that arse of a Morris. One of these days, when I get a bit bigger, I'll be visiting him. I can live with him beating on me, but I'll beat the ever-living crap out of him for beating on you. Have you checked out Emil's background? You told me you never did that with Morris."

"Thanks for looking out for me, son," Myrna replied. "You'll never know how much that means to me. I've already checked out Emil's background and from what I've gathered, it's all good."

In the upcoming days, Myrna tried her best to foster a good relationship between Emil and Rob. It turned out to be somewhat of a difficult task. Being a bachelor in his thirties, Emil had never had to deal with children and was very uncomfortable in reaching out to Rob. Rob got along well with older men in general, especially with Jed, Michael and those he grew up with on the ranch. He did, however, have a bias against Emil as he thought he was trying to replace his beloved dad. In addition, his bad memories of Morris didn't help the situation any. Despite his feelings of uneasiness, he chose to keep his concerns to himself rather than harping away about his feelings to his mom.

Rob worked an hour or so after school delivering papers. In addition, he, Ada and Jacob still worked a half day Saturday for Jed.

One evening when Emil was visiting, he offered Rob a couple of hours work after school at the lumberyard. The offer was made in kindness, but it didn't bring the intended results.

Rob didn't answer, but vigorously shook his head.

"You'll never get ahead in life delivering papers," Emil added. "Working in the store would give you good work experience. You could even work part-time on Saturdays and put in more hours in the summer break."

"I like doing my own thing," Rob responded, his voice strained. "Besides, Jed has Jake, Ada and me work for him or his boss Saturday mornings doing carpentry stuff. Next summer, I'm headed back to the ranch. Michael, Dad's old boss, said he'd give me a job for two months this coming summer."

Myrna had been looking daggers at Emil, attempting to signal him to lay off, but Emil did not have his antenna engaged and continued on undeterred.

"If you calculate the cost of train fare out to the ranch and back, you'd probably make more money working for me."

"I couldn't give a damn about the money thing," Rob countered. "Michael will pay my way out there and back and besides, I love the ranch. That's where my dad is buried and that's where his spirit came to me, Michael and Aunt Edith."

"Yes, we often think we see things when someone near to us dies," Emil replied.

"Don't be ignorant," Rob shot back, his voice rising. "You weren't there. My dad came to visit me one day at the cross. Michael was there and he too saw Dad. Edith also saw my dad's spirit the same day he was killed."

It would not be a winning day for Emil. Rob leapt to his feet and headed to his room.

"You've got to try to be more sensitive with Rob," Myrna said, once Rob had left. "Rob wasn't the only one who was visited by William's spirit. Both Michael and Edith saw William's spirit too. You couldn't ask for more reliable people than them."

"A few days before I left for Ontario, I went out to the ranch and then out to the cross that marked the spot where William was killed. I so needed William's council that day and as I sat by the cross, I was asking for his guidance. The words were no sooner out of my mouth when a huge raven landed on the cross right beside me. I'm confident that it was William that came in that bird to give me assurance that moving to Ontario was the right thing for Rob and me to do."

Emil smiled and shrugged his shoulders. Myrna recognized by the look on his face that he didn't believe in anything that was of the paranormal.

"I'm not one to interfere, but do you think that maybe Rob could stand to be coached not to use such rough language, especially when speaking to an adult?" Emil added quietly. "Maybe we should change the subject."

Myrna was a big hit with Emil's mom, Elsie. Elsie had been a teacher and she and Myrna had much in common.

While Myrna and Emil were courting, Rob spent a lot of time at the Lewis place.

The feelings that Ada and Rob started having for each other at the ranch, intensified over the coming year. Jed was a good chaperone though. One day when alone with Rob, he mentioned he was aware that Rob was having feelings for Ada. "Rob," he said with a grin. "When you're with my daughter, just remember to keep your pecker in your pants."

Rob smiled and nodded.

In early July, Rob was western bound to spend the school break working at the ranch. He had wanted Jacob and Ada to accompany him again, but Jacob was working with his dad. As Eva had started working at the hotel again, Ada stayed at home and did the housekeeping and cooking.

Rob was now well into puberty and really enjoyed working full-time. He was a welcome addition to the ranch crew. The regular hands marveled while working with Rob how he could keep right up with them.

When Rob was alone with the single hands, they teased him about Ada and asked him why he hadn't brought his girlfriend back for the summer.

One afternoon, when out on the range with a couple of hands, one of the cow punchers who used snuff offered Rob a pinch. At first Rob turned the offer down, but after a bit of friendly pressure from the two cowboys, he took a large pinch of snuff and placed it under his bottom lip. Within minutes he was dizzy and his head started to spin. It took a couple of hours before he felt normal again. It was his first experience with snuff and he vowed it would be his last.

Rob dropped in on Edith for a couple of weekends. He told her of the experiences he and his mom had with Morris and Emil. "Morris was such a total asshole. Why Mom ever fell for him, I'll never know. I guess she was lonely. Anyway, her new boyfriend, Emil, seems like a pretty good sort. He couldn't hold a candle to Dad, but he seems kind to Mom. It sounds like they will be getting married fairly soon."

At the end of August, Rob was on his way back to Ontario. Although he enjoyed the summer's work, he was looking forward to being back home with Ada and Jacob, especially with Ada. Over the summer, they had exchanged a number of letters.

Back at home, things were going fairly smoothly for Myrna and Emil. They had visited Eva and Jed a couple of times. Jed knew Emil from his work as a carpenter and thought well of him.

Just before school started, the Lewis' got bad news from Jed's folks in Tennessee. His mom phoned that Jed's dad had a heart attack and had been hospitalized.

Jed took the train back to Tennessee. Although Jed's dad, Abe, was recovering, the doctor advised him that in the future he'd have to cut out all heavy physical work. Abe was in a bind as Jed was his only son. As heavy work was out of the question, he was at a loss as what they should do with the farm and wondered if Jed would be interested in coming home to take over it's operation.

Jed advised his dad that he'd talk things over with Eva and then they would jointly decide whether or not to accept the offer. When Jed returned home, he and Eva had an ongoing discussion of the pros and cons of moving back to the States.

Once Rob was back home, Ada, Jacob and he were back in school and again spending their free time hanging out together.

One day in mid September, Rob was looking most glum as his mom, Emil and he were eating supper.

"Is something bothering you?" Myrna said. "You seem down in the mouth. I know you're having some problems with one of your teachers. Is that it?"

"Not really," Rob replied with a sigh. "I'm afraid my worst dream is about to come true. As you know, Jed went back to be with his dad when he had heart trouble. When Jed got back home, he said that although his dad was holding his own, he wouldn't be able to do any heavy work anymore. Anyway, Ada just broke the news to me that they've decided that they're going to be moving back to the States. Jed's folks want Jed and Eva to take over running the farm. What a bummer. How on earth will I ever find friends like Jacob and Ada again? It will be especially hard on me losing Ada."

"I know it's going to be hard for you, but you can certainly correspond by writing each other and who knows, maybe the odd time you can take the train down to visit them."

Shortly before the Lewis' were to leave, an incident occurred that tested Rob's mettle. For the most part, Darin had given Rob his space since the altercation they had several years before. With Ada now being a real knock-out and a very close friend of Rob, out of spite, Darin thought he'd make a play for her. He planned on doing it more to prove his bravado to his male chums than because of an emotional or physical attraction towards her. His timing would prove a bit off.

At the end of a class one afternoon, the students were milling about in the hallway on their way to their next class. Darin had been boasting to some of his male counterparts that this was the day he was going to make a play for Ada. As Ada was walking past him, he called out, "what's the rush, Babe?" and put his arm around her waist.

"Leave me alone," Ada cried out. Before she could break away, Darin had his other arm around her with his hand on her breast.

Rob heard Ada call out and came running.

Darin had Ada pinned. While he was trying to smooch her on the neck, his hand had moved from her breast to her leg. He was glancing over at his buddies hoping to get a thumbs-up for his daring antic and didn't notice Rob rushing up.

Rob grabbed Darin by the hair and yanked him away from Ada. Before Darin could react, Rob hit him a dandy on the side of his head.

Initially, Darin thought he'd impressed his friends with his advances towards Ada, but now he had been clobbered by Ada's protector. In order to save face, he felt he had to prove himself against his attacker. Shaking his head to try to clear the cobwebs, he bellowed, "You always liked to throw your weight around, asshole. I'm going to beat the ever-living crap out of you!"

Although Darin was a year older than his rival, he was ignorant of boxing techniques. Rob not only possessed tenacity, but over the years, Jed had taught him and Jacob basic boxing skills. In addition, a couple of years back, Jed had introduced Jacob and Rob to weightlifting. Even though a bit younger than his rival, Rob was very strong and had lots of stamina.

Minutes into the fight, Darin had yet to land a damaging blow. Rather than him beating the crap out of Rob, Rob was beating the crap out of him. His nose was bleeding. One of his eyes was swollen shut and turning black and his face was red and puffy. As Rob continued to beat on him mercilessly, Darin was staggering.

In desperation, recognizing that the fight wasn't going his way, Darin hollered, "take this" and threw a wild haymaker at Rob. Rob ducked low and the haymaker sailed harmlessly over his head. With Darin being off balance, Rob caught him with a hard-right-overhand to the side of his jaw. Darin reeled backward and collapsed, unconscious. The fight was over. One of the girls who witnessed the fight raced to the principal's office. Darin was still out cold when principal, Ian Dane, came running up.

While Ada filled Ian in on what happened, Darin was coming to.

"Your sexual advances towards Ada will not go unanswered," Ian shouted. "Get to my office. I'm calling the police, the superintendent, Ada's folks, your folks and Rob's mother. I also want Rob, Ada and any of you students that witnessed the incident to come to the office."

It was not a good day for Darin. While they were waiting for the police to arrive, Ian had the students who had witnessed the fight write out their observations of the whole affair and then let them return to their classes. Their accounts all jived with what Ada had told Ian. When Larry King and the police arrived, they read the accounts the students had written. After hearing from Ada, Rob and Darin, the officer was all for laying sexual assault charges against Darin. Jed and Eva arrived a bit late and were briefed on the incident. Jed was enraged that Ada had been violated. Eva had her hands full keeping Jed from tying another licking on Darin. Although initially Larry King thought Darin deserved being charged, after talking to Darin's buddies, he learned that Darin had initiated his assault of Ada on a dare. It appeared to all that his intent was not to take sexual advantage of Ada, but to prove his bravado to his cronies. They decided rather than laying sexual assault charges, Darin would be expelled from school. In addition, a restraining order would be placed on him forbidding him from having contact with Ada or Rob.

"Thank you so much for defending Ada," Jed said to Rob as they were leaving the principal's office. "From what everyone says, you beat the tar out of him. We're so proud of you. I wish I had been there to give you a hand. Job well done! We'll have to keep a watch out for Darin's old man, though. From what I gather, both Darin and his old man are real assholes."

Darin's mom and dad were out of town when the incident occurred. When they returned, the superintendent advised Darin's folks on what action the school division had taken. Rather than accepting the decision of the police and superintendent, Darin's dad contacted a lawyer with the hopes of bringing action against the school board. Once his lawyer examined all the facts, he advised the Browns that from what was witnessed by the students, Darin could have been charged with sexual assault. Had charges been laid, he could have ended up in reform school.

Rather than taking the advice from the lawyer to cool it, Horace chose to take matters into his own hands. In a School Parent Advisory Council meeting, he raised the issue of the superintendent expelling Darin from school and ranted and raved about the unfairness of the action. All in all, he made a capital ass of himself.

Jed and Eva attended the meeting. As the meeting was breaking up, Jed caught up to Horace in the hallway and stepped in front of him.

"It was my daughter your son took advantage of," Jed began. "From what I gather, Ada's friend, Rob, knocked the crap out of your son. Had I been there, the little bastard would have been taken to the hospital."

"Out of my way," Horace barked. "I have nothing to say to you."

Had Eva not been with Jed, Horace would have been on the way to the hospital from the Jed-inflicted bruises. She now stood between the two gentlemen.

"If I were you, Mr. Brown, for the sake of my health, I'd leave as fast as I possibly could. I don't know how long I can hold this man of mine at bay. If he loses his cool and starts in on you, I can guarantee you a hospital stay. I've seen him in action both in and out of the ring. Let me assure you it isn't a pretty experience for his opponents."

Without making any comment and with a terrified look on his face, Horace stepped around Jed and made a quick retreat. When the whole issue was published in the local paper, the community held both Darin and his dad in distain. In a fit of anger, Horace quit his job and he and the family moved back to the States.

Rob was desperately hoping that there would be a change of plans for the Lewis family, but such was not the case. On a Friday, in early October, Eva told Myrna that they'd be leaving next week.

Myrna had a small going away party for them. Rob and his mom bid Jacob, Ada, Jed and Eva goodbye at the railway station. Their parting was especially hard for Rob and Ada as over the last year they had become very close. As Rob hugged Ada goodbye, both of them were in tears. Then the Lewis' climbed the steps of the coach. The train pulled out and they were on their way down South.

CHAPTER 15

THE REST OF the school year was pretty heavy sledding for Rob. Up till now he only had Jacob and Ada as close friends. With them gone, he found himself living a lonely existence. He half-heartedly tried to make some new friends, but was not having much success. As his mom and Emil were now a twosome, without Ada's and Jacob's friendship, loneliness was Rob's constant companion.

Although Emil's relationship with Rob continued to improve, Emil felt somewhat threatened by Myrna's and Rob's memory of William. He recognized he had big shoes to fill.

"When you're talking to Rob, it's best to not say anything negative about his dad," Myrna said one day. "He's very loyal to his dad's memory and as you can imagine, no man can measure up to his father."

"I gathered that much," Emil responded. "I recognize I'm in a delicate situation with Rob. I'll be extra careful."

Myrna also coached Rob on trying to get along with Emil and to always be polite with him. Over time, her efforts at smoothing out things between Emil and Rob began bearing fruit. Although relations weren't as yet at a buddy-buddy level, neither one was rattling the other one's chain anymore.

Myrna was pleased that both were making a concerted effort to get along.

With the news of Myrna's new relationship with Emil, all her fellow teachers expressed happiness for her. She assured them that her relationship with Emil would not be a repeat of the Morris fiasco.

Although Myrna was happy to have a new relationship, she still harbored feelings of betrayal to the memory of William, her first love. The more Emil pressured her to get engaged, the more uneasy she felt. One evening in early winter when she was alone in the house, she called out in desperation to William to give her a sign that marrying Emil was the right thing to do.

All the windows and doors in the house were closed and it was a calm night. Something made her look at the wind chimes that were by one window. To her astonishment, the chimes began to jangle. For several seconds, they played a melodious tune. As quick as they started to sway, they stopped.

"Thank you, darling. That's so wonderful of you to contact me again when I needed your counsel so much." Although Myrna told the wind chimes incident to Rob, she decided to keep William's miraculous visitation from Emil.

Myrna and Emil announced their engagement at Christmas. In April, on the long weekend, during the school Easter holidays, they would take the train to Niagara Falls and be married there in a quiet ceremony. Both Myrna and Emil encouraged Rob to accompany them. At first, he thanked his mom and Emil for the invitation, but told them it would be easier for him if he stayed at home. However, when he found out that Jed, Eva and Ada would be coming up from Tennessee to attend the wedding, he quickly changed his mind. Jacob was not feeling well so would stay at home. With his own money, Rob bought a train ticket to Niagara Falls.

Ada sat with Rob at the ceremony and they held hands. Unlike his mom's marriage to Morris, this wedding was a happy occasion for all. It made Myrna so grateful that the Lewis family was happy with her choice. By Emil's track record, Jed and Eva were confident that he would treat Myrna and Rob well.

For the rest of the long weekend, Rob and Ada were inseparable. They went for many long walks to the falls.

Once back from the wedding, Rob was very lonesome for his dark female friend. The two were now corresponding by letter on a regular basis.

Relations between Rob and Emil continued to remain cordial. Both stepfather and stepson were doing their best to be amicable with each other.

At the end of June, Rob was again on the train heading West. When he got to the station in Medicine Hat, Edith was there to greet him. The next day, Michael was on his way into Medicine Hat to pick up Rob.

It soon became obvious to Michael and the crew at the ranch that young Rob was growing into quite a man. "It's just like having a young version of his dad working with us," Dave commented to Michael one day. "Last year, he was getting some size to him, but now he's a strapping young man."

"Yes, you're right. The young lad is as strong or stronger than most any of us. Give him another few years and he'll be as big and powerful as his dad. Would William ever be proud of him!"

In his spare time, Rob would often ride out to the cross that marked the spot where his dad drew his last breath. He'd sit by the cross on the old block, just to be close to where his dad had died and where his dad's spirit had visited him many years before.

A week before Rob left for Ontario again, Mildred phoned the ranch that Eric had a bad stroke that paralyzed his right side. Although the stroke didn't impair his ability to speak, he was now confined to a wheelchair or bed.

Accompanied by his Grandma Mildred, Rob had visited his grandpa a few times since he and his mom came East. More often than not, Eric was either under the influence of alcohol or suffering from a hangover and of course the house was always a pig-sty. Mildred made it known to one and all that her ex-husband was an irresponsible old booze hound.

With Eric now totally reliant on others for his keep and with the cost of hospital care high, Mildred, Ken and daughters Becky and Beth moved him to a small house in town once he could be safely discharged from the hospital. They hired Marian Richards, a retired nurse, as a live-in caregiver. To cover expenses, they sold the farm to the neighbor who had been renting their land. After helping their mom move Eric into town, Becky and Beth would have nothing more to do with their dad.

Although Marian was kind to a fault, she kept Eric on a short leash. At first, she allowed him only one drink of rye per day. Strangely, after a couple of weeks, he accepted the new limits to his drinking and was no longer pestering her for more booze. Stranger still, a short time later, he completely weaned himself off alcohol. A new era was on the horizon.

Once Rob was back home, he and his Grandma Mildred visited Eric. It was a complete change of venue for Rob as his grandpa now was a sober man. He asked Rob to drop in sometime and play a game of checkers with him.

"It's sure different visiting Grandpa now that he's not on the booze anymore," Rob commented to his grandma once they had left. "I can't ever remember Grandpa not being drunk or hung over."

"Yes, it's a real miracle alright. Marian says he hasn't touched a drop of whisky in over a month. Why, oh, why couldn't he have gotten off the booze before? Think of all the years he's wasted. I only visit him out of my feelings of duty. I used to love him dearly, but any feelings I had for him have all dried up. I just can't forgive him for all those wasted years and what his boozing did to our family. Had he even shown the slightest bit of effort in trying to lick his drinking problem, I'd have never divorced him and married Ken. It's all too late now though."

A week later, Rob was on his way to see his grandpa. He felt quite nervous as he knocked on the door. He really didn't know his grandpa that well. This would be his first one-on-one visit with him.

"Your grandson here to see you, Eric," Marian called out as Rob stepped inside.

"Thanks for looking me up," Eric replied from his bedroom. "Come on in. I have the checkerboard ready."

Eric was in his wheelchair at a small table. There was another chair on the other side of the table. Rob sat down and the contest began. They played five games. Rob was amazed at Eric's skill. His grandpa won four of the five games they played and Rob was pretty sure that his granddad had let him win that one game. Rob was astonished at the change that had come over Eric since he'd dried out. It was a case of Doctor Jekyll-Mr. Hyde. Before, he dreaded the visits as his grandpa had always acted like a drunken old sot. To his amazement, he now found that his grandad had a brilliant mind and a great sense of humor.

Despite the change that had come over Eric, other than Mildred's and Rob's visits, the rest of the family would have nothing to do with him. Rob would always bike over to his grandpa's house every Sunday afternoon for another checkers tournament. By the end of six months, Rob's skill had improved to the point that now he was winning about a third of the games.

Rob was always astonished at the depth and insight his grandpa had on a host of topics. He looked forward to their weekly conversations as much as their checker tournaments.

Rob had a fair amount of money saved up from working at the ranch. During the Easter break, he took the train down into the States to see Jacob, Ada and their folks. It was a bittersweet visit. Although he had a great time with his two friends, Jacob was not doing all that well.

"I've had these horrible headaches for the last while," he told Rob. "Last week we went to see a specialist and the news wasn't good. They x-rayed me and the doctor said I had an inoperable tumor on my brain. He figured it was cancerous. It's the pits, but they said there was nothing they could do. At times, life can sure be a proper bitch." Despite his horrible diagnosis, Jacob tried to remain in good spirits.

In spite of the grim news from Jacob, the attraction between Rob and Ada was becoming stronger. She always looked up to Rob. In the past, he was the big strong friend who never let anyone take advantage of Jacob or her, but now, romantic feelings towards Rob were building.

To say that Rob fell under Ada's spell would be an understatement. She had changed from the tomboy Jacob and he used to roughhouse with to this beautiful sexual being. This time, when their eyes met, it was like the flash of fireworks. With Jed as the chauffeur, Jacob, Ada and Rob spent many hours sightseeing in the family's newly purchased car. One evening, Rob and Ada went for a long walk. Jacob was feeling under the weather so stayed at home.

As they were walking, Rob reached over and took Ada's hand.

"Do you mind?" he asked awkwardly.

"Not at all," Ada whispered, "We held hands at your mom's wedding and ever since you came down here, I've been waiting for you to take my hand."

"Why do we have to be so far apart?" Rob said glumly.

"I guess until we're both through school, we could continue to write letters."

In the growing darkness, Rob took Ada in his arms. As he held her tight, he rubbed his face against hers.

All too soon, Rob had to head back home. The threesome made a pact to keep in closer contact by writing letters.

Once he got home, it was back to the old grind for Rob. Although separated by over a thousand miles, Rob's heart was back in Tennessee with his sick friend and the young dark-skinned lady he'd held in his arms.

CHAPTER 16

A FEW DAYS AFTER returning, Rob was over at Eric's place to play checkers. It was close to a year now since they'd started having their checker tournaments. Eric seemed unusually quiet. They only played one game when he set the checker board aside.

"Let's talk," he said. "I imagine Grandma Mildred has told you a lot about me and my drinking days."

"Yeah, sort of," Rob replied. "Grandma and I visited you a few times when you were on the farm. You were pretty well hammered most of the time."

"Yeah, I know. I was wasted most of the time. I've got to be honest with you. Ever since my accident, I've acted like a proper jerk."

"Grandma said you used to be a very hard worker and were very dependable. She said that you used to have a drink or two the odd time, but then all of a sudden, for no good reason you went to pot and became a real booze hound."

"She's right for the most part. For the last twenty or so years, I guess I've been a waste of skin. The part about me having no good reason to become a booze hound is dead wrong though. I had a reason why I drank so much, but I just

169

couldn't get up the courage to tell what it was. Believe me, it's hard for me to tell you all of this now. Try to understand that as a young guy, physically I was strong as a bull. I was a follower though and not a leader. I guess you could say I was emotionally weak."

"I've noticed that for the last while my mind has been slowing down and I've started to get these real bad headaches. A few nights past, I had a dream that I was soon going to die and that it was time to tell all. It's pretty heavy stuff, but now I know its time to spill my guts. You're the only one of the family who gives a damn about me, so if you'd care to listen, I'd like to tell you my story. You must promise to tell no one until after I've croaked. Do we have a deal?"

"If it would help you, Grandpa, go ahead. I promise to keep it to myself until after you're gone."

Rob reached over and shook Eric's outreached hand.

"Okay, but you'll have to try understand how hard it is for me to bare my soul to you."

"I understand, Grandpa. Go ahead."

"You see, back when I was in my mid-twenties, I was working the winter away from the farm in a lumber camp in northern Quebec. Your grandma and I had only been married for a couple of years. Pierre Richard was my workmate. We were fellers, cutting down and limbing the trees. Later, the logs were skidded to the river bank and in the spring, they'd float them down the river to the sawmill. We were back in the bush some three or four miles from the main camp, had our own little cabin and did our own cooking. Other than having a bad temper, Pierre was an okay sort. Seeing he had more experience at bush work than I had, I let him take the lead and everything went fairly smoothly."

"At nights, we'd sometimes get into political arguments, but nothing too serious. Pierre had a violin and would play old jigs and the like. He was not too bad on the violin and even though I'd get my fill of his playing, I never complained."

Rob smiled. "I know where you're coming from. Last summer at the ranch, one of the hands had a guitar. He played it hour on end in the bunkhouse. It got to be a real pain in the butt."

"I hear you. Anyway, one afternoon while I was out working in the timber berth, limbing, Pierre took the toboggan and headed to the main camp for supplies. He got his hands on a bottle of whisky and by the time he got back to camp he was feeling no pain. We forgot about supper and both of us got into the booze in earnest. Before long I too was feeling no pain, but I was nowhere near as wasted as he was."

"After a bit, he grabs his violin. He was none too co-ordinated and stumbled. He banged the violin up against the table and a string broke. He blew his cool and the drunken fool blamed me for playing around with his violin when he was not around and tightening one string too much. I told him I hadn't touched his stupid violin and he shouted that I had. I got fed up with him and told him he was nothing but a drunken little frog. The fight was on. When he was sober, he would never have dared get into a tussle with me as I was much bigger and stronger than he was. He came at me, fists just a flailing, calling me all sorts of crude names. I pushed him back, but that only made him madder. When he came back at me again, he had the steel poker in his hand and said he was going to brain me with it. Anyway, he swings this poker at me. I ducked and he missed. When he swung the poker the second time I ducked again and he missed me again. I saw my opening and caught him a dandy on the side of his jaw. Pierre fell backwards full force. The poker went flying and he hit the back of his head a terrible crack on the sharp edge of the open cook stove oven door."

"When I looked at him, he wasn't moving. I tried pouring a cup of cold water on his face to bring him too. To my horror, I then saw he wasn't breathing and his eyes were open in a death stare. I tried for several minutes to get some life back in him, but nothing worked. What to do? What to do? I knew it wouldn't look good if I reported we had an argument and a fight and I hit him so hard that he died. I finally decided that all I could do was to get rid of his body. It seemed to me that was the only choice I had. After all these years, I'm still unsure whether or not it was the right thing to have done."

"Man, that must have been scary. Just thinking on it makes me queasy. What the hell did you do?"

Eric was breathing heavily as he continued.

"Well, I sat there a spell racking my brain, wondered what I could do with his body. Then it came to me. We used to get our drinking water from the river about a quarter of a mile away. I loaded Pierre on the toboggan, put our cream can, axe, bailing pail and his mitts on board and headed for the river. We had a 2-foot by 2-foot hole cut in the ice. I cleaned the new ice out of the hole and slipped poor Pierre into the opening. The current pulled him away. Then I filled the bailing pail with water and let it sink to the bottom of the waterhole. I wanted to make it look like he fell in while he was trying to retrieve the pail. I left his mitts and everything else by the waterhole."

"My God, what a bind to be in," Rob interjected. "You did what you had to do. I mean, what else could you have done? The way I see it, if I'd been in your shoes, I'd have done the same thing you did."

"Anyway, I headed back to the cabin, walked back to the main camp and got a hold of the boss. By now I was sober."

"We got a problem," I told him. "Pierre came back to our cabin late this afternoon, pretty drunk and went down to the river to get water. When he didn't come back after an hour, I went looking for him. The toboggan, cream cans and his mitts were at the waterhole, but there was no sign of him. Seeing he was pretty drunk, I figure he must have fallen into the waterhole and drowned."

"I stayed in the main camp overnight. In the morning, someone went to notify the police. The police officer arrived late in the day. The next morning, three of us plus the police went back to the cabin. After looking things over, the police asked me a bunch of questions. I showed him the bailing pail you could see at the bottom of the waterhole. I guess he was satisfied that there was no foul play because in his report he called it an accident. The police figured the river current carried Pierre's body away and if they ever did find the body, it wouldn't be until next spring after the melt."

"Another fellow came to take Pierre's place. As he was young and inexperienced, I took the lead. Although we got along well, for the rest of the winter I went through hell with the horrible memory of what I'd done. Keeping busy helped keep me from going crazy. In the middle of March, we shut things down for the year and I came home."

"Some time later I checked in with the police. When the ice was gone, they had done a bit of a search, but found nothing. As near as I know, they never did find Pierre's body. The police said they had told Pierre's kinfolk that his death was an accident."

"I, of course, also told your grandma and everyone else that it was an accident, which in a way I guess it was. Anyway, that's what I kept telling myself. Some time later, I asked a doctor if a person hit themselves hard on the back of the head if it could kill them. The doctor said if a person is hit hard right where the neck and head come together, it can be fatal as it can sever the spinal cord. As time went on, I found the only way I could live with the horror of killing Pierre was to work so hard I didn't have time to think about it. For something close to twenty years I worked like one possessed and I seldom touched booze. As near as I know, no one in the family has ever suspected anything. They just thought I had become a workaholic."

"What a bitch of a thing to have to live with," Rob interjected. "You're right in calling it an accident, though. That's really what it was."

"I half-assed managed for many years. Your dad was born and then your two aunts. I was always thinking and suffering some about Pierre's death, but I might have been able to live with it if it hadn't been for my accident. I believe your dad was 17 the summer my accident happened."

"Your dad and I were putting up hay. Once we got a rack full of hay, we'd pull up to the front of the barn and fork the hay into the barn loft. Anyway, I was up in the loft carrying the hay in once your dad forked it up to me. I was standing at the edge of the loft opening. Your dad was a bit off with a fork full. I reached out with my fork to get it, lost my balance and fell out of the loft. I landed astride the wooden cross piece at the front end of the rack. The pain to my crotch was unreal. I bled some and they took me to the hospital. My knackers turned black and blue. The doctor patched me up, but said as no bones were broken other than giving me something for the pain, there wasn't much more they could do for me. I was swollen up down there for a long time. Every time I had to take a leak there would be some blood coming out. It took me several weeks before I could start doing a little work. During that time, my past started to really haunt me again and I got quite depressed."

"I can sympathize with you, Grandpa. Years ago, when mom was married to that arse of a Morris, he beat on me so hard that I was peeing some blood when I took a leak. All I can think of is that your life went from bad to worse."

"Believe me, it does get worse. Before this accident, I always managed okay in bed. You know; the sex thing. Well, after I'd healed up, one night I decided it was time to give the sex thing a try. Damn, I couldn't believe it. Nothing happened. My poor tool just hung there like a wet noodle. Your grandma thought I tried too soon after my injury. At any rate, I lay off trying to have sex for maybe two weeks or so. Before I tried it again with your grandma, I sort of tried to get things up there by hand. You know what I mean. Things hadn't improved. It still hung there like a wet noodle. As you can imagine I was really pissed off. So, a week or so later, I got in touch with my doctor and told him about my problem. He referred me to a specialist in the city."

"I told the specialist about my accident. After he examined me, he sat for quite a spell, shaking his head and reading my doctor's report."

"'It's like this,'" he finally said. "'When you fell, you did a lot of damage to the nerves and blood vessels at the base of your penis. Everything is healed now, but everything has to work just right for a man to get an erection. I'm sorry, but from a medical point of view, I don't have a good answer for you. This means that unless a miracle happens, intercourse is out of the question for you. It's been some time since you had your accident so you've healed as much as you're going to heal down there.'"

"The first thing I did after seeing the doctor was to buy a bottle of rye to try to drown the horrible reality that I would be impotent for the rest of my life. From there on out I was drunk most of the time up until this last stroke. During that first year, on my own, I tried everything possible to get my poor tool up, but nothing worked. I could get excited thinking about sex, but it was still the wet noodle thing. I know it was hard for some people to figure me out, but as I saw it, with me being drunk, nothing much of the sexual thing would be expected of me. Ever since I got back from seeing the specialist, I slept alone. Your grandma thought I was sleeping alone because I was drinking so heavily. By sleeping by myself, I figured that no one would know what my problem was. I imagine you think my reasoning was kind of stupid, but not only did being drunk all the time take the pressure off me not being able to get things up, it helped dull my thinking on Pierre. I guess, if I'm honest, from the time of the accident, my life has pretty well all been down hill. It's been a waste of time."

"What a total piss off your life has been," Rob said, shaking his head. "First there was your accident with Pierre and then falling out of the barn loft and injuring your crotch. I can see now why you turned to booze."

"The family may have wondered why it wasn't too hard to wean myself from the booze after the stroke. I'm partially paralysed now so nothing much of the sex thing could be expected of me. I don't have to hide behind the bottle anymore. While I was boozing, to cut costs, I made my own small still on the farm and brewed my own poison."

"Well that's my story. I hope you don't hate me too much for telling you all the horrible things that happened to me."

"Yes, I think I can understand now where you're coming from, Grandpa. It's a shame you didn't have the balls to come clean on it, but I'm asking myself if I had been in your shoes, would I have done anything differently? Admitting that you're impotent would not be easy to do, especially when you're still fairly young. I guess whether you told all or didn't tell all, you'd still think of yourself as a loser. What a screwed-up life you've been forced to live."

"When I get home, while it's still fresh in my mind, I'll make notes on all you told me. If and when you do croak, I don't want to get your story wrong. For you, there's truth in that old saying, 'life's a bitch and then you die.'"

The next Sunday afternoon when Rob visited his grandpa, the checkerboard was no where in sight.

"Let's talk," Eric said. "I had the strangest dream last night. It's been many, many years since my fight with Pierre, but the silly arse was there in my dream. As near as I can recall, it's the first time that I've dreamt of him. There he was, playing the fiddle again. He wasn't any worse than he had been, but he certainly wasn't any better. Anyway, he was in good spirits and said, 'see you soon.' Now I'm not really into the paranormal thing, but the dream makes me wonder if my time is just about up."

For the rest of Rob's visit, Eric talked non-stop of all the good times he and the family had before he started drinking.

Eric's dream was right on. Six days later he died in his sleep.

The funeral was small with just family and a few neighbors attending. After the minister read a short eulogy, Rob asked if he could say a few words.

"I guess most of us remember Grandpa Eric as a drunk," he began, "but he was able to quit the booze quite some time ago. I started visiting him every Sunday afternoon. Shortly after he swore off drinking, we started playing checkers and he beat me most of the time. A few days before he died, I was visiting him and he told me he had a dream that he was about to die. He told me the story of why he drank so much and that his drinking had ruined not only his life, but had been very hard on his family. Sometime later, I'll tell the family his story of why he was such a boozer. All I can say now is, 'Bye Grandpa. I wish you an easier life the next time around.'"

With the interment over, the immediate family gathered at Mildred's and Ken's place. After they had lunch, Mildred turned to Rob.

"Would this be a good time to tell us the gist of what your grandpa told you about why he became a drunk?"

"Alright," Rob replied after a long pause. "You'll have to remember that some of this is pretty rough stuff. I made some notes on his story. I didn't want to get things mixed up."

"Grandpa said his story started the winter he worked in northern Quebec in a logging camp."

"Yes, I remember," Mildred interjected.

Rob wove the tale of Pierre's death, Eric's injury when he fell out of the barn and him turning to alcohol to numb the pain of being impotent. Every family member was in shock as they tried to absorb the horrible, incredulous, sad tale.

"When Grandpa finished his story, he told me he had three regrets. His first regret was that he hadn't been strong enough to tell the story to his family. His second regret was that he couldn't tell it to my dad. His third regret was that Pierre had died. He made me promise not to tell the story to anyone until after he died. This is the first time I've told anyone. I told him that once he had passed on, he'd be able to tell his story to my dad. 'That would give me such peace of mind if I could,' Grandpa said."

For a long time, everyone sat in stupefied silence.

"Thank you so much for that information, Rob," Mildred finally blurted out. "Not only were you able to find out why he drank so much, but to your credit, even though he had been a drunk for many years, for the last months of his life, you were a big enough man to befriend your grandpa."

"I think I speak for everyone when I say Eric's story shocks us all out of our minds. If only I had known, if only I had known. You see, after the accident when he turned to alcohol, I assumed that his drinking was what made him want to sleep alone. I should have been smart enough to figure it out, but before God, I never dreamed it was his impotence that caused him to turn to the bottle."

"If only any of us would have known," Becky added. "Poor Dad had to suffer for all these years because he didn't have the strength to tell us his story. It's so sad that he had to spend all those years with the guilt of killing his workmate, not to mention the agony of being impotent. I guess all of us can learn from what happened to Dad. All that keeps going through my mind is what Mom said. If only we would have known. If only Dad had found the intestinal fortitude to tell us."

"Yes, but the death of his work-mate aside, we've got to try to look at this impotency thing from a man's point of view," Jerry, Becky's husband interjected. "The real reason he turned to booze was that he couldn't live with the thought of having to tell his wife that he was impotent. From any man's point of view, it would be extremely hard having it made known that you're impotent, especially when you're still fairly young."

"I think we should let dead dogs lie," Beth added. "I firmly believe the story should end here with us and then die with us."

Everyone except Emil nodded.

Not being family, Ken remained silent. Although Emil didn't agree with Beth, he too remained silent. After discussing Rob's tale, the immediate family decided that it would be best to take Beth's advice and let dead dogs lie.

"I really question not going to the authorities with this confession," Emil began when he, Myrna and Rob got home. "I mean, shouldn't we report a suspicious death?"

Seeing the color coming to Rob's cheeks, Myrna barged in.

"You and I are not even family so I think we'd be wise to keep mum like the rest of the family said they'd do," Myrna added. "What earthly good would an investigation do now? We have to remember that both Eric and Pierre are dead. A judge wouldn't even consider the case seeing all they would have to go on is Rob's word of what Eric told him of an incident that happened 40 years ago. Pierre's family were told by the police that his death was accidental and in away, it was. Besides, all it would do now is rile up a bunch of people."

"Mom's right," Rob added. "Going to the police now wouldn't prove a thing. They'd only have my word to go on and as Mom just said, that would never stand up in court."

Emil was about to respond, but then recognized that it would be wiser to keep peace in the family rather than waxing eloquent. He bit his tongue and remained silent.

Rob pined for his Grandpa Eric a lot. In the last year, other than the odd visit from Mildred, Rob was the only family member who would have anything to do with the old lad. Rob often went out to Eric's grave, just to be close to him.

While Rob was grieving the loss of his grandpa, his relationship with Emil was improving. Rob was no longer delivering papers and would help Emil out in the store occasionally. Myrna was elated that Emil, Rob and she had become a cohesive family.

Although Myrna was happy in their marriage, Emil was starting to put pressure on her to start their own family. Emil's mother was also doing her own lobbying. Emil was her only child and she made it known to Emil that she longed for her 'own grandchildren.' Although she maintained that she had accepted Rob as her step grandchild, her interaction with Rob certainly didn't show it. Their relationship remained cool.

At first, considering the debacle of her marriage to Morris, Myrna was opposed to the plan of starting another family. In addition, she had her career, was well into her thirties and Rob was now past his mid-teens. She wasn't enthralled with the idea of going back to changing diapers, quitting her job and trying to find a babysitter when she went back to work.

The pressure from husband and mother-in-law continued unabated. She thought long and hard about how having a baby would impact on Rob, but felt most awkward in broaching the subject with him. Seeing that she truly loved Emil and that he treated her so well, she finally gave up the fight. Two months later she found out from her doctor that she was expecting. Although Emil and Elsie were ecstatic, Myrna was very concerned at what Rob's reaction would be.

After many days of anguish, Myrna finally decided that it was high time that she told Rob of her pregnancy.

"I'm a bit uneasy about breaking this news to you, Rob," she began when Rob got home from school. "I found out from the doctor yesterday that I'm expecting."

"God Almighty, I don't know what to say, Mom," Rob finally blurted out, slumping down at the kitchen table. "Were you planning this?"

"Sort of," Myrna responded. "When we married, I told Emil that I wasn't interested in having any more children, but although he cares for you a great deal, he desperately wanted us to have another child."

"Emil and I get along really well now, but this is pretty shocking. I've got to take some time to think this one out." Shaking his head, Rob got to his feet and headed outside.

Although very shocked with the news, Rob remained civil with both his mom and Emil. Over the next week or so he did a lot of pondering on how the birth of the baby would impact on him. As he still longed for his old home on the wind-swept prairie, he had made up his mind that once he'd finished his schooling, he would live out West.

"I'll be heading to the ranch in another two weeks," he said to his mom one day in mid-June when they were alone. "I've been thinking about my plans for when the baby arrives and my plans for the future. I'd like to go to school for another year, but after that, I plan on working at the ranch. Michael and Maud have asked me to come to the ranch and work for them full-time once I'm through school."

"I've been feeling more than a little down of late. You see, I still miss Dad something awful. Then, I lost Jacob and Ada a couple of years back and now it looks like Jacob is terminally ill. We were such close friends. Anyway, since they left, I'm not having any luck in making new friends. It seems I don't have that much in common with the kids at school. To top it off, Grandpa's gone. Even though he was a drunk for many years, after he sobered up, I had such a good thing going with him."

"It's good for you guys that you got married. I really mean that, Mom. Emil is so much a better man than that dumb asshole, Morris. From what I see he treats you very well, but now with the baby coming, I just don't know how I'd be able to handle things."

"I've been thinking that I'd like to finish my last year of schooling back in Medicine Hat as I have no close friends here. Once I'm through with my schooling, I'll be going to work for Michael and Maud. I've talked to Edith about staying with her if I went to school in Medicine Hat. She said I'd be welcome as long as you agreed."

"You see Mom, your heart is here in Ontario and it always has been. My heart is still at the ranch. That's where Dad is. With Ada and Jacob living here, things were pretty good, but with them gone, I'm really lonely again. I wish you, Emil and the baby the best, but I think it's time for me to move back to Alberta and do my own thing."

"But you still have one more year of high school left." Myrna replied tearfully. "Couldn't you stay here with us a little longer? Don't you and Emil get along better now?"

"Yes, we get along really well now, but remember, Mom, as I just said, Ontario is in your blood. Alberta and the ranch are in my blood. Remember, I'll be staying on out West and working on the ranch once I've finished high school."

"I know, but I just feel so responsible for you wanting to head back to Alberta," Myrna lamented. "If I hadn't gotten pregnant, maybe you'd still want to stay here."

"Not really Mom. It would just have been a matter of time before I headed West. You've got to listen to me, Mom. I don't seem to be able to get through to you. Many, many times I've told you that my heart's out West. I'm happy for you and Emil and I know I'll miss you guys a lot, but I've been thinking on this for a long, long, time. The more I think on it, the clearer it's becoming that heading West is the way I should go."

For the next few evenings, Rob, Myrna and Emil discussed Rob's proposal to head back to Alberta. Though both Myrna and Emil stressed to Rob that he was an integral part of their family and always would be, the more they discussed it, the clearer it became to all of them that even though separation would be painful, in the long run it would be best for Rob.

At the end of June, Rob, Myrna and Emil were at the train station.

"You're so much like your dad, so much," Myrna said as Rob held his mom in his arms. "You have his size and his makeup. Like him you're stubborn, but kind. Write as often as you can."

"Remember our home is your home," Emil added.

As the train pulled out of the station, Rob waved back to his sobbing mom and Emil.

CHAPTER 17

E DITH WAS AT the train station to welcome Rob. They spent an enjoyable day together discussing Rob's plans. Rob would work July and August at the ranch before returning to stay with Edith and take his last year of school at the Medicine Hat High School.

Rob truly enjoyed his summer work and without question, the ranch crew enjoyed having him aboard. This summer, not one of the hands could match him for strength.

"Look at the young lad swing a post maul," Michael commented to Wilfred one day when they were replacing fence posts. "He's getting close to being the man his dad was."

"Well, pretty close," Wilfred replied, "but I think he's still a little shy of his old man. I'll never forget the time William flattened Andrew back in Montana. Being hit by his right hand was like having a horse kick you in the face."

Since visiting Ada and Jacob at Easter, Rob and Ada were exchanging letters every week or so. Jacob was still feeling under the weather and wrote when he had the strength to do so.

Down in the States, things were starting to look up for Jacob. When an old aunt of Jed's was visiting them, she suggested that

Jacob try using frankincense to see if it would cure his cancer. A friend of hers had been dying of brain cancer and had used it. Within a year, her cancer had disappeared. Having nothing to lose, Jacob gave the frankincense a try. Miraculously, with each passing day, he was feeling better and the headaches were subsiding. He was soon back at school, getting caught up in his school work. Rob was overjoyed with the good news from Jacob.

Once his work on the ranch was done for the summer, Rob was at Edith's place, back in school. He insisted on paying Edith room and board.

Rob had his own battles to overcome. The Ontario curriculum was quite a bit different from the Alberta one. Although up till now, Rob had been able to get by in math, he had never been that proficient at it. Algebra was really giving him problems. In addition to his school problems, Rob missed Ada, Jacob and his mom and even missed Emil. In midwinter, he learned that he had a new brother, Emil Junior. Letters from Ada and Jacob and his mom helped some, but still he felt alone.

Edith had suffered depression in the past and picked up on Rob's dour mood. She spent many long hours trying to help Rob have a more positive outlook on life. By late spring he was doing somewhat better.

Back in the States, the news from Jacob continued to be good. When he was checked out by his specialist six months after starting on the frankincense, the X-rays showed that the tumor had shrunk to a quarter of its size. A few months later the x-ray showed no sign of a tumor. Everyone was amazed at Jacob's turnabout. When Jacob told Doctor Gilespie about the frankincense, the doctor smiled an all-knowing smile and shook his head.

"We know less about cancer than we know about it, son. I don't want to make light of this supposed frankincense cure you've been talking about, but from my professional point of view, I rather doubt it had much to do with eradicating the tumor. You see, sometimes for reasons that completely baffle the medical community, cancer will go into remission or as in your case be completely eradicated from the body. All I can say is the best of luck to you. Check in with us again in six months."

Rob was elated when he got the good news from Jacob.

Despite dealing with depression, Rob managed to pass all his exams, squeaking by in math.

Myrna and Emil offered to send him a train ticket so he could pay them a visit once school was out. Rob thanked them for their offer, but had enough money left over from last summer's work to buy his own ticket. Although Rob felt somewhat awkward visiting his new brother, he spent an enjoyable visit with his mom, Emil and Emil Junior.

A week into his visit, it became abundantly clear to him that his home was no longer in Ontario, but on the windblown prairies. He knew that his mom's heart would always be in Ontario. Although he had good visits with his mom, Emil, his baby brother and relatives, with Ada and Jacob gone, that old gut feeling he first had when he and his mom moved to Ontario was returning. He remembered the feeling his mom experienced on the ranch after his dad had died. He now felt the same way about Ontario. It was like he was in a foreign country.

By mid-July, he was back in Alberta, working at the ranch. Over the next few months he was fitting right into the ranch work and really enjoying himself. Corresponding with Ada, Jacob, and his mom kept his spirits up. As winter was usually a slack time at the ranch, Rob took two weeks of holidays.

The Lewis clan had invited him to spend Christmas with them and he cheerfully accepted their invitation. Towards the end of December, he was on the train heading south. Ada, Jacob and Henrietta, Jacob's girlfriend, were at the station to greet him. The foursome spent Christmas and Boxing Day with Jed and Eva. All in all, they had a whale of a holiday.

"There's one thing I can't figure out," Rob commented to Jed one evening after the four young people had returned from a local party. "I'm sure not complaining, but everywhere we go everyone is black. Do the whites not want to mix with you?"

"With the odd exception, socially, whites will have little to do with us," Jed replied. "Down here, most of our churches are segregated, as are our schools and colleges. It's almost like we live in two different countries. Now, from my own experience, when I lived in the northeastern states, there was much less discrimination. It's more like it is in eastern Canada. Down here, Rob, you are an anomaly. I guess you always were. The color of one's skin means nothing to you. Years ago, you beat the ever-living crap out of a white goon who made sexual moves on Ada. Our family will never forget that. Years before that you decked the same arse for picking on Jacob, just because of the color of his skin."

"That's why we love you." Ada interjected. "You're so fair. Now I don't know if you've picked up on it, but in addition to the prejudice we endure, some of the black people down here will have nothing to do with whites. In some strange way, they must think they're getting even with the whites for all the abuse they're suffering."

Things occasionally got pretty hot and heavy between Ada and Rob, but they did their best to control their primal instincts and were more or less successful.

Ada and Jacob would be through school in June. The Tennessee curriculum was different than the Alberta curriculum, requiring them to take an extra year to get their college entrance. Ada was wanting to go to teacher training college while Jacob was planning on working with his dad full-time.

Before Rob left the ranch, he had talked with Maud and Sue. Maud told him that with her wanting to slack off from the kitchen end of things, they were hoping to get a young girl to help her in the kitchen come summer.

"I was wondering about Ada," Rob had interjected. "Would there be a chance she could get work with you this summer?"

"If Ada would be interested, we'd be more than happy to have her on board," Maud replied. "She worked here with me in the kitchen years back when you three young ones visited the ranch. She was such a conscientious hard-working girl. Have her give me or Sue a call."

During his visit, Rob told Ada of his talk with Maud regarding the possibility a summer job for her at the ranch. He advised her that she should contact Maud or Sue.

All too soon, it was time for Rob to leave. As they parted at the train station, Rob was holding his dark beauty tight. "I so wish we were closer, but that's the way it is," Rob whispered.

"On the positive side, we can hopefully look forward to being together next summer."

In early January, Ada contacted Maud and Sue about working for them in the summer. They wrote Ada that they would be looking forward to having her come. Once she had finished school, Ada advised Sue and Maud that she'd be in contact and take the train up to the ranch.

In late May, Ada phoned Rob regarding her plans for coming to the ranch.

"I'll be through school next week so should arrive early in the second week of June. I'm so looking forward to seeing you and being at the ranch again. Jacob said he'd love to come back to the ranch with me, but he'll be busy helping Dad. He said he has had enough of school and doesn't plan on going to college this fall. I've made application to a local all-black college to take my teacher training, come September."

When Ada's train pulled into Medicine Hat at 10 am, Rob was there to pick her up in his newly purchased Model-T Ford. Ada stepped off the train into Rob's arms. After their long embrace, Rob had Ada close her eyes.

"See if this brings back any old memories for you," Rob said, holding a small bottle up to Ada's nose.

"Oh, that's so beautiful. It smells like lilac."

"It's White Lilac perfume," Rob replied. "Remember, years back in Ontario when you, Jacob and I went for a walk and came to that grove of white lilacs? That was a few months before you moved away."

"Yes, I'll never forget that walk. You picked me a bouquet of the lilac blossoms and they smelled so beautiful. I took them home and put them in a vase in my room. I kept them there even after they had wilted and dried up."

Ada took the perfume from Rob. She daubed a little behind each ear and on her neck.

"We'd better hit it," Rob said. "Sue said to make sure we're back for dinner."

The crew at the ranch were all glad to see Ada again. Once dinner was over, Ada jumped in and insisted that she help Sue with the dishes while Maud sat and brought her up to speed on the comings and goings at the ranch.

Every second week, the help at the ranch had a three-day weekend off. Michael, Carl and Paul saw to it that Rob and Ada had the same weekends off.

After her first week at the ranch, Maud and Sue were tickled pink with Ada's hard work ethic and ability as a cook. Ada had apprenticed well under her mom's guidance. She was not afraid to do more than her share of the chores. Once the day's work was done, Ada and Rob were never far apart. They would either be out horseback riding or be touring the local haunts with Rob's Model-T Ford.

"I can see why this open prairie has gotten into your blood," Ada commented to Rob one evening when they were out riding the range. "Just look at it. The Cypress Hills as a background to the east and then miles and miles of windswept prairie to the west, north and south."

When I'm though college, I'd love to come back here to live."

"As Mrs. Burke?" Rob asked with a sly smile.

"It will be Mrs. Burke if I have my way about it and if you'll have me," Ada replied reaching over and taking Rob's hand.

"I wouldn't have it any other way. I'd be so proud to call you Mrs. Burke."

After work on Friday, Rob and Ada drove into Medicine Hat to visit Edith.

"I'm so glad to see you again," Edith said as she gave Ada a hug. "Rob was right when he told me you had grown into a beautiful lady." Ada blushed as much as it was possible for a dark-skinned girl to blush.

They spent an enjoyable evening, looking at old photographs. Edith and Rob told Ada many of their old ranch adventures. They visited until well past midnight.

As it was Rob's and Ada's weekend off, Edith insisted they spent the night with her rather than driving back to the ranch in the dark. By noon the next day, Rob and Ada were off to visit Fort Walsh on the east side of the Cypress Hills. Suppertime found them back at the ranch.

Early Sunday morning, Ada packed a big lunch. They saddled up their mounts and spent the day riding the range. By one pm they were back at the cabin in the bush they had visited years before. It was a fairly warm day so they just got the stove lit to have tea.

After eating their dinner, Rob's suggestion that they rest for a bit was met with a nod and a smile. The cabin had a small bed. They lay down and soon the two young hot bloods were into some pretty heavy stuff.

"Please stop," Ada called out. "If we don't stop now, I'll say, 'let's go for it.' Remember, we promised each other we wouldn't go all the way."

With a sigh, Rob reluctantly took his hands away from the promised land and moved away a little from his beloved.

They were back to the ranch for supper. The single hands were on their best behaviour when Ada was around. Just as they had done with Rob's dad years past, they speculated on where the couple had spent the night, but as with William and Myrna, the hands kept their speculations to themselves.

As the weeks passed, Rob and Ada were becoming very close. When they were by themselves it was a constant struggle for Ada to monitor her boyfriend's basic nature and keep his hands from wandering to where they shouldn't be wandering. To his credit, although he longed for intimacy with his beloved, Rob did not put undue pressure on his lady friend. In addition, Jed's admonition made years past of keeping that certain part of his anatomy in his pants, was always on his mind. They now talked openly of spending the rest of their lives together.

"I've really fallen in love with this country," Ada began one day when they were out riding the range. "I'd like to take my teacher training back in Tennessee. After that I'd love to move back here, be with you and teach in the area close to the ranch."

"I'm all for it. With you in college, maybe you could spend your summer breaks up here at the ranch and we could be together again."

"I don't see why not. If Maud and Sue will still have me, that's something we can look forward to."

All too soon for their liking, the end of August had come and it was time for Ada to head South.

"You don't know how much I like your suggestion of me coming back out here next summer," Ada said as Rob held her in his arms at the train station. "Now we can both look forward to that."

"It will be hard to be separated from you for so long. Maybe if all is going well, I can drop down again to see you at Christmas."

"That would be wonderful," Ada said as she climbed up the steps of the train.

Rob was soon on his way back to the ranch. There was a loud bang when he drove over a rock on the road. He stopped, got out and checked the underside of the car for damage, but it appeared that all was well. He was about to get back in the car when he spotted a huge raven circling overhead. Finally, the big bird swooped down and landed on a fence post, less than twenty feet from Rob. The raven gawked at Rob as if to say, "Who are you?" It croaked a couple of times, hopped in the air and winged its way back into the hills. Rob thought the bird was pretty cheeky. The visit of the raven was constantly on his mind. On his next days off he dropped in on Edith and told her about the raven's strange visit.

"The raven plays a big part in the native religion and beliefs," Edith replied. "As you know, my grandmother, your great grandma, was native. "I was named after her. She lived with us for the last five years of her life. Grandma Edith and I became very close. She talked to me a lot about the old native beliefs. According to Grandma Edith, the raven was held as sacred. The natives believed that the raven was a messenger of both good and bad news, and a predictor of dramatic transformation in one's life. It was a great helpmate, teacher and guide. The raven was also believed to be a fierce protector."

"We lived on a farm and had a teepee in our back yard. Grandma preferred sleeping in the teepee in the summer and I often slept with her. She always said that spring water was better for her than our well water. Back of our yard some quarter of a mile was a spring on the edge of a forested area. Many times, she and I would walk out to the spring to fetch a pail of water. The last few months she was alive, she was too weak to walk, so I'd go and get the water for her."

"Grandma Edith was now bed ridden and nearing the end. She was out of spring water and asked me to bring her some. I was sauntering along, half way home with the water when a raven, making a lot of squawking, flew low over me heading towards the house. About fifty feet in front of me it landed and hopped in the direction of the house. When I took no heed of its antics, it repeated the whole procedure. Finally, I clued in that the raven was trying to tell me something and I raced home. Grandma was laying in bed, close to the end and gasping for breath. Mom was holding her hand. I handed her a glass of her spring water. Mom lifted Grandma's head up so she could drink. She whispered, 'thanks,' then took a big swig. With a smile on her face she lay back on the pillow and breathed her last."

"When I looked out the bedroom window, I noticed that the raven was perched on the top of the tree in our front yard. A week or so after Grandma's funeral, I stopped at her grave to plant some flowers. On top of the disturbed soil was a large black feather."

Rob often thought of Edith's story of her grandma and the raven.

Things were taking a predictable pattern. Rob was enjoying his work. In her letters to Rob, Ada said she was enjoying college. Rob and Ada exchanged letters every week. By early December, however, Rob was noticing a worrisome change in Ada's letters. Although still newsy, it seemed to him that they were losing some of their warmth.

Finally, in mid-December he phoned Ada to see about coming to see her at Christmas.

"I'd really like to see you, but I don't know if it would be much of a holiday for either of us," she replied. "My courses in college are tougher than I thought they would be. Our midterm exams will be right after Christmas and I'll be spending the holidays cramming for them."

Rob got a sick feeling that something was amiss and terror was starting to build in his gut.

"Your letters used to be so warm," he continued. "Now they seem to have cooled off some. Is there anything more that I should know about?"

"Not really, dear," Ada responded after an awkward pause. "It's just that I'm so overwhelmed by my studies. Hopefully things will let up soon."

There had been a lot of static on the line and before Rob could reply, the phone went dead. When Rob contacted the phone operator, she advised him they had lost all communications into the States.

Rob was very disappointed with not being able to see Ada. He decided instead to spend Christmas with his mom, Emil, his wee brother, Grandma Mildred and Ken. He was a bit on edge with the Ada thing and talked it over with his mom. Myrna tried to convince Rob that Ada's feelings for him were not cooling down. It was just that she was under a lot of pressure with her studies.

While at his mom's and Emil's place, Rob phoned Ada and the rest of the Lewis clan to wish them a Merry Christmas. Again, when he talked to Ada he was unnerved, as much of the warmth seemed to have gone out of her comments.

Once back on the ranch, Rob's worry over his relationship with Ada continued unabated. Her letters were still newsy, but if anything, were becoming more emotionally distant. When Rob wrote Ada about her coming again to the ranch for the summer break, her reply had Rob break into a cold sweat.

She wrote, "I'll just have to see how things work out."

In March, Rob got a letter from Jacob that further raised his anxiety. He wrote that there was a guy by the name of Norman who was trying to shine up to Ada. Jacob said as near as he knew, Ada hadn't yet dated him. He wrote that in his and his dad's view, Norman was a full-blown, big-mouthed jackass.

Rob was having a very difficult time as the letters from Ada continued to be quite distant and cool. Despite numerous inquiries, Ada kept the same old line that her studies were more demanding than she thought they would be. Now she was only writing every other week.

Finally, in late June, Rob had enough and he wrote Ada a letter blasting her out of the water. Before he could mail the letter, he got a letter from her.

Rob's heart skipped a beat when he read, Dear Rob, rather than the usual, Dearest Rob. With fear building in his gut he began reading the rest of her letter.

Dear Rob.

I'm feeling so bad about writing you this letter. I should have done it at Christmas, but I just couldn't seem to be able to get up the courage. I've put it off long enough. I guess it's high time I told you all. I would still like to stay your good friend, but another young man has come into my life. Norman and I met some months ago at our church. Norman is a nephew of our senior pastor. He's also attending the all-black college that I'm going to. I'm crying now as I write you this letter. You will always hold a special spot in my heart. You were there through thick and thin, always defending Jacob and me as we were growing up. I will forever hold those memories dear to me and until I met Norman, you were the only man in my life. I hope this letter won't upset you too much. I will close by saying I will continue to pray for your success and happiness. It's my hope that we can still stay good friends

Your old pal,
Ada.

The letter shattered Rob's dreams. His worst fear had come true. With a heavy heart, he read the letter several times. He vacillated between being heartbroken and being enraged.

"What in the world happened?" he muttered in total disbelief. "We were talking about getting married last summer and now this. Why, oh why, is this happening to me? Why has the universe turned against me? With Ada gone, what have I got to live for?"

For a couple of days, he stewed in abstract emotional agony. He just couldn't bring himself to phone Ada. Finally, in the throes of an enraged fit, he penned her a short note.

Dear Ada,

I'm really pissed off with you and your letter. What in the world happened? Last summer we were planning our life together and now this. You've betrayed me. Go ahead and have a good time with that asshole of a Norman. The last time Jacob wrote me he mentioned that this Norman character was trying to shine up to you. Dummy that I was, I trusted you. Don't waste your time praying for me. The prayers of a traitor only bounce off the ceiling. All that keeps going through my mind is why you would do this to me. From what I gather from Jacob, not only he, but also your dad thinks that Norman is a full-blown jackass. I can now see that loyalty means absolutely nothing to you. Save your phony tears for someone else. Don't you dare ever contact me again. It breaks my heart, but I guess I'll just have to write you off as a bad experience.

Your heart-broken, peed off old boyfriend.
Rob

CHAPTER 18

E VERY TIME ROB re-read Ada's letter, he sank a little
deeper into despair.

"Damn the universe for letting this happen to me," he
mused. "I just can't get it through my head. For the life of me,
I can't get it through my head. What in hell happened to the
future we were planning together? A few months back when
Ada was here, she told me that a year or two in the future
she wanted to move to Alberta to be close to me and be my
wife. When we first started writing after her visit, we wrote
openly of our love and in the future of getting married and
now this. It just doesn't make sense. Damn my luck. What did
I do to deserve this?"

When Rob told Michael and Maud of his 'Dear John' letter,
they did their best to offer him their support. On his next
days off, he headed to Medicine Hat to see Edith. With a
disconsolate look on his face, he handed her the letter.

"My heart goes out to you," Edith responded after reading
the letter from Ada. "Life always seems to throw curves at us
when we're least expecting them."

Over the next few days, Edith spent many hours attempting
to help Rob deal with his grief. Despite her attempts, Rob
seemed unable or unwilling to climb out of his cesspool of

self-pity. Over and over he'd lament: "Why me? Why me? What did I do to deserve this?"

Rob was still feeling very down when he headed back to the ranch.

After hearing his sad story, Paul, Carl and the rest of the crew did their best to buck Rob up. Although their support helped him some, Rob was still feeling very depressed. It was Dale, though, a new hand, that started Rob on the path to near destruction.

Dale had only been working on the ranch for a few months. Although a good worker, he was a binge drinker. He was circumspect in that he only drank when he was away from the ranch on his days off. Knowing the strict rules of no liquor on the ranch, he always made sure he was sober when he returned after his three-day weekend. Michael, Paul and Carl were aware of Dale's weakness with liquor. Although pleased with his work, they kept a close eye on him. They were now careful to be sure Dale's and Rob's days off did not coincide. Michael felt responsible for Rob and in view of his depressed state, did not want Dale introducing him to liquor.

Dale had gone through many failed relationships with the fairer sex and a multitude of misfortunes. Hearing of Rob's derailed relationship, Dale reached out to him. The two puddle glums had many discussions on how fate had individually dealt them many low blows.

"I imagine you've been told a few stories about my drinking," Dale began one day when he and Rob were by themselves.

"Yes, a few."

"I'll level with you. There's no question that I like a bit of liquor now and then. It helps me deal with all the crap I've been dealt in my life and I've had my fair share of it."

"Yes, life can be a proper bitch," Rob agreed. "Just when I thought things were on the upbeat for me and Ada, the rug is pulled out from under my feet. It seems it's always been that way with me too. I'm feeling like lukewarm crap."

"Have you ever tried liquor to help lessen the sting of things? There are those who figure it's my downfall, but I'll lay odds that those who criticize me haven't had the hard things to deal with in their lives that I've had."

"You might have a point there, but as I was growing up, I saw what too much liquor could do to a person. My grandpa was a real booze hound. It ruined his and his family's lives. Michael hates alcohol with a passion because his first wife drank herself to death. I know my dad never touched the stuff because of what it did to Grandpa. To be honest with you, I've had a few drinks and other than not liking the taste, it never did anything for me."

With the passage of time, Rob was trying to get a handle on his feeling of despair over losing Ada and though Dale still went on his off-ranch benders, he laid off trying to get Rob to turn to the bottle to ease his pain.

Rob's anguish deepened when he got a letter from Jacob informing him that Ada and Norman were engaged. Jacob stated that, that in his view, Ada's boyfriend was nothing but a manipulative loser. He and his dad had tried to talk some sense into Ada, but she refused to heed their advice. Although Ada did not write anymore, Rob still had the hope, faint though it was, that by some miracle, she would come to her senses and fate would somehow bring them back together. With Ada's engagement, though, he now had to recognize that his dreams would never come true. Rob was overwhelmed with despair as he tormented himself with the realization that Ada had slipped away and there wasn't a thing that he could do about it.

Over and over again in his mind's eye he could see this Norman character being intimate with his beloved.

"What can I do with this emotional agony I'm going through to end this unbearable pain?" he asked himself time and time again.

The thought of suicide even crossed his mind. Finally, feeling he was at wits end and with no more resolve left, he made the agonizing decision to follow Dale's advice and try to see if booze would help lessen his pain. Recognizing that he was not yet 21, he gave Dale the money to buy him some whiskey the next time he was in town.

When Dale was in Medicine Hat on his days off break, he bought a couple of bottles of whiskey for Rob. He returned to the ranch at midnight at the end of his break. He hid the whiskey in the back of Rob's car and covered the bottles with a blanket.

Rob never touched the booze until his days off. Rather than going to Edith's place, as he usually did, he took a hotel room in Medicine Hat and proceeded to drink his pain away. He drank the whiskey straight. Although he disliked the taste of whiskey intensely, he drank heavily and was soon quite wasted.

"Maybe Dale has the right idea," he thought. As he lay on the bed in his hotel room, the ceiling seemed to be spinning. "Yes, Dale is right. This stuff does lessen my pain some." Unlike most people, Rob was one of the few who never got sick to the stomach from drinking heavily.

On his days off, Rob finished the two bottles. He headed back to the ranch late at night, pretty well hung over. When he sat down for breakfast, he was sure that no one could smell liquor on him, but Michael caught a whiff of Rob's breath. He had a good nose for the smell of liquor and was suspicious that Rob had been boozing.

"You stop in to see Edith?" Michael asked.

"No, I went to Redcliff and spent some time with an old school friend," Rob lied, without making eye contact.

And so, Rob's binge drinking career began. Now, on his days off he would always drop in on Edith before he'd begin his boozing, just in case Michael or Maud would contact her inquiring about his whereabouts.

While under the influence, Rob's pain was somewhat numbed, but it returned in full force once he sobered up again. Instead of trying to work his way through his emotional pain, Rob was now looking forward to his days off drunk. His pain aside, Rob was getting addicted to the temporary numbing of his anguish that the liquor brought.

Because Rob looked much older than his age, he discovered that he had no problem in buying his own liquor. Although Dale had his suspicions that Rob too was now drinking on his days off, he never talked about it to Rob. Seeing he had bought

Rob liquor and brought it to the ranch, he thought it wise for the sake of his own job to say nothing and know nothing.

As he looked on Rob as a grandson, Michael was getting more and more concerned for Rob. From dealing with an alcoholic wife, he was well acquainted with the smell of whiskey on one's breath. He continued to smell booze on Rob's breath every time he returned to the ranch from his days off.

"I'm really concerned for young Rob," he said to Maud one evening. "I'm positive I can smell whiskey on his breath when he comes back from Medicine Hat."

"Yes, I've smelt it on his breath too, but what can one do? We can keep the hands from drinking here on the ranch, but unfortunately, we can't control what they do when they are off the ranch."

"I hope Rob isn't on the slippery slope that could take him into becoming an alcoholic," Michael continued. "We know he's suffering a lot from depression over losing Ada. Being depressed is how Kate's downfall began. She, like Rob, had a problem that she thought whiskey could cure. Instead of curing her problem, the liquor killed her. I'm going to have a talk with Rob."

"We've got to talk," Michael began in earnest a few days later when he and Rob were by themselves. "Are you drinking on your days off? I'm sure that I can smell whiskey on your breath when you come back to the ranch."

"Yeah, a little. I'm still feeling so down over losing Ada and I'm drinking a bit to control the pain."

"And how much is a little? A 26 ouncer or two?"

"Yeah, something like that."

"Well, we can't control what our men do off the ranch on their three-day break, but I'm very concerned for you, son. You're one of my best men. Your dad, rest his soul, was the best man I ever had. He hated booze every bit as much as I do. If your dad were here and knew you were drinking, he'd kick your ass right through your hat."

"Yeah, I guess he would," Rob replied, looking at the ground. "I'll have to try a little harder to stay off the stuff."

For the next month, Rob didn't touch a drop of the poison. Edith did her best to bring him out of his funk, but her efforts didn't seem to help. Rob continued to flail about in his own cesspool of self-pity and rail on the powers that be for the rough straits he found himself in.

Shortly after they finished fall round up and just before his days off, Rob got a letter from Jacob. Ada had included a note for him in Jacob's letter that drove him deeper into despair. She wrote that Norman and she had set their wedding date for early July of the next year. Ada again thanked him for always being there for her when they lived in Ontario and wished him well.

After reading Ada's letter, the little resolve that Rob had left, vanished. He took her note out back of the barn and burned it. When he got into Medicine Hat, he dropped in on Edith and cried the blues to her. After a short visit, he got a hotel room, went to the liquor store, bought some whiskey and proceeded to get hammered.

This second bout of drinking became more intense than his first bout. Now as soon as he got to town on his days off, after paying Edith a short visit, he'd be into the sauce with a vengeance, never drawing a sober breath the rest of weekend. Although he longed for a drink while working, he remained circumspect in not bringing alcohol to the ranch.

For some time, Myrna had been worried sick with what was happening with her son. He seldom wrote his mother anymore, but whenever he did, he was constantly harping away about Ada's abandonment and his pain. Edith, Maud and Michael continued to spend countless hours trying to get Rob to think more positively, but it didn't seem to help. In desperation, Edith wrote Myrna on how Rob's emotional condition was deteriorating and his reliance on liquor to ease his pain. Myrna felt helpless. What with still teaching full-time, running the house, supervising young Emil's babysitter and looking after her young son after work, her plate was full. In November, she sent Rob a letter imploring him to spend Christmas with them. As of mid- December, she hadn't received a reply.

A few days after getting his mom's letter, Rob was in Medicine Hat on his days off. As usual, he was feeling very low. After getting to the point that he was feeling no pain, he went down to the bar and poured out his anguish to Molly, the barmaid. After listening to Rob for a spell and sympathizing with him, Molly said, "Let's go to your room and talk some more. I've just finished my shift."

Molly was in her mid-thirties. Although she was on the plain side, she had an attractive body. Unbeknownst to Rob, she had the reputation of being quite a floozy.

As soon as they got to Rob's room, Molly began making advances towards Rob. Almost before he knew what was happening, they were undressed and on the bed. Rob had never had sex with a woman before and it was over almost before it got started.

"That will be ten dollars," Molly said as she was getting dressed.

"I don't understand," Rob replied, completely taken aback.

"Well, do you think I do this for nothing? "she responded coldly.

Rob reached in his wallet for his last ten-dollar bill. Without making eye contact, he handed it to the dame. Molly didn't even say thank you. She just stuffed the bill in her dress pocket.

"Anytime you need my services, just leave word at the bar. If I'm not working, I'll look you up." Having said her piece, she headed out the door.

Not only did Rob feel the depression coming back, now he felt mortified over what had happened with the barmaid. He sat on the bed, nursing another drink, feeling so rotten, so used.

Unbeknownst to Rob, not only did Molly have a bad reputation, she had a big mouth.

Being a slack time at the ranch, Dale had taken some time off and was also in town. The afternoon after the Molly incident, he dropped up to Rob's room for a visit.

"I was talking to Molly this morning," Dale began. "She's quite the slut. That's her business I guess, but from what I hear the dumb dame has the clap. It's best to give her a wide birth unless you want to get infected."

"God Almighty," Rob blurted out. "I had her here in my room last night."

"Yeah, she told me that. Were you shagging her?"

"I'm afraid so."

"Did you use a safe?"

"Oh, my God, no."

"If I were you, I'd get checked out by a doctor. Maybe you'll be lucky, but the doctor will have a better idea about what you should do."

The news about Molly sobered Rob up in no time flat. Later, when he broke the news to Edith, he was relieved that she didn't give him a hard time. She phoned Doctor Glassford for him. The doctor agreed to meet Rob in the hospital in a half hour.

Doctor Glassford listened intently as Rob told him the tale of being intimate with Molly.

"As you don't live in town, I don't imagine you've heard of Molly's reputation," the doctor replied. "It's a well-known fact in the community that Molly is not only promiscuous, but as you learned, charges for her services. She did have gonorrhea some years back, but she was treated and given a clean bill of health. Under normal circumstances I wouldn't be talking to you about such a confidential matter, but since you were sexually involved with her, I feel obligated to try to put your mind at ease. It's risky for me to be talking about Molly, so bear in mind if you tell anyone else what I've just told you, I'll deny having spoken to you. And please, son, for your own welfare, use a condom if you engage in casual sex in the future.

Not only will condoms protect you from sexually transmitted disease, they prevent unwanted pregnancy. If it would put your mind more at ease, you could make an appointment with me for next month and I'll check you over."

Rob breathed a sigh of relief and thanked the doctor for his help.

For his next days off, it was 'the same old, same old.' Up till now, his boozing wasn't interfering with his work. Although he wasn't drinking any more, he certainly wasn't drinking any less.

On the spur of the moment, Rob decided to take up on his Mom's offer to spend Christmas with her and Emil. On December 20th he was on the train heading back to Ontario.

Myrna had advised Emil over and over again not to challenge Rob on his drinking. By and large it was a good visit. Emil Jr. was enamored with his big half-brother. Rob dropped over to visit both his grandparents. He did not touch a drop of liquor during his visits.

The day before Rob left for Alberta again, he and his mom had a good talk. Little Emil was having his afternoon nap and Emil Sr. was at work.

"I'm so concerned that you've started to drink," Myrna began. "Your dad hated liquor with a passion because it ruined his dad's life."

"Yeah, I know. There are just so many things that have happened to me that are getting me down. Losing Ada is number one. I just can't seem to get over her abandoning me."

"I feel so helpless. Is there anything I can do or say to help you through this rough time?"

"Not really, Mom. I know it's hard on you, but it's best to try not to put pressure on me. In time, I hope to get a handle on things. All I can ask of you is to please be patient."

Soon Rob was on the train heading back to Alberta. Once the train pulled away from the station, he took out the small flask of rye he had in his inside overcoat pocket and had a stiff one.

Once back from visiting his mom, Emil and his baby half-brother, Rob made an appointment to see Dr. Glassford. The tests showed he had no sexually transmitted disease.

CHAPTER 19

A FTER HIS SABBATICAL on drinking while in Ontario and being checked out by Dr. Glassford, Rob had just started to seriously hit the bottle again on his days off when he had a horrific accident.

In mid-morning, he was heading to the town of Irvine with a team and wagon to pick up supplies. As he headed down into a small ravine, a deer jumped in front of his team. The horses bolted to the side of the trail and the team and wagon headed down into the ditch. The wagon overturned and Rob was thrown overboard. He hit his head and side hard on the frozen ground and was knocked unconscious. Although tangled in their harness, neither horse was injured. With the wagon overturned, the team was unable to move.

By the luck of the draw, three ranch hands from a neighboring ranch were heading for town. They were driving a car and only a few minutes behind Rob's rig. They managed to get the unconscious Rob into their car. While the one hand drove Rob back to the Francis spread, the other two hands untangled the team, righted the wagon and followed the car back to the ranch with the team and wagon.

Rob finally began to surface by the time they got to the ranch. In addition to his head injury, he had what appeared to be some broken ribs. Michael drove Rob to the hospital and notified Edith about the accident. Rob floated in and out of consciousness on the way to Medicine Hat. Once in the hospital the doctor attended to his broken ribs. Rob's blood pressure was very low and when he surfaced, his speech was slurred and slow. He'd be conscious for a few minutes and then slip back under. Recognizing the seriousness of Rob's injuries, Michael and Edith stayed by his bedside for the rest of the day. Finally, in late afternoon, Rob became more alert and was able to talk to them a little.

"What happened?" he asked. "I remember a deer jumping in front of the team and from that time on, everything else has been kind of fuzzy."

"Well, you were thrown off the wagon when it overturned and knocked unconscious when you hit the frozen ground," Michael replied.

Rob was having a lot of trouble getting his thinking straight and at times what he said made no sense. He was experiencing severe headaches and X-rays showed that he had a small crack in his skull.

Over the next few days, although Rob's thinking and speech were getting back to normal, he was still having bad headaches and experiencing a lot of emotional instability. Not only did he have quick bursts of anger, but bouts of weeping would quickly descend on him. Doctor Glassford advised Rob that it was common to have these emotional swings after a severe head injury and that it might take him some time to get back to normal. In addition, he added that his cognitive thinking could be a bit off and there might be some significant temporary memory loss.

Once out of the hospital, Rob stayed with Edith for a few weeks. Although his headaches were becoming manageable with painkillers, the emotional trauma over losing Ada only intensified and he had long weeping sessions. Doctor Glassford was aware that in the past Rob had been a heavy binge drinker. He advised him that it could be quite dangerous for him to go back to alcohol, at least until his mental condition was back to normal.

Rob wanted desperately to get back in the saddle. To that end, three weeks after his accident, he got Edith to drive him back to the ranch. She had to drive slowly as the slightest bump would trigger a headache. In addition to his headaches, his ribs were still a little sore. Everyone was glad to see him.

Right after breakfast, Rob and Carl were to head out to check on the cattle. Carl quickly saddled up and was waiting for Rob outside the barn. When Rob didn't show, Carl went back into the barn. Rob was standing by his horse, bridle in hand, looking most perplexed. He had made many unsuccessful attempts to put the bridle on his horse.

"Damn it, damn it, damn it," he cried out. "For some stupid reason, I can't remember how to put this bloody bridle on this horse." He was shaking his head in frustration.

While Carl bridled the horse, Rob threw on the saddle. He neglected to cinch up the belly strap though and just stood there looking very confused. Carl waited a bit and then went over and cinched up the belly strap. As they trotted out to the cattle, Rob's headache returned with a vengeance and they were forced to walk their horses.

"I think maybe you're forcing yourself a bit," Carl said. "There's no question that you'll definitely have to lay off riding a horse for awhile. You'd better walk your horse back to the building site and rest for a bit. We'll find some other chores you can do that won't bring on these headaches."

Rob slowly turned his horse around. His headache was so severe that he had trouble getting back to the building site. After dinner, he was forced to go to the bunkhouse and rest.

And so it went, day after day. Many of the tasks he had been so proficient at before his accident, he could no longer remember how to perform. Other tasks that he could do would bring on a vicious headache. Rob felt totally frustrated as now he had to give up on any work that involved horseback riding. Carl and Paul were very longsuffering with Rob and only assigned him work he could handle.

To add to his physical problems, the emotional trauma he had been going through over losing Ada and the guilt he felt over the Molly caper continued to add to his anguish.

By early spring, Rob's headaches had all but subsided. His memory, although a little hazy at times, was returning to near normal. His depression though, had definitely not lifted.

He was now again drinking heavily on the weekends when he was off work. His heavy drinking was further adding to his emotional imbalance. Rob now had a bottle or two of whiskey stashed at the ranch and in the evenings, would occasionally head out to his cache and take a snort.

Although still living on the ranch, Michael and Maud had pretty well retired. The day-to-day operation of the ranch was now in Carl's and Paul's hands. Although Maud was there if needed, Sue had taken over in the kitchen. Michael and Maud continued to spend countless hours with Rob, attempting to give him counsel and encouragement. Rob was always polite with them, but continued to wallow in his pool of self-pity.

Edith was also doing her level best to get Rob to see the positive side of life. Her attempts, like Michael's and Maud's were not bringing the desired results.

By early summer, things were going nowhere fast for Rob. On his days off, as usual, he would be heading into Medicine Hat, staying at the hotel or with a drinking buddy. One morning, before he left for town, he had a strange feeling he should phone his mom. Neither Maud or Michael were in, but he used the ranch phone. His mom brought him up to speed on the local affairs and then inadvertently dropped a bombshell.

"I don't know if you knew this, but Eva just wrote me that today is Ada's wedding day."

"My God, this is all I needed." Rob replied. "Thanks Mom, for really making my day. Now I can really be on a downer. Her marrying that bastard rat of a Norman. Why, oh, why, do I have to deal with this pain? I curse the day I was born. What have I got to live for?"

Rob quickly ended the phone call and headed to his car. He stopped at the hay stack where he'd hidden his booze and retrieved a bottle.

He was soon on his way to Medicine Hat. The beautiful July day had turned sullen. Rob was raw inside. From Jacob's last letter, Rob knew that Ada was getting married soon, but now that the day had arrived, he felt like crap. As he drove his car into Medicine Hat, he was nursing the bottle of hooch he had at his feet, constantly taking a swig or two. By the time he got into town he was feeling no pain. The next two days were a confused blur as he never drew a sober breath. Although the news of Ada's wedding had thrown him for a loop, he had a morbid curiosity as to how the wedding went. On Sunday afternoon, he was debating whether or not he should phone Jacob to get an update on the wedding. After stalling for some time, he finally resolved the problem by pouring himself another drink.

Rob was feeling so raw that before he left for the ranch late Sunday afternoon, he bought a couple more bottles of whisky from a bootlegger. As he drove back to the ranch, he was anything but sober. He added the whisky to his other cache of liquor he had in the hay stack.

With the liquor close at hand, Rob had reported to work a number of times on the tipsy side. Carl and Paul were suspicious that Rob now had some booze hidden away somewhere on the ranch. They felt stymied, as Rob was paying no heed to their warnings. Up till now, though, because of his depression, they were reticent to take action.

Things finally came to a head Friday morning, the last week in August. Rob had not made it in for breakfast. When he showed up for work, he was well past the tipsy state. He was intoxicated. Just the day before, Wilfred had found Rob's stash of booze hidden at the base of a hay stack.

"You can't go to work in the condition you're in," Carl said to Rob. "You're drunk. You could hurt yourself or someone else. You had better go to the bunkhouse and sleep it off. Yesterday, Wilfred found your cache of whiskey."

"I'm sorry," Rob mumbled. He slowly turned around and started walking back to the bunkhouse.

"Just look at Rob," Paul said to Carl. "The poor guy's staggering." They watched Rob trying to walk to the bunkhouse without going off the path.

After giving Rob a few hours to sober up, Carl and Paul dropped in on him.

"This is a very hard thing for us to have to do," Carl began. "Paul, Michael and I have warned you countless times about drinking while you're at the ranch. This is the fourth time you've showed up for work with a fair shine on. Before you were a bit tipsy, but this morning you were drunk. On other occasions, we've smelled booze on your breath in the morning, especially when you came back from town. With Dad's blessing, we were going to make you a junior partner with us, just like your dad was. We can't do that now because you refuse to get a handle on your drinking. Though it breaks our hearts to do so, as of today we have to let you go. You'll be more than welcome back if you can swear off the sauce and swear off it for good."

"That's okay guys," Rob muttered, staring at the floor. "I was sort of expecting this. Nothing much matters for me anymore. Damn Dale's hide for getting me that first bottle. I guess its chicken shit for me to blame him. I'm to blame. Even though he convinced me to try the damn stuff, I got to take responsibility as I asked him to buy it for me. Anyway, I feel like such an asshole. Why couldn't I have died when I had that accident on the way to Irvine? I'll put my few things in my car and hit the road. Thanks for putting up with me as long as you have."

"Dale is no longer with us," Paul continued. "As of yesterday, we let him go too. On his last days off, he was boasting to one of the young hands that he got you started on booze. When Dad found out that he started you drinking, he was torn right up with him and fired him on the spot. I've never seen the Old Man so totally lose it. I had to step in because old as Dad is, he's still a tough old hombre. I was afraid he would hammer the pee out of Dale."

"Here's your pay," Paul said handing Rob an envelope. "We'll more than welcome you back if you can lick the booze thing."

"Could you stop in to see Mom and Dad before you go?" Paul continued. "We've just come from their place and they're both pretty upset." Carl and Paul shook hands with Rob and left.

As soon as Rob had his few belongings in the car, he stopped to see Michael and Maud. He stepped inside looking like a whipped dog.

"I'm sorry for all the pain I've caused you," Rob began, fighting for control. "It's my fault. I've become nothing but a drunken arse. You guys, Paul and Carl have been more than fair to me. Hopefully, someday, I'll be able rid myself of this horrible depression and cure the drinking thing. God only knows the pain I'm going through."

Michael slowly got to his feet, wrapped his arms around Rob and both of them wept.

"Years ago, we lost your dad and now we're losing you," Michael finally blurted out. "Maud, Carl, Paul and I so hoped you would become part of our operation. The offer is still there though. We beg you to try to get some help. When you get your act back together, you're more than welcome to come back."

Maud too was crying as Rob hugged her good-bye.

Before heading out, Rob stopped at his dad's grave.

"I'm sorry for what's happened, Dad," he whispered, "I feel so ashamed of myself. I wish I could be as strong as you were. Please don't think lowly of me. I hope someday to make you proud of me again."

With that, Rob got into his car and headed down the road into Medicine Hat. He was fearful it would be the last time he'd see his beloved ranch, his beloved home.

As soon as Rob left, Maud phoned Edith and told her that Rob had to be let go.

Before he dropped in on Edith, Rob stopped at the liquor store with the intent of replenishing his stock of booze. He was stepping into the store when he met Dale.

"Well, it finally happened," Rob began. "I got run off for coming to work drunk. I hear you got run off too."

"Yeah, me and my big mouth. I was feeling no pain one day here in town and let slip to one of the young hands that I got you your first booze. Somehow that word got back to the ranch. Well, as you can imagine, when old Francis found that out, he fired me right on the spot. He was so mad I thought he was going to work me over. Anyway, such is life, such is life. What are you going to do now?"

"I haven't a clue."

"I'm not sure either, but I met an old friend who just got back from working on Vancouver Island. He said there was lots of work there logging. He gave me the phone number for the outfit he worked for. He said they were always looking for help and the pay was really good. If you've got nothing else in mind, maybe we should give them a call and see if they're hiring. I could phone them Monday morning."

"That sounds good to me. I was going to tie one on today, but maybe I should hold off on that and hang out with Edith for a day or two. There will be plenty of time to get into the sauce if we find out we have work.

"Well, I finally properly screwed things up," Rob began hesitantly when he met Edith at the Old Folks Home. "When I reported for work this morning, I was a little bit on the tipsy side. I'd better be honest. I was drunk. Paul and Carl had no choice but to fire me."

"Yes, Maud just phoned me and told me what happened. I'm so sorry that it had to come to this. How are you feeling about it?"

"Well, I'm sure not blaming Carl, Paul, Michael or Maud. They did what they had to do. When you're riding the range, handling livestock, or working with farm equipment you can't be drunk. I can tell you one thing. The damned universe is really doing a number on me."

"I'm not sure what I'll do now, but I was just talking to a friend. He said there's lots of work on Vancouver Island, logging. He's looking for work too. He's going to phone a logging outfit on Monday to see if they'd have work for us. I guess there's also the possibility of going to work at the brick plant in Redcliff. After what's happened to me, though, I think it would be better to move away for a spell."

223

Some time back, Edith had given up on trying to counsel Rob as he was most determined to wallow in the 'Poor me,' 'Why was I born,' 'The universe is against me,' mode. It helped both of them to call a truce on the counselling sessions.

Monday morning, Dale phoned the logging company on Vancouver Island. He contacted Tom Foot, the foreman for the sawmill division of the logging company.

"My buddy and I are looking for work," Dale began. "We are from Alberta and were working on a ranch near Medicine Hat.

"We can always use good help," Tom replied. "The work is physically demanding, but we pay well. As logging and sawmill work can be dangerous, we have a zero-tolerance level for booze in the work camp. Town is not many miles away. What our workers do on their days off is no concern of ours as long as they show up to work sober. We work 10 hours a day and have a fifty-hour work week. Things are shut down from noon Saturday until Monday noon. This gives the guys who've gone to town time to get back. We have a thirty-day probation period. If you're a good worker, you stay on and get some benefits. If you're not up to snuff, we let you go. As I've mentioned, we pay well. We can discuss that and the accommodations we have for the workers when you sign up."

Both Rob and Dale told Tom they were eager to start working as soon as possible. Tom took down their personal information and promised them work as soon as they got there.

Monday, after Edith got off work, Rob talked to her about his new job offer. She was tempted to begin on another round of counselling, but seeing her track record in the past had yielded nothing, she chose instead to spend a non-confrontational evening with Rob.

Tuesday morning, Edith drove Rob to the train station. He would leave his car and his few belongings at Edith's place for now.

"You have a chance to turn over a new leaf," Edith said on the way to the station. "Try to stay off the booze."

Rob smiled, but did not reply.

After Rob hugged Edith goodbye, he and Dale bought their tickets to Vancouver. They were soon on the train heading West. Both gentlemen had a 26 of rye in their carry-on bags. They made sure it wasn't too noticeable, but as soon as the train pulled out, they were into their respective bottles of booze with a vengeance. It wasn't long before both gentlemen were getting pie-eyed. As the miles slipped by, they were soon into their 'Poor me,' 'Why me,' cesspool.

CHAPTER 20

AFTER ARRIVING IN Vancouver, they took the ferry to Victoria. The company bookkeeper met them at the dock, drove them to the sawmill and introduced them to Tom, the sawmill foreman. He was an older chap, not too tall, but heavy-set. After introductions were made, he got right down to business.

"We can use you in our logging end of things, setting chokers, Dale. I was talking to the logging foreman and he said they were needing help. You're wiry and slim. You should fit right in there."

"It's been a while since we hired someone as husky as you, Rob," Tom continued, spitting out a wad of chewing tobacco. "We're steam-powered and for the most part, we're sawing Douglas Fir for bridge and trestle timbers. As we're just a medium-sized mill, we hand-pile the timbers. In the last three months, we've gone through five pilers. They weren't lazy, but just couldn't handle the heavy lifting. Those who stayed on with us had to be moved to other positions. Let's go to the cookhouse. We're having our morning coffee break. I'll introduce you to Linton. You'll be working with him piling. He's worked for us for three or four years now."

"You'll find Linton to be a good-natured fellow. He's about 40 and just a little shy of your size. Linton is tough as nails and strong as a bull."

While Tom was introducing Rob to Linton, Dale was on his way to the logging camp some three miles removed. After Tom supplied Rob with a lumber apron and gloves, Rob joined Linton piling.

Both Tom and Linton were tickled pink with Rob's strength and stamina. He had no difficulty in keeping up with his share of the work.

"I was half-expecting another dud," Linton said to Rob as they were eating dinner. "Tom told me he was bringing in another piler for me, but I figured it would be the same old thing. Man, oh man, I'm used to doing all my own share and a good bit of the other guy's share of work. I know I'm a pretty strong old half-breed, but I really have to pour it on to keep up to you. What a relief to get a man as tough and strong as I am! The way you handle those heavy timbers, you might well be a bit stronger than I am."

"I have a wife and two young sons back in Washington State," Linton told Rob one evening after work. "I'm only here because the money's good and they treat me like I'm human. Where I come from, back in the States, us breeds are treated like mules. I try to get back to see the wife every couple of months or so. I won't be taking off for another three or four months. The Mrs. is expecting. I should be there when the baby comes. I'll stay at home for a few months to give her a hand with the baby. My job is always waiting for me when I come back. Seems they can't find anyone tough enough or stupid enough to take my place."

"You coming into town?" Rob asked Linton at the end of the shift Saturday morning. "I think I'll go to town and knock back a few. One of the guys told me they have a flop house a guy can stay at for fifty cents a night if he can't get a ride back to camp."

"No, I'll be staying in camp. I don't hit the bar no more. Years ago, before the kids was born, the Mrs. and I used to drink way, way too much. I learned the heavy drinking thing from my old man, I did. Well, one night, my wife June and I was partying and we was into some over proof rum. She drank too much too fast and damn near died. She was passed out and was breathing kind of funny so we called the doctor. He came and got June to the hospital. The doctor said she had something called alcohol poisoning. At any rate, she barely pulled through. So, when she got back from the hospital, we both said 'that's it for our boozing days.' June and I haven't touched a drop since, and that's got to be close to ten years now."

"You go ahead, but to save your butt, don't have too much booze on your breath when you come back. Old Tom can smell whiskey half a mile off. If he smells it strong on a guy, that's it. And just another word from your old half-breed workmate. It's none of my business why you drink, but remember, booze never helped no one. Since we stopped drinking the Mrs. and I bought our own house on a small farm. In a couple of years, it will be paid for and then I'll stay at home, be with the wife and kids and try to do a little farming."

Because Linton was a teetotaller, Rob thought it best not to go into the wherefores and the whys of his own drinking habit.

Work was going well for both Rob and Dale despite their warped mindsets. They continued to do their binge drinking on their days off. They both chose to continue to wallow in their 'Why me' thinking, but religiously shut things down early Sunday evening to save their jobs.

Rob was hoping that his depression would ease in a new location, but as he refused to get to the root of his problem, if anything, his depression was intensifying. Like on the ranch, he was still living for his days off when he'd try to drink away his pain.

At the end of four months, with Linton's wife's due date fast approaching, he left to be with her for a few months. Linton's replacement, Lyle, was a hard-working kid, but nowhere as physically capable as Linton or Rob. Rob now found he had to take some of Lyle's share of the work on his own shoulders to keep things rolling.

Tom was aware of the situation and always lauded Rob for carrying the bigger part of the load. Usually at the end of the shift there were enough unpiled timbers to keep Rob and Lyle going for another 20 minutes or so. Tom always tried to join in to help them finish off.

Three weeks after Linton left, Adam, the mill boss's nephew was there to brief the crew Monday at noon before they began their shift.

"As of today, there's a big change," Adam began. "Tom had a heart attack on Saturday, just when he got to town. He's doing well, but will be in hospital for some time. I'll be looking after things for him until he returns."

For the next while Rob and Lyle laboured on. As per usual, they stayed an extra 20 minutes after the shift ended to get caught up. Rob had asked Adam if he could give them a hand, but he indicated it wasn't in his job description.

Three weeks after his heart attack, Tom appeared just as Rob finished getting caught up after putting in an extra half hour.

"Well, how are things going and where is Lyle?" Tom asked.

"Things are going not too bad," Rob replied, "You know, the same old, same old. I sent Lyle back to the bunkhouse at the end of the shift. He's feeling under the weather."

"Adam doesn't give you guys a hand cleaning up?"

"No, he says it's not expected of him. How are you making out?"

"I'm still feeling pretty weak so I'll be in the office for the next while. Adam will stay on until I'm up to snuff. Sit for a spell and let's talk."

Tom and Rob sat across from each other on timbers.

"This is really none of my business, but I hear you do a fair amount of drinking on the weekends," Tom said.

"Yes, a bit."

"I was talking to Dale the other day, He was in the hospital getting a bad cut sewed up. He filled me in on your girlfriend troubles."

Rob nodded, but didn't reply.

"Maybe I shouldn't be blabbing about this. You see, very few people know it, but I'm also a binge drinker on weekends. I have a small shanty in town that I go to for privacy. Years ago, my wife and our two kids died in a house fire. In the morning, I stoked up the fire in the heater and left for work. Dummy that I was, I left a jug of coal oil near the heater. Somehow the heater must have got too hot, the coal oil exploded and started the house on fire. The wife and both kids died. Even though it's more than 30 years past, I still can't forgive myself. I'm constantly living with the horror of their deaths. It seems the only way I can live with my pain and guilt is to get hammered on Saturday and Sunday."

"I know where you're coming from. For me, I just can't get over my girlfriend abandoning me for some useless asshole. I too get a bit of relief by boozing it up on the weekends."

"I fully understand."

"I'll tell you what," Tom continued. "There is no way I dare lift a hand now with my bad heart, but seeing Adam was above helping you guys get caught up at the end of your shift, I'm going to get Lloyd, the bookkeeper, to give you and Lyle an extra half hour of pay each day. You both earn it."

For the next while, things went by without incident. Tom would occasionally check in on Rob and Lyle, but was still not feeling up to snuff and spent most of his time in the office. As they were sitting down for dinner on Monday, Adam caught up to the crew in the cookshack.

"Bad news, guys," he began. "Early this morning Tom had another heart attack and passed away. We're going to hold the funeral Friday afternoon in Sook. We'll be shutting down the mill and provide transportation for anyone who wishes to attend the service. It's a heavy blow for all of us, but I guess that's how things go. As of today, I'll be taking over Tom's position permanently."

As they were heading to the cookshack for afternoon coffee, Adam caught up with Rob. "Lloyd and I were with Tom just before he passed on. He gave us the names of the guys he wanted as pall bearers if he didn't make it. You were on his list."

A month after the funeral, changes were on the way.

"Harold Biggs, the owner of the logging sawmill operation met with Lloyd, Fred, the foreman of the logging operation and me," Adam began when he stopped in on Rob and Lyle. "We were going over the books and noticed that Tom had authorized you fellows getting an extra half hour pay each shift."

"Yes, you're right." Rob replied, "Tom started that up. As you've seen, Lyle and I are hard pressed to keep up and we have to stay an extra 20 minutes or so to get everything cleaned up ready for the next day."

"Well, Biggs was not happy with the extra pay you guys were getting so that will be cut out. Biggs also said if our over-all productivity at the sawmill didn't pick up, he might have to cut wages back a bit."

Rob and Lyle shook their heads and went back piling.

Over the next few days, Rob and Lyle were thinking seriously of pulling the pin if things didn't improve. Lyle received a letter from his mom informing him that his dad was sick. If his dad's condition didn't improve, she would need him back home on the farm to give a hand with seeding.

With each passing day, Rob's depression was getting worse. He was now tempted to sneak a bottle of booze back from town to ease his emotional pain.

Just before the morning coffee break on Friday, Rob and Lyle were working their rumps off trying to keep up and Lyle got a bad nosebleed. Rob had him sit a spell and carried on by himself.

"What the hell is going on here?" Adam shouted. He was making his morning inspection and noticed Lyle sitting on a timber.

"Lyle has a bad nosebleed so I told him to sit a spell," Rob called out. "Could you grab his gloves and give me a hand to catch up?"

"I'm the one who gives orders around here." Adam shot back. "As of Saturday morning, you're fired, Lyle. I'm tired of watching you slack-assing it."

"I have news for you, you flabby-assed excuse for a man!" Rob hollered, stopping a few inches from Adam's face. "As of right now you're short two pilers. Tell old Biggs that we're not mules. Tell him to take his job, neatly fold it and place it in a spot where the sun doesn't shine. You're nothing but an ignorant asshole for picking on a guy who is in physical distress. For two cents I'd knock that smart-assed look off your face, but you're not worth getting myself in trouble over."

"But you guys can't quit like this. Without you piling, the whole sawmill will have to shut down."

"You should have thought of that before you started flapping your gums," Rob replied. "As soon as his nosebleed stops, Lyle and I are headed to the bookkeeper for our checks."

By the time Rob and Lyle got to Lloyd's office, the mill had shut down.

Lloyd was smiling as he made Rob and Lyle out their checks. "Poor Adam knows bugger all about managing men," he said. "He's headed over to the logging division to see if he can get a couple of men to come and pile. A minute or two before you got here, the dumb asshole was here trying to stop me from settling up with you guys. I told him to go suck eggs. Get your stuff packed up and I'll drive you into town."

When Lyle arrived in town, he phoned his home in Manitoba and learned that his father's condition was not improving. His mom asked him to come back home as soon as he could to help out on the farm. Lyle took the ferry to the mainland and from there would take the train to Manitoba.

Once Rob was dropped off, he headed to the bar. Dale was already there. "They're going to be shipping me to a hospital in Victoria tomorrow," Dale began. "I'm to have a hernia operation in a couple of days."

"I'm heading back to Alberta," Rob responded. "Lyle and I just quit. Tom, our old foreman was a good sort, but he had a heart attack and died. The new foreman is a real arse, so here I am."

For the rest of the day the two bingers got totally hammered. Soon they were right at it again, crying over all the misfortunes and disappointments that life had dealt them.

The next day, a very hungover Rob caught the ferry to the mainland and then the train back to Alberta.

After Tom's death, when things started to go bad, Rob wrote Edith that he might quit. He also contacted the brick factory, just out of Medicine Hat at Redcliff to see if they had work. He gave them Edith's phone number. If work was available, he advised them to leave word with Edith.

Edith was at the train station to welcome Rob home. The brick plant had phoned her to have Rob contact them as soon as he was in the area. They said they thought they'd have work for him.

Soon they were back at Edith's place and it was the same old 'Poor me' story she'd heard countless times before. The longer he talked, the more morose he became.

"If I get on with them at the brick factory, I have no idea how it's going to pan out," Rob said. "I can assure you that I'm getting tired of fighting this crap all my waking hours."

Edith had heard that same kind of story many times. Before he left for Vancouver Island, she had given up on trying to help Rob, but now, out of compassion, she felt that she had to try again. She did her best to counsel Rob in the evening and the next day when she got off work. As per usual, she couldn't seem to get through to him as he was in that old 'Poor me, 'Why me,' 'The universe is against me,' mindset.

Thursday morning, Rob drove to the brick plant in Redcliff. He was offered a job starting Monday. Rob met Mark, a fellow who had just started working at the plant. He suggested that Rob check out the same boarding house he stayed at. Rob did so and got a room. After checking in at the boarding house, Rob drove back to the Old Folks Home and told Edith about finding work. He spent the weekend with Edith and as she expected, he was constantly lamenting about his lot in life.

Soon Rob was at work. Although the work was physically demanding, Rob was enjoying his new job. Rob's friend, Mark, was also into liquor and like Rob, was a binge drinker on his days off work. He hadn't let his drinking interfere with his job though.

Mark had a lot in common with Rob. It was the same old agenda that had played between Rob and Dale. Like Rob, Mark had his own personal demons and he also used liquor to try to ease his pain. The two fed on each other's anguish, constantly bitching over the poor hand that fate had dealt them.

For the first week on the job, Rob was very careful not to touch a drop of liquor. But soon, with a drinking buddy close at hand, he was back on the sauce. To save on the cost of whiskey, some time back, Mark got in touch with a local yokel who made excellent moonshine at a fraction of the cost of the store-bought liquor. Although the twosome had a snort or two after work, they kept their serious consumption of the spirits until the weekends.

Rob was doing well for the first few months on the job even though he and Mark continued to be weekend binge drinkers. As Rob was still feeling guilty about his drinking, he had pretty well cut off all communications with Edith, Jacob, his mom and the folks at the ranch.

Rob knew little of Mark's past, but he thought it strange that Mark never invited him to his room. He always had some excuse why they should drink in Rob's room. Rob also thought it strange that Mark always insisted on buying the moonshine. He also wondered about the large wad of big bills Mark kept in his money belt.

Their friendship came to a sudden end a few months later on a Saturday evening. The two had been drinking. Neither of them was feeling any pain when there was a loud knock at Rob's door.

After quickly gulping their drinks down and hiding the bottle under the bed, Rob slurred, "Come on in."

An RCMP officer stepped inside.

"Well, we meet again," the officer said to Mark. "It's taken us a while, but we usually get our man. You're under arrest for robbing a bank in Winnipeg. We've just been in your room and found a wad of marked bills."

Turning to Rob he continued, "I'm Constable Frank. We've executed a search warrant on this man's room. The name of Mark is an alias. His real name is Sebastian Turcott.

"Sorry, Rob," Sebastian said as the officer hand cuffed him.

"Has Sebastian ever given you any cash?" Frank continued. "We got some of the marked money from the guy he bought moonshine from."

"No, he never has given me any money. He always insisted on buying the liquor himself and always refused to let me help pay any on the liquor he bought."

"We've also done a check on you, Rob. Other than your drinking habit, we've found nothing amiss with you. Did you not know of Sebastian's past? He's been in and out of jail for the last fifteen years."

"No, I never told Rob about my past," Sebastian interjected.

"This is all news to me," Rob added.

"When Sebastian's case comes to court there's a slight possibility that we may need you for questioning," Frank said to Rob. "If you're going to be gone for any length of time, drop in at the precinct and give us an address where you can be reached at."

"If you insist on continuing your drinking habit, young man, I'm afraid that you'll have to buy your liquor," the constable continued. "We've confiscated several bottles of liquor from Sebastian's room. "We've also arrested the bootlegger for selling unlicensed alcohol. You're still young, Rob. Take a little advice from an old cop. If you want to get anywhere in life, try to take it easy on the booze. Heavy drinking never helped anyone."

Rob was in shock, but as soon as Sebastian and the RCMP left, he reached under the bed, brought out the hidden the bottle and poured himself a stiff one.

Over the next few days Rob was on a real downer. To add to his feelings of despair, with his drinking buddy gone, he was feeling very lonely. To offset the loneliness, he just drank a little more on his days off. As his supply of cheap booze had dried up, Rob's drinking habit was now getting quite expensive.

The owner of the brick plant, in an attempt to increase productivity, hired Brian as the new foreman and the jobsite atmosphere became very strained. Physically, Brian was a small man with a Napoleon complex. He was a yeller and was constantly at the workers to put out more.

As Rob was very physically fit, not only did he keep up with his quota, he helped the less physically capable workers. Leroy, one of Rob's co-workers, was one of the men that Rob helped. Leroy had just been discharged from the TB sanatorium and was none too robust.

One Monday morning, even with Rob's help, Leroy was having difficulty keeping up. Brian was making his rounds and noticed that Leroy wasn't moving as fast as he thought he should be.

"You're going to have to start pulling your weight around here," Brian yelled at Leroy. "You've got to put out more than you have been, or you'll be looking for a new job."

"I'm just trying to catch my breath," Leroy gasped. "I've only been out of the sanatorium for a few weeks."

"Tell your problems to someone who cares. If you can't keep up you shouldn't be working here. This is not a babysitting work place."

"Hold the show," Rob called out, striding over to Brian. "Leroy is doing the best he can. He just got out of the TB sanitorium. When he gets a little behind, I give him a hand so he can get caught up. Before you were hired on, Lee dropped by a couple of times and thanked me for doing more than my share to keep things rolling. You have any problem with that?"

Brian's temper flared. "You mind your own damn business and stop breathing on me," Brian shouted, pushing Rob back, hard. "You'd better pull up your socks too. You smell like a brewery. This isn't the first time you've come to work smelling this way."

The next thing Brian knew, he was air born. Rob grabbed him by his coveralls, lifted him clear of the floor and pinned him against the wall.

"If you ever get physical with me or anyone else in this plant again, I'll work the snot right out of you." Rob plunked Brian back on the floor and went back to work.

Brian hustled into the boss's office. In a few minutes, he was back. "The boss wants to see you in his office," he said to Rob. After delivering his message, Brian made a quick retreat.

Soon Rob was standing before Lee, the owner of the business.

"I recognize that your work record with us has been really good, Rob," Lee began. "You more than carry your own weight. You have to appreciate that you aside, our overall productivity here at the plant has been really abysmal. That's why we hired Brian to shake things up a bit."

"Although to my knowledge you've never been drunk on the job, Brian tells me he smelt liquor on your breath a few times. Then, Brian learned you were fired from your second last job for showing up to work drunk. I never asked this of you when you hired on, but do you have a drinking problem?"

"Well, I do admit that I lost my second last job due to being under the influence a bit," Rob replied. "I do drink some on my days off. I'm suffering a lot from heavy emotional stuff from my past. I drink a little to ease my pain. I may have the odd drink in the evenings during the week, but the only time that Brian could have detected liquor on my breath would have to be on Monday mornings."

"We can't control what our workers do off work, but you should know, because of our company policy, we have zero tolerance for our workers being under the influence while at work. For reasons of safety, we simply can't abide it. Other than having the smell of liquor on your breath, you have a good work record with us and yes, of his own admission, Brian did admit that he gave you a small shove."

"Your admitting to having a drinking problem at your second last job doesn't really apply to your job here. We are concerned that you occasionally come to work smelling fairly strongly of liquor, but that aside, your assault on Brian and your threat to him are more than we can overlook. I'm afraid we have no choice but to let you go. Seeing you have a good work record, if you were to be dead sober when you came to work and accept Brian's authority, there's a good chance we'd hire you back on in the future."

"I think I understand," Rob said. "I was just sticking up for a man who is recovering from T.B. For your information, Brian was harassing and threatening him. Anyway, I guess what's done is done. When will my check be ready?"

"Stop back at the paymaster in an hour. He'll have it ready for you by then. I'm sorry it had to end this way, Rob. You're a good worker."

After picking up his check, Rob left the brick plant feeling lower than he'd ever felt in his life. To top things off, the light drizzle that was falling was adding to Rob's feeling of gloom.

"You're really doing a good job on yourself, you dumb turkey," he muttered as he headed back to his boarding house. "This is the third job you've lost in the last couple of years. One job down the tube because you came to work drunk, your job at the sawmill lost because you couldn't get along with the foreman and this one lost because you came to work smelling like a brewery, lost your temper with the foreman and got physical with him. Just what the hell are you going to do now? Talk about an idiot. Three jobs lost because you're out of control."

Although disgusted with himself for the high price he was paying for his drinking, Rob returned to his room and proceeded to get absolutely wasted.

CHAPTER 21

F OR SOME REASON, this time the liquor did not lessen his pain. It only accentuated it. For several hours Rob sat on the edge of his bed nursing a drink and writhing in emotional agony. He awoke the next morning, hung over and beside himself with anguish and self-loathing.

"What the hell have I got to live for?" he moaned. "Ada is married to someone else. I'm addicted to liquor. I have no friends and now no job. Edith, Mom, Emil, the ranch crew and everybody else I know think I'm a loser and I am. I really am. I have turned out to be an alcoholic bum, just like my grandpa. I have nothing left to live for."

The more Rob wallowed in his pool of self-pity, the more hopeless his situation became. Finally, unable to bear the pain any more, he drove over to Edith's place and poured out his anguish to her.

After listening to Rob go on for an hour with the 'Poor me,' 'Why me' lament, she finally had enough.

"I care for you a great deal, Rob, but save me from this 'Poor me,' 'Why me,' 'Why was I born' stuff," she began. "I've heard your tale of woe many, many times before. Nothing that I've ever said seems to help you. Feeling sorry for you and sympathizing with you doesn't help. Trying to get you to see the light of day doesn't help. Blasting you out of the water doesn't help. I'm about at wits end with you, Rob. I have one last suggestion. If it doesn't work all I can do is offer you my sympathy and let you carry on destroying yourself. That's what you seem bent on doing."

"I have a dear friend whose bad breaks in life are many times greater than yours and yet he's the most positive person I've ever met. I knew you were having trouble and talked to Ruben about your problems a few weeks past. He said if and when you were ready, he'd be willing to talk to you. Will you go see him?"

"I can see that I'm wasting your time," Rob replied keeping his eyes on the floor. After a long pause, he continued. "If it would make you happy, I guess I could see him, but let's get realistic. We both know I'm way beyond help."

"I phoned Ruben after you phoned me. He said if it would help, you could drop in on him tomorrow morning."

"Whatever," Rob replied, shaking his head.

"You know how to get to his place? Ruben lives three miles east of town in a small white house. He's just off the main road on the south side."

"Yeah, I've driven by his place before."

Rob got to his feet and left.

"Well, that was a waste of our time," he mumbled as he sat in his car. "Now what?"

Still feeling in a hopeless state, he left Edith's place and drove back to Redcliff.

Before heading back to his room, he stopped at the post office to check on the mail. There was a letter from his mom. He quickly browsed through the family news. When he got to the last paragraph in the letter he cried out, "God Almighty!" His mom had written: I assume you no longer stay in touch with Ada since she married. I just found out that Ada now has a baby daughter.

"Oh, dear God!" Rob bellowed, crumpling up the letter. "Ada has had that bastard Norman's baby. My God, why couldn't it have been my baby? Why oh why was I born? I'm at the end of my rope. I can't take anymore. I want out, I want out, I want out so badly. There's no more hope for me. There's nothing left to live for. No one cares. I've just got to get up courage to end this horrible pain. Oh God, I want to die so badly!"

Rob kept his Dad's old 44 colt revolver in a small carrying case behind the seat of his car. The 44 had been very special to William. He never carried it and stored it on a shelf over the door. He often cleaned and polished the revolver. When William died, Myrna gave the gun to Michael for safe-keeping. Once Rob began working at the ranch full-time, Michael gave the revolver back to him.

Rob's mind was no longer functioning properly. Mole hills had suddenly become mountains. He rifled behind the seat and with trembling hands, retrieved the box that housed the revolver.

"There's no hope left for me," he cried out. "I'm going to end it all at the spot where Dad died." Strangely, once Rob had made the decision to end it all and began planning out the details for his death, a lot of pressure and anguish left him.

He decided to take a short cut across the open range to the spot where his dad had died, rather than driving close to the ranch buildings. When he arrived at the cross, he sat on the wooden block by the cross and began writing his suicide note. The drizzle had turned to light rain, smudging his writing. He was forced to go to his car to finish his suicide note.

> To Michael, Maud, Edith, Mom, Emil, Jacob, Jed, Eva and the rest of my family and friends:
>
> No one knows the pain I'm in. I can't take any more. Please forgive me for what I have to do. Thank you all for your help over the years. Please bury me beside my dad. I'm sorry I turned out to be such a loser.
>
> Rob

He folded up the note, placed it on the passenger seat, grabbed the sack the gun was in and went back to the block. As he sat there, memories began flooding his mind. He remembered riding the range with his dad when he was five years old, picking strawberries with his dad back where the forest abutted the ranch, listening to the stories his dad had read to him at bedtime, how cold his dad's body was when he touched his forehead after he died and then how warm his dad felt when he visited him just a few feet from where he was sitting.

"Please forgive me, Dad, for what I have to do," he moaned. "God only knows how much I'm suffering. I just can't stand this horrible pain anymore. I got to end it."

Rob was in so much emotional agony that he didn't notice a raven, several hundred feet in the air, slowly circling the cross.

He pulled the carrying case out of the sack, opened the case and retrieved the 44 Colt. The gun felt cold and awkward in his hand. He slowly loaded it. The gun barrel glistened from the drizzle. It took every ounce of strength he had to place the end of the barrel against his chest. For the family's sake, he thought it would be less messy to shoot himself in the heart rather than in the head. It was a single action revolver. Once cocked, it took little effort to pull the trigger. With his eyes closed tight, he cocked the 44 with his thumb and then tried to pull the trigger. Nothing happened. His forefinger froze, refusing to squeeze the trigger.

"Damn it anyway. Why won't my finger pull the trigger?"

Rob made three more attempts, but no matter how hard he tried, he couldn't get his forefinger to squeeze the trigger. He quickly changed hands, but the left forefinger, like his right one, would not squeeze the trigger either.

Strangely, the revolver no longer felt cold in his hand. He'd have sworn that the gun barrel felt warm. In disgust, Bob aimed the 44 at the base of the cross and pulled the trigger. The gun fired, blowing a small hole in the bottom of the cross.

He sat on the block, in total mental anguish. "Damn it all!" he cried out. "What a loser you are. You screw up everything you try."

And then it happened. Just as he put the barrel of the gun against his chest again for another try, a vision flashed before his eyes. He saw Ada on her knees, tears slipping down her face. He'd have sworn he heard her voice pleading, "Oh, dear God, don't let Rob kill himself!" As quickly as the vision appeared, it disappeared.

"Now what the hell was that vision of Ada all about? My tortured mind must really be playing tricks on me."

Rob was in deep shock. He finally jumped to his feet, put the 44 back in its case, put the case in the sack and laid it all on the block. In a daze, he headed over to his car, crumpled his suicide note and tossed it out on the grass. He started the car and began driving back to the main road. Never in his life had he felt so hopelessly lost, so down, so alone.

"Damn it all to hell!" Rob exclaimed a couple of miles into his return trip back to the main road. "I forgot that bloody gun. The 44 and case is back on the block beside the cross."

Rob quickly made a U-turn and headed back the two miles across the range to the cross. When he arrived at the cross, to his dismay, the gun, case and sack were not on the block and nowhere to be seen.

"Now how the hell can this be?" he muttered. "This is unreal. I definitely remember putting the 44 in it's case, putting the case in the sack and leaving it all on the block before I took the note and threw it on the grass." Rob found the crumpled-up suicide note, but despite a long search around the block, the gun, case and sack were nowhere to be found.

Just as he was about to call the search off, he noticed something close to the base of the cross. He stooped to pick it up.

"My God," he cried out. "It's another agate."

"What in hell is this all about?" he said as he got into the car again and headed back to Redcliff. "What in the world is happening to my mind? First, I can't pull the trigger, then I see Ada and hear her pleading for me not to kill myself, then the gun disappears and then I find another agate a few feet from where I found the agate when Dad's spirit visited Michael and me years ago. There's got to be something strange going on in my head. How the devil could all of this be happening?"

Once back in his room, to ease his pain, he reached for his bottle of whisky. Rob had never before gotten sick to the stomach while drinking, but this time, after a couple of stout swigs of the whiskey, he rushed outside and threw up. He felt nauseous the rest of the evening. For several hours, Rob sat there, writhing in agony. Finally, at eleven he took three sleeping pills and drifted off into a troubled sleep.

At seven am, Rob was awake, feeling like death warmed over.

"Now what?" he whispered. "Just what the hell do you do now, you stupid idiot? Oh crap, I forgot that I promised Edith that I'd look this Ruben character up. I guess I'd best get at it. I just know it will be a waste of time, but I'd better keep my word. Really what have I got to lose?"

Rob started his car and headed out to Ruben's place. By eight am, feeling very apprehensive, Rob pulled into Ruben's yard.

"Come on in," Ruben boomed out when Rob rapped at his door. "You're just in time for coffee."

Rob was taken aback by the strength of Ruben's voice. From Edith's description of Ruben, he expected his voice would be much weaker.

"Maybe I could get you to grab an empty cup. They're sitting next to the coffee pot. Pour yourself some coffee, help yourself to the muffins that are on the counter and bring one for me. If you take any trimmings in your coffee, you'll find the canned milk and sugar in the cupboard. Could you top up my coffee too? I have macular degeneration with only 10% vision left. Because of my poor eyesight, I quite often pour as much coffee on the table as in my cup."

Rubin was a small, old, elf-like fellow. He was bald and had a very distinctive purple birthmark that ran all the way from the left side of his bald head down his face, neck, his left arm and hand. Rob also noticed that his left side was not well developed.

"My God," Rob thought, "Edith is right. Ruben is far from being a handsome man."

Rob poured himself a cup of coffee, topped up Ruben's cup and brought over the tray of muffins and the sugar.

"Well I'm glad you had the intestinal fortitude to come to see me," Ruben continued, taking a sip of coffee. "It's hard talking about our emotional problems. Edith has told me some about your state of mind. I've suffered depression myself as a young guy. I know from experience that being depressed is no picnic."

"I'd like to make one thing clear before we start, though. I'm not a psychologist. Over the years, though, I've been able to help a number of people who were suffering depression.

I can't give you any guarantees, but I think you're a good candidate to be able get back on the beaten path again. Edith told me of your childhood and how you were the defender for your two friends in Ontario who had been picked on by their classmates. Remember this. Happiness and peace of mind comes from within. I may be able to show you a better way, but it will be up to you whether or not you want to take that path."

Rob sat in a stupor, staring at the floor, trying hard to stay focused, but reliving the horrors of his failed suicide attempt. "I'm so down," he whispered, "so down. If I'm honest, I can't think of any reason to keep living."

"I hear your anguish, Rob. Hopefully, we can get you into a more positive mindset."

"Years ago, like you, I was in the depth of depression, feeling down and confused about what life was all about. A guy who had spent close to forty years in a wheelchair and a little crippled lady in her eighties helped me out of my depression. So, the floor is yours, Rob. Take as much time as you need to tell me about the pain and joy that life has brought your way. As much as you feel comfortable in sharing with me, try to tell me your whole story."

"Well, okay. The way I got things figured, the Powers That Be are out to get me. Things couldn't be more hopeless for me. About all I can say is that life is really doing a number on me." Rob took a big swig of coffee and continued to stare at the floor.

"Before you go any farther, Rob, let me be blunt," Ruben replied. "This convoluted view that people have that somehow the Cosmos is against them is pure poppy-cock. We all have crises in our lives. It's how we handle our problems that separates the wheat from the chaff. We are here in this life to learn from all the decisions we make, the good, the bad and the ugly. So, go ahead, but save me from this 'Poor me' stuff. Just tell me your story."

"All right," Rob said, shrugging his shoulders. "I guess I should have known better. Edith told me that you wouldn't stand for the 'Poor me' line."

"Anyway, as Edith no doubt has told you, my dad was killed by a grizzly bear when I was five years old."

"Yes, she mentioned that to me. Go ahead."

Rob nodded and went on and on, weaving a negative tale of how much pain he had experienced in his life.

"So just yesterday I went to the spot where the grizzly killed Dad. I was so down that I tried to shoot myself, but my attempt was just another one of my failures. As hard as I tried, my forefinger just wouldn't pull the trigger. Then my mind started to really play tricks on me. I'd swear I had a vision of Ada, my old girlfriend. She was on her knees, pleading for God to keep me from killing myself. My mind has never gone bonkers like this before."

"I feel so helpless. It seems that everything I put my hand to is a failure. God help me. I'm at the end of my rope." Rob bit his lip and sat there, looking most dejected.

CHAPTER 22

A FTER A LONG silence, Ruben replied "If I were to give you a report card, Rob, I might give you a failing grade for trying to kill yourself, but I'd give you a 'Passing with Honours' grade for being unable to pull the trigger. No, your mind wasn't going bonkers. Somehow the Almighty got the news to Ada that your life was in peril. I believe you actually heard her voice. Not killing yourself will be the most successful thing you have ever done. Edith told me about your dad's spirit visiting you at that cross when you were five. Now you may think this malarkey, but I'll lay odds that your dad was also there yesterday at this same spot where he came to comfort you many years before. When you tried to pull that trigger, it was him and Ada's prayers that paralyzed your finger. The Powers That Be knew it was not your time to go."

"I don't know. I hope you're right. I'm just feeling so down, so down. The harder I try to figure it all out, the more confused I get. If only there was some magic pill that I could take to get rid of the pain."

"I think we can find an answer for you, Rob," Ruben replied. "Years ago, I had a co-worker who attempted suicide by jumping off a bridge into the middle of a river. He couldn't swim and planned on drowning. It was unbelievable, but he managed to swim the 150 odd feet to the riverbank, fully clothed, with his shoes on. Later, when he tried to swim

253

again, he had a swimming suit on and was in water that was about five feet deep. He sank like a stone. It was a miracle that he was able to swim to shore fully clothed. Like you, it wasn't his time to go."

"It was so strange," Rob said. "After my finger froze, I aimed the gun at the base of the cross and it fired perfectly. When I put the gun back to my chest, again my finger refused to pull the trigger. I just can't figure it out."

"As with my co-worker, it wasn't your time to go, Rob. God paralysed your finger. As you were telling your story, one thing really stood out for me. By Edith's account, you had many good things that happened in your life, but for all intents and purposes you ignored them and only concentrated on the negative. Hopefully, we can get you to see life as it really is, some bad, but an awful lot of it really good."

"God, I hope I can find my way out of all the pain I'm suffering."

"Have faith that a new day is dawning for you, Rob. I, like you had a lot of heavy things to contend with. With the help of a number of very positive people, I was able to turn my negative outlook on life into a positive one. Hopefully, we can do the same for you."

"By what my uncle told me, I was born in rural southern Ontario. You had a beautiful relationship with your mom, Edith and also with your dad up until his untimely death. I had no relationship with my dad, my birth mother or my stepfather. My dad was a farmer and died six months before I was born. My mother was pregnant with me and two months after my dad's death, she married a guy who was a professional gambler. As I understand it, my mom was a former barmaid. I was abandoned a few hours after I was born."

"Being given up by your mom is pretty heavy stuff. When did you find out about all of this?" asked Rob.

"I think I was about eight or nine when Uncle told me. Uncle said that at my birth, when my mother and stepdad saw I was deformed, they must have decided they didn't want me. They knew where my uncle George lived. They brought me to his place in the middle of the night and left me crying and hungry in a cardboard box, on his doorstep. There was a note attached to me. From what Uncle George said, he awoke to a knock on the door and the sound of a baby crying. When Uncle got to the door, he saw a buggy pulling out of the yard. He saw that I was in a bad way. George gathered by reading the note that the birth had happened sometime in the afternoon. My uncle said he had to think fast. He was sure it was a backroom delivery as the umbilical cord was still attached to me. He was pretty sure I hadn't been fed. He rushed me to a neighbor's place. Mrs. Cowan, the neighbor, had just given birth to a baby and nursed me along with her own baby until I was six months old. I owe my life to her and my Uncle George. Over the years, Uncle George and I tried to find my birth mother, but were unsuccessful."

"What horrible people to abandon you. They sure didn't have any heart. It's hard to believe a mother could give her baby up like that. It was like they were throwing you away."

"Yes, that's about what they did. Dear Uncle George acted as both mother and father to me. I was deformed on my left side and as you can see was covered with birth marks. Despite my infirmities, I guess I was a healthy tyke. Uncle was a farmer and he had a lot of outside work to do, often with horse-drawn implements. Since he was my only caregiver, everywhere he went, I had to go. He put me in a blanket-lined apple box that he would attach to the implement he was using. I learned to sing from Uncle because whenever I'd get cranky, he'd sing to me. Sometimes he'd serenade me to sleep. Other times he'd sing to me when we were out in the fields. The horses seemed to like his singing too."

"Man, that must have been heavy sledding for your uncle. You know, the responsibility of not only making a living, plus looking after you full-time. Do you ever remember him getting down?"

"Uncle was a very strong man, both physically and emotionally. He may have had his down times, but I was unaware of them."

"When I started school, I had a rough time. We lived on a farm, two miles from the village where the school was. The neighbors drove their kids to school with a team and buggy and would stop to pick me up. Kids can sure be cruel and some of them picked on me because I looked odd. Orville was the worst. I was clumsy because of my one weak side and not all that steady on my feet. One day at recess, we were out on the playground and Orville tripped me. When I fell down and cut my lip, he laughed at me. I told the teacher about it, but she didn't do anything. I told Uncle about being tripped and showed him my cut lip after I got home from school. He asked what the teacher had done. When I told him that the teacher hadn't done anything, he said he'd handle it. When I was bullied before, Uncle would take it up with the teacher. Sometimes the teachers would intervene, sometimes they wouldn't."

"It was like that for my friends, Ada and Jacob back in Ontario. They were black and some kids picked on them because of their colour. I stood up for them when they were given a rough time."

"Yes, Edith told me about you defending them."

"Back to my tale. I was sure surprised the next morning when there was a knock on our classroom door. Before Miss Zelling could get to the door, Uncle barged in and walked over to Orville's desk. It was quite a sight to see. Uncle was a big man, over six feet tall and very husky."

"'Some of you kids have been bullying Ruben,'" he began loudly. "'This is going to stop.'" When Orville grinned, and muttered something under his breath, Uncle reached down and plucked him from his desk, lifted him up and pinned him against the wall. Poor Orville's feet were two feet off the floor. Uncle held him against the wall with his left arm and put his big right fist right under Orville's nose."

"'From what I gather, you're the one who tripped Ruben and gave him a bloody lip,'" Uncle roared. "'This will be your one and only warning. If you ever pick on Ruben again, I'll make mincemeat of you.'"

"It was too much for Orville. Still pinned against the wall, he wet his pants and started to cry. Uncle let Orville down and turned to Miss Zelling."

"'I'm sorry I had to take things in my own hands, but Ruben told you about Orville tripping him and giving him a bloody lip and you did nothing. I'll take the young fellow home and get him a change of clothes. Once he changes his clothes, I'll bring him back.'"

"When they were in the buggy, Uncle asked Orville where he lived."

"Orville told Uncle it wouldn't do any good to take him home because these were the only clothes he had. Orville said that his mom worked at the hotel and they didn't have much money because his dad ran away from his mom and him."

"Uncle found out what size of clothes Orville wore, took him to the general store and bought him two pairs of pants, two shirts, a jacket, some underwear, socks and a pair of shoes."

"When he stopped at the hotel, Uncle told Orville's mother what had happened at school and showed her the clothes that he had bought. She was in tears and thanked Uncle over and over again. As he and Orville were leaving, Uncle handed her a fifty-dollar bill. I guess then she really started crying in earnest. Uncle took Orville to his house and after he changed to his new underwear, pants and shirt, he took him back to the school."

"You know, the kindness Uncle showed to Orville and his mom made such a difference to Orville and also to me. We became friends. I was good at school work. Orville had problems in that area so I often helped him with his assignments. Orville became my protector. Uncle also continued to look out for Orville and his mom, bringing them meat, milk, eggs and garden vegetables every week or so."

"I guess Orville looked out for you, like I became Jacob's and Ada's protector," Rob replied. "I knocked the crap out of a guy who was giving Jacob a hard time, just because of the color of his skin. Years later, I whaled the tar out of the same asshole when he tried to make moves on Ada."

"Both Edith and I are proud of you for looking out for your friends. Always remember that showing kindness is all that really matters in life. It's powerful medicine."

"Academically, I had no problems in school, but because of my deformities, despite Orville being my bodyguard, I was sort of ostracized by a lot my classmates. I was always on the outside looking in. Uncle George was a very positive sort and always tried to lift me up when I'd get down."

"As soon as I finished high school, Uncle helped me get a job at a small factory that built farm machinery. Lynn Carpenter was their bookkeeper and I worked under him learning to do books. Like at school, I was forced to put up with a bit of guff from some of the public because of my odd looks. When I turned 20, Lynn suggested that I take a two-year course in bookkeeping at the Regional College. The company would pay for my tuition and board and room as long as I returned to work for them. It worked out well. Once college was over for the year, I worked the summers at the factory."

"One thing that always amazed me about Lynn was although he'd been confined to a wheelchair for over forty years, he was always cheerful."

"I'd been with the company for some five years when I really started feeling depressed. I was doing well at my job, but even though I tried to fill my spare time with hobbies, life seemed empty and meaningless to me. I longed to have a relationship with someone of the opposite sex, but as I looked anything but normal, I was not having any luck in that area. "

"I turned to liquor when Ada abandoned me," Rob added. "I felt so totally alone."

"I can see where you're coming from. In my view, we were meant to be with a mate," Rubin said. "I spent most of my life longing for one."

"Lynn could read me like a book. One day when I was really feeling rough, he said that I was looking kind of glum and asked if I was feeling down."

"Yeah, I sure am," I mumbled. "It's hard to be cheerful when you're feeling like lukewarm crap."

"I know what you're talking about," Rob interjected. "I've been feeling like crab for the last few years. Why would a guy who was paralyzed be cheerful? It just beats the hell out of me."

"We'll get to that, Rob."

"Lynn said that when he was young, he too was depressed. He suggested that I drop over to the house after work to talk things over."

"Seven-thirty found me at his door. Lynn's wife poured us coffee and then left for a ladies meeting. "

"Lynn asked if I was comfortable in sharing my story."

"Alright," I replied. "For sure, I felt like I was at a confessional."

"I bared my soul to Lynn, revisiting all the hurts I'd experienced in my short life. As I was spinning my tale of woe, Lynn was constantly nodding his head. After I'd finished my spiel, Lynn sat quietly for quite a spell before responding."

"He said he could sympathize with me over my pain as he had experienced many hurts himself with his disability."

"He said when he was eighteen, he and his cousin had a runaway with a team and buggy. He was thrown off the buggy, breaking his back. Lynn ended up being paralyzed from the waist down. As he was recovering in the hospital, he was an angry young man and supremely pissed off with life. Not only was he surly with the staff, when his friends visited him, he constantly ranted and raved over his plight. He said that he was well on his way to becoming an angry, bitter, sour codger."

"When they transferred him to the rehabilitation ward, something wonderful happened that changed his life. Lynn met an 11-year-old Metis girl who was wise way beyond her years. Barb lived on a farm and was helping her dad cutting hay. She was severely injured when she was run over by the mower. Barb's right arm was severed at the elbow and her right leg was so badly cut up that it had to be amputated just below the knee. By Lynn's account, Barb was a cheery little lady. Not once did she moan over her lot in life and never took Lynn to task for his negative outlook, other that saying, "'Cheer up, Lynn.'" She hobbled along on her peg leg, visiting Lynn every day. She would bring chocolate milk that they shared. Because of Barb, his negative outlook on life was starting to soften and he was beginning to get a hold of himself. He said he would never forget the day Barb was discharged. Her mom and dad were there to pick her up."

"She walked over to Lynn and put her small left hand on his chest. "'You're getting better, Lynn,'" she said softly. "'Remember, you have lots of power here. Keep on using it.'"

"Barb's last words were like being struck by a bolt of lightning for Lynn. Here she was a crippled little girl, reaching out to a guy who so badly needed to see the positive side of things. Her words on using his inner strength became Lynn's mantra. Once discharged from the hospital, he enrolled at college in bookkeeping and business administration. It was in college that he met Helen, the girl who became his wife. Life handed him a big set-back, but by following little Barb's coaching he believed that Helen and he had done not too badly. Lynn and Helen decided to support orphans as something they could do to help the less fortunate."

"Once Lynn finished his story, I sat in silence for some time, almost hypnotized by his tale," Ruben continued.

"You've given me a lot to think about," I said to Lynn. "The story of little wise Barb is most remarkable."

"I'm starting to see how it can work," Rob said. "Little crippled Barb helped get Lynn back on track and Lynn was trying to help you."

"Your getting it Rob, but back then, even with Lynn's coaching, I still had a way to go."

"The day after hearing Lynn's tale and before I could fully digest it, I had my own crisis. Over the last few years my bum leg was getting quite unreliable. In our factory warehouse we had a steep set of stairs. I was coming down the stairs when my leg gave out. I fell several feet and broke my left hip."

"I was in hospital for several weeks. Although I thought a lot on Lynn's story, I was still suffering some from depression as life still seemed empty for me."

"One day a nurse asked me if I'd care for a visit from Nell. She explained that Nell was an elderly lady who regularly visited patients in hospital, trying to cheer them up."

"That would be fine," I replied.

"A few minutes later the nurse returned, wheeling in an old black lady in a wheelchair. It looked like Nell was suffering badly from arthritis as her hands were all gnarled and bent out of shape and she was hunchbacked. She appeared to be well into her eighties. She was wearing sunglasses, but as it was a bright summer day, I thought nothing of that."

"After introducing herself, she asked if I was feeling a bit down. I assumed that the nurses had told her of my depression."

"When I told her that I wasn't feeling up to snuff, she asked me if I'd be comfortable in sharing my story with her."

"Again, it felt that I was at a confessional as I told her of the pain in my life and feeling that life had no meaning for me."

"I know where you're coming from," Rob interjected. "I feel that way every time I have to tell my story."

Ruben nodded and continued. "Nell smiled and said she had a story to tell me and then a bit of advice to give me. By pulling with her feet she got her wheelchair in closer to me."

"She said her life began on a cotton plantation in the southern states and that as a young girl she had been with a group that traveled the underground-railroad from a life of slavery in the South to freedom in Canada. Nell told of the horrible things that happened to her and her family under slavery. Once she reached Canada, she was able to get an education and eventually became a grade one teacher."

"Her advice to me, though spoken kindly, was somewhat blunt and at first it made me upset. In her view, the negative attitude that I had would get me nowhere. She added two other things that she said would help me. Nell said that at times we have to figuratively give ourselves a good stout kick in the butt and instead of feeling sorry for ourselves, start reaching out to others less fortunate than we are."

"Then she went on to her other point. Nell put her poor old gnarled hand on my shoulder and told me that God has given each of us great inner strength. She said we should thank God each day for that strength and ask the Almighty for help in accessing it."

"It's remarkable that her message was sort of in the same vein as what Barb told Lynn," Rob added.

"You're right, Rob. The messages from the two ladies were almost identical."

"At first, I found Nell's comments difficult to take, but with each visit from her, I began realizing that there was merit to her simple message. I attempted to try to think more positively."

"Nell dropped in on me twice a week for my stay in the hospital. Her visits were always a ray of sunlight for me. She was always so positive and supportive. On her third visit she said it was time she told me that she practiced what she preached. From the time she was on the run in the underground railroad, she had evolved a simple daily ritual that had been her mainstay throughout her life. Each evening before going to bed she'd go to her own personal space. She would thank the Almighty for the strength he had placed within her and ask for help in accessing that strength. She added that old and crippled as she was, she still practised her ritual every night."

"Do you think there's something in Barb's, Lynn's, Nell's and your story that would help me?" Rob asked quietly.

"I think you're getting it, Rob," Rubin replied. "Yes, I think you're getting it."

"I'll never forget my last visit with Nell. It sticks out in my mind as if it happened yesterday. I was to be discharged that afternoon. It was an overcast day with light rain falling, but when they wheeled her in to say goodbye to me, she was still wearing those sunglasses. I held her poor old gnarled hands in mine and thanked her for all her visits. She wished me well and then she was wheeled away."

"She's quite a saint," I said to the nurse, "but why does she always wear those sunglasses?"

The nurse shook her head and put her hand on my shoulder.

"'I thought someone would have told you,'" she replied quietly. "'Dear old Nell has been blind for the last five years.'"

"That really was mind boggling. Here this crippled old blind lady had such a big heart that she overlooked her own infirmities to reach out to others. Her example will stick in my mind to my dying day."

"Once out of hospital and back at work, I was doing much better. I told Lynn of my visits from Nell and how positive they were for me."

"So, there you have it. A little Metis girl got Lynn back to a positive mind set. Dear old crippled Nell got me back on the positive trail and now I'm trying to get you back on track."

"Wow," Rob responded. "Like you said, all of this really blows one's mind. The more I think on it, the more I'm persuaded that there's still hope for me."

"There is indeed, Rob, there is indeed."

"Like Lynn and Helen, I started supporting an orphanage and that really gave me a purpose in life. The Bible instructs us that it is more blessed to give than receive. I soon came to realize how true that was."

"My next challenge came when Harry, a fellow in his early thirties was hired on to our workforce. Harry was quite mentally challenged. He was our errand boy. With Lynn's blessing, I took it on myself to mentor him. Harry was a very conscientious sort and we got along admirably. He was unable to read or write. His vocabulary was very limited, but he tried his very best and did contribute positively to our overall operation.

"I learned that he desperately wanted someone to read to him. I began reading to Harry in the evenings after work. Harry had a room in his mother's rooming house. She was delighted that Harry had found a new friend. After supper, I'd drop in on him and read to him for a half hour or so. Over the time Harry worked for our firm, I read him hundreds and hundreds of books. In addition to the reading, Harry insisted that I sing for him. His favorite book was Pilgrims Progress; his favorite song, Mocking Bird Hill. I vouch that over the years of his employment with the company I read him Pilgrims Progress at least fifteen times and I must have sung Mocking Bird Hill to him close to a couple of hundred times."

"That must have taken a lot of patience on your part," Rob said. "I suppose, though, in a way, I did the same thing in defending Ada and Jacob. Then, when it came to working, being big and strong, I always helped those who couldn't keep up."

"Yes, according to Edith, you have a track record of helping others. Now you need to help yourself."

"It did take a lot of patience on my part to be there for Harry, but it was so rewarding to see what my help meant to him. Another thing I soon realized was how good it made me feel, reaching out to someone who so desperately needed help. Sadly, Harry's health gave out when he was in his early forties. I never did find out what took him, but his mother thought it was somehow related to his mental condition. The last day he worked, he was unable to talk and the next day he had to be hospitalized. I was honored to be at Harry's bedside holding his hand at his passing. He had been comatose for the last week or so with his eyes shut. Suddenly he gripped my hand, opened his eyes, smiled and passed away. It was a privilege for me to deliver Harry's eulogy."

"A couple of years after Harry's death, Lynn had a massive heart attack and passed on. I became the head bookkeeper. I was thriving at my job, but my eyesight was beginning to give me trouble. I still was supporting orphans and every other Saturday I'd take the train to the orphanage and you guessed it, read to the young kids."

"It was like you sort of apprenticed helping others with looking out for Harry and then just kept at it with visiting the orphanages," Rob interjected.

"Yes, I guess that's a good way of putting it. It really started when Uncle took me under his wing. Then with Nell's and Lynn's help I got into the same helping game. Anyway, Uncle and I still had a close relationship. We saw each other every two weeks or so and I spent my holidays with him."

"After being with the company for thirty plus years, changes were on the way. I still was holding my own, but now was really struggling with my eyesight. A big bombshell came when Uncle told me he was thinking of moving to Alberta. A year before, Jane, an old adventurous girlfriend of his, in her sixties had moved up here to Medicine Hat to teach school. Uncle had been up a couple of times to visit her. They had been very close for many years. When she was diagnosed with cancer, dear old faithful Uncle, with my blessing, decided to move out here to look after her. He sold his farm and machinery, moved here and bought this land. Despite being in his seventies, he faithfully looked after his beloved for the better part of a year before Jane took her leave."

"It seems to me that your uncle George spent all his life looking out for others."

"Indeed, he did, Rob, indeed he did. After Jane's passing, Uncle came back to Ontario to see me. My eyesight was now so bad that I knew my days as a bookkeeper were numbered. He suggested that I move out to Alberta and live with him again. I had a fair amount of savings from my years of working and Uncle was financially comfortable. He was renting this newly purchased land to a neighbor."

"Before I could make a decision, my employer made it for me. They sold out to a much bigger company. I took early retirement and moved out here. Uncle and I had a good three years together, but then his health started to fail. Realizing he was close to the end, he willed all his property to me. Two days after his eighty-first birthday, he died in his sleep. I missed him terribly. I still do for that matter. He was the father I never had."

"That must have been terribly hard on you to lose your surrogate father. My dad's death was very traumatic for me. It still is heavy for me for that matter."

"Yes, losing Uncle was very hard on me. I spent many months grieving his death. Edith told me of the heavy time you had with your dad's death. Anyway, I carried on although I was legally blind. I kept a few chickens and tried to grow a garden. Neighbours were very kind to me and were always there to give me a hand. When I'd have to do business in town, they would give me a ride. They always dropped my mail off."

"Then one day, Edith dropped in on me and a new chapter of my life began. Dear Edith learned about my vision problem and the saint took it upon herself to help this poor old creature out. Although we'd never met before, we learned that we had grown up in Ontario, less than fifty miles apart. Age-wise, I was just a few years older than her."

"Yes, Edith is a real saint. She helped raise me and has spent countless hours trying to help me out of the doldrums. I'm feeling guilty now that I didn't try a little harder to help myself."

As it was getting late in the morning, they took a tea break. Ruben took Rob outside for a short tour of his yard, ending up at his garden.

"Dear Edith pretty well planted the garden by herself. I helped as much as I could, but being practically blind, she did the most of it."

As Rob thought about how little crippled Barb reached out to Lynn and then how blind Nell had reached out to Ruben, a flame of hope started flickering in his chest.

"The longer we talk, the more I'm beginning to feel that there's hope for me." Rob said.

"There is indeed Rob. You're seeing the light now."

"I guess in a way, Edith acted as your surrogate parent the same way Uncle George acted as my surrogate parent."

"Yes, she truly has been my surrogate Mom. I owe her so much. Although I can't complain about my birth mom, Edith helped raise me and has always been there for me through my low times."

"It's easy for all of us to get off-track, Rob. Your assignment now is to help yourself get back on-track again."

As for me, I still practice the ritual that Nell had discovered. Every evening I go to my private spot and verbally thank the Almighty for the strength He's invested in me and then ask the Creator for help in accessing that strength. I'm confident Barb's and Nell's advice will work as well for you as it did for Lynn and me. Are you willing to give it a try?"

"I will," Rob whispered, "I will. I'm seeing things much clearer now. Thank you so much Ruben. How will I ever repay you for all of your help?"

CHAPTER 23

WITH RUBEN'S GUIDANCE, Rob made dinner. Ruben was low on groceries so after dinner, Rob drove him into town and helped him do some shopping.

As they shared their lives, Rob realized how far he'd wandered off the path. Now, with Ruben's guidance, he was determined to renew his life.

"I have a further suggestion for you," Ruben said as they were eating supper. "I have a dear native friend who turned his life around. Eli had worked on the railroad as a brakeman for many years. He, like you, got into liquor. He had left the reserve years before. When he was told by his boss that he'd be let go unless he stopped drinking, he headed back to the reserve to get help. An elder gave him a spiel and then advised him to go to an ancient spot that had a strong spiritual significance to the local natives. There were ancient native hieroglyphic carvings in rock outcrops close to the north bank of the Milk River. Eli went there and told me that he felt something like a surge of power come into him. Whether real or imagined, what Eli experienced was the turning point in his life. He returned to work and as near as I know, has never touched another drop of liquor. Eli is now retired and lives on an acreage a few miles out of the small hamlet of Milk River. I don't know if you want to go that route, but if you do, I'm sure Eli would be happy to go to the carvings with you."

"Sure, I'd be willing to give it a try."

Ruben got Eli on the phone and made arrangements for Rob to pick him up at ten the following morning.

"I don't mean to intrude, but are you and Edith a twosome?" Rob asked after they had eaten supper.

"Well, that depends on your definition of what a twosome is," Ruben replied with a grin. "You see, for all my adult life I longed to have a relationship with the fairer sex. Being that I'm anything but handsome and physically disabled, I'd about given up until Edith came my way. On our first meeting, we shared a lot of the pains and disappointments plus the good times and blessings that we had experienced. On Edith's third visit, something very beautiful occurred. I remember it as if it happened yesterday. She invited me into the bedroom. She lay down fully clothed and invited me to lie down beside her. I did so and she wrapped her arms around me. Now you may think it odd, but it was the most wonderful feeling I'd ever experienced. I was so overcome with emotion that I shed a few tears. Edith shed a few tears too. She, like I, had pretty well given up hope of ever finding a good partner."

"Edith comes out on her days off and helps me with my chores. At any rate, Edith is retiring from the Old Folks Home in a few months and the two old fogies plan on getting married. She loves it out here even though we don't have electricity. We'll probably spend the summers out here and the winters in her house in town."

The evening, like the afternoon, was a time of sharing. When they first met, Rob was only sharing the rough times he had experienced, but now he was also talking of all the good times in his life.

Later in the evening, Rob phoned Edith to give her an update on the day's events. She was overjoyed that they were making progress on dealing with his problems.

"Tomorrow's the start of my days off, but I think I should head out to the ranch," Edith said. "Michael is very low and Maud would like me there with them. They don't expect him to last long. I'll try to get out to see you and Ruben late tomorrow or the day after. It all depends on how long Michael holds on."

Four am the next morning found Rob on the road, heading to Eli's place. He was told that the roads, though passable, were no more than upgraded trails in places. As gas outlets were still few and far between, Rob took along a small drum of extra gas. It was a beautiful day. There was a chinook arch to the southwest with a soft wind blowing. Rob's thoughts though were with his old buddy, Michael. As he drove along, he was thinking about all the good times they had riding the windswept range. The roads were better than Rob had anticipated and by 9:30, he pulled up to Eli's house.

Eli invited Rob in for coffee. Soon Rob and Eli were on the road heading to the sacred carvings.

"Ruben probably told you a bit about what booze did to my life," Eli began once they were on their way.

"He told me you were about to lose your job."

"Well, not only was I going to lose my job, the wife told me if I didn't lay off the bottle, she was going to leave me. It was so strange. At that time, though I'd heard a bit about those carvings, I didn't really believe that they would have any power. Seeing I was about to lose my job and my wife, I figured I had nothing to lose. I guess I'll never know what it was that was so magic about that spot, but as I sat there, this strange feeling of happiness came over me. It lasted for quite a while. After I'd left the Sacred Rock, I lost all my craving for booze. I haven't touched a drop of booze since my visit there."

"I sure hope it helps me out," Rob replied. "Like you, I've had a bad bout with the bottle."

They stopped the car several hundred feet from the rock outcrops. Eli led Rob to the spot where he had meditated and then went back to Rob's car.

Rob sat cross-legged on the ground and gazed up at the ancient hieroglyphics carved into the sandstone. As Eli had instructed, he tried to stay focused on the writing and purge his mind of all other thoughts. For a half hour, he stared at the writing. Suddenly, he felt the air grow warmer and a feeling of elation spread through his whole body. The feeling lasted for a few minutes. Just as the sensation started to wane, he saw Michael's face flash onto the stone wall. In a few moments, the vision vanished. On a whim, Rob pulled out his pocket watch and noted the time. After sitting for a few more minutes, Rob went back to the car.

"Well did anything happen?" Eli asked eagerly.

"Yes, something really strange happened." Rob filled Eli in on the remarkable things that had occurred. "I saw the face of my old boss, Michael Francis on the rock carvings. Michael has terminal cancer and is on his last legs. I wonder if his spirit visited me."

"That could well be," Eli replied. "Yes, that could well be. As we've both found out, this is a very powerful place."

Soon they were back at Eli's place. Eli invited Rob in for dinner. After eating, Rob thanked Eli's wife for the meal and Eli for taking him to the Sacred Rock. As he drove along back to Ruben's place he was constantly dwelling on the vision of Michael. A few miles into his return trip, Rob stopped the car and walked into a bluff of trees that was adjacent to the road.

Looking skyward he called out, "Thank you God Creator for the strength you have placed within me. Give me the ability and the self-discipline to access that strength."

By seven pm, Rob was back at Ruben's place and telling him of his adventure.

"I should check in on the ranch," Rob said. "That vision of Michael's face makes me wonder if something has happened to him."

Paul was very somber when Rob got him on the phone.

"There's sad news," Paul began. "Dad passed away this morning."

"My condolences to you and the rest of the family," Rob replied. "This is hard to believe, but I saw a vision of Michael's face flash before me. I looked at my watch and it was 11:05. I was by the Milk River at the spot where there are old native writings and pictures carved into the rocks. The vision of his face on the rocks was so real."

"Oh my God," Paul replied after a long silence, "You see, a few minutes before Dad passed on, he opened his eyes and said, 'Rob is going to be okay. I know that he's got his liquor problem licked. I just know that.' "He then said goodbye to all of us. 'Rob will be coming back to the ranch.' he added turning to Carl and me. Mom kissed him goodbye and then he stopped breathing. We recorded his death at 11:10. I just can't get over Dad coming to you in a vision and then a few moments later, just before he died, telling us you'd licked your drinking problem."

"We would like you to be a pallbearer, Rob. We haven't set a day for the funeral yet, but we'll have it here at the ranch and we'll bury Dad next to your Dad."

Rob broke down as he was extending his condolences to Maud. "I'd be honoured to be a pallbearer," he finally whispered to her. "I'll be out as soon as I can."

Once off the phone with Maud, Rob talked to Edith. She said she'd soon be out to Ruben's place.

"What a blow," Rob said after getting off the phone. "When Dad died, Michael became my surrogate father."

As Rob was reiterating what Michael had said just before he passed on, Ruben was constantly nodding his head.

"There's no question in my mind that Michael's spirit left his body just before his passing to visit you and to give Edith and your extended family assurance that you would be alright. I have no doubt of that. It's so strange. One soul passing into the next dimension while your soul being re-born."

Rob and Ruben continued sharing their stories till midnight.

"It's too late to phone the eastern states now," Ruben said, looking over at the clock. "If you'd care to, you can sleep here tonight again. Tomorrow morning, I have one last assignment for you. It will be a tough one that will test your mettle. In the morning, you should phone Ada and make peace with her. I know it will be hard, but only by making peace with her will you get deliverance from the anger you've been harboring towards her over these last years. From my perspective, it's something you should do before Michael's funeral."

"I don't think you could have asked me to do a tougher assignment," Rob replied after a long pause. "It will take all of my strength, but I know you're right. I know that to heal I have no choice but to do it. Tomorrow's Saturday. She teaches so she should be at home. I don't know if she's moved, but if I can't get her, I'll phone her mom so I can make contact with her."

Rob was so apprehensive over the pending phone call he knew he must make that he had difficulty getting to sleep. At seven the next morning he gathered up courage and made the call. Ada answered the phone.

"Ada, this is Rob. It's high time I got in touch with you again. I'd like to apologize for being such an idiot and writing you that snotty letter a few years back forbidding you from ever contacting me again. I was hurting really bad, but that was no excuse. I've been having a horrible time of it, but with the help of a friend, I believe I'm now getting back on track again. Hopefully we can turn over a new leaf." Pausing to gain strength he continued, "I'd like to congratulate you on the birth of your daughter. How are you and Norman making out?"

Rob could hear Ada sobbing.

"Oh Rob, I've been constantly praying for this day. Oh my God, I'm so relieved to hear your voice. A couple of days ago, I was just about at the point of giving up on us ever getting together again. I was by myself marking papers in school that afternoon. I felt a very heavy burden for you and I was constantly praying for you. Suddenly, I had this most terrifying vision. It just came as a flash. I saw you holding a gun to your chest. I dropped to my knees and prayed for your safety for several minutes. And then, don't ask me why, suddenly I felt at peace. Oh, dear Rob, I'm just so overcome. Thank you so much for contacting me. God only knows how relieved I am. Like you, I've had an awful time too. I guess its time we both found out what happened to us."

"You're right, Ada. What is so mind-bending is that I really had a gun against my chest. My finger couldn't squeeze the trigger though and then I had a vision of you on your knees pleading to God for me not to kill myself."

"Oh my God, Oh my God! The Creator does answer prayer!"

"Let me tell you my story," Ada continued. "I know this is a poor excuse, but you and I had been separated for quite some time and I was desperately lonely. Many of our church members were encouraging me to take up with this Norman character. He was a smooth talker and had most everyone at church including me convinced that he was a sterling character. Dad and Jacob thought him a phony, but sadly, I didn't listen to them. Somehow, Norman and both pastors found out that after I sent that letter, you were doing some heavy drinking. Norman was the senior pastor's nephew. Both the senior pastor and the youth pastor were encouraging me to drop you because of your drinking and take up with Norman. They kept harping away about you being a drunk. Norman went on and on about how much better a choice he was than a drunk. I must be honest with you, Rob. I was just weak and for sure I wasn't thinking. As I relive those troubled times, I rue the day that I ever had anything to do with that creep. I wasn't as strong as I should have been. The rotter turned out to be an unfaithful jerk."

"It sounds to me that you've had every bit as rough a time as I've had," Rob said. "So, what happened?"

"I'm getting to that. Our wedding was certainly not what I'd hoped it would be. I couldn't get over how Norman tried to get all the attention directed to himself. As I lay in bed the night of our wedding, I was weeping while Norman was snoring. It suddenly hit me that I still loved you. Although his lovemaking was crude, what really was getting to me was his need to put me in a subordinate role and for him to be the top dog in everything."

"As time passed, his attempts at lovemaking did not improve. I say attempts because they were just that, attempts. It seemed to me that he thought sex was just to satisfy the man."

"Why, oh why, did I write you that stupid letter forbidding you from contacting me again? If only I had kept the lines of communication open, it would have saved both of us a lot of heartache."

"It gets worse. One morning, two months into our marriage, I came home unexpectedly. It was raining and the roof in my classroom sprang a leak. My class was cancelled for the rest of the day. Before I left in the morning, Noman said he wasn't feeling well so wouldn't be going to work. When I stepped into the porch, I saw an umbrella and a pair of woman's rubbers. I tiptoed to the bedroom door. It was open a crack. When I peeked inside, my heart just about stopped. To my horror, I saw Norman cuddled up to another woman. They were in bed, both asleep. I tiptoed back to our kitchen and phoned

Dad. He was there shortly. Dad never did like Norman and was against me marrying him. He thought him a flake."

"Without any fanfare, Dad barged into the bedroom and caught them right in the act. Poor Norman got the beating of his life from Dad. He really worked him over. The woman he was sleeping with grabbed her clothes and made a hasty retreat. After the bruising he got from Dad, Norman had to get some medical attention to get patched up."

"Good for your dad," Rob replied. "I'm certainly proud of him. Had I been there, the bastard would have had a few more lumps on his head."

"Anyway, a week or so later, Norman and the youth minister who had married us asked for a meeting with me. You see, as I mentioned, before I got married, Norman constantly claimed to be a very devout Christian. Lloyd, the youth minister, bought his claim, hook, line and sinker. Lloyd had done his best to convince me that being a Christian, Norman would be a far better match for me than you would be."

"I agreed to meet them, but unbeknown to them, I had Dad there with me. Dad and I had done a little sleuthing and found out that this wasn't the first time Norman had cheated on me. In fact, we found out that prior to meeting me he had a track record of being promiscuous. We had a couple of notes from the women he had been promiscuous with after we were engaged. Of course, when we met, the minister said that up until this incident, Norman had been a good Christian. He said that Norman was led astray by the devil and he, Norman and Daniel the senior pastor had just met a few hours ago and Norman had re-committed his life to God."

"When I asked Norman about the other women he had slept with after we were engaged, he maintained this was the only time it had happened. The stupid youth minister chimed in that he was sure this was the only time Norman had been unfaithful. Then Dad read the notes proving Norman's unfaithfulness, after we were engaged. Norman sucked in his breath and stood there, unable to get one word out. Needless to say, the minister had nothing more to say either."

"What a sleezy character that Norman was. It sounds like the youth minister wasn't the brightest pebble on the beach either."

"You're right on both counts. Dad grabbed Norman by the arm. 'You have thirty seconds to get out of Ada's house,' he bellowed at Norman. 'If you're not out in thirty seconds, I'll hammer the snot out of you again.'"

"As you can imagine, Norman and the minister made a hasty retreat. It was my apartment and a few days later, Norman came back with a friend to get all his stuff. When he tried to turn on the charm with me, I told him to get lost and threatened to call Dad. That put the run on him. A month later, we were divorced."

"Thank God you got yourself out of that mess. I just can't get over how stupid it was of me not to stay in contact with you."

"It certainly was good to get rid of him. You've heard about my daughter. I adopted Roberta a few months after I was divorced. She was quite a mixed-up little person when I got her. She had been in a couple of foster homes and it just wasn't working out for her. I realized the little tyke needed a good home. Mom offered to look after her during the day while I was teaching. Adopting Roberta helped ease the pain of losing you, my first love. It also helped ease the pain of my failed marriage. Roberta was originally named Bobbie, but I changed that to Roberta. She is named after you, dear."

"After Norman and I were divorced I dated our new youth minister a few times. He was more interested in me than I was in him, but he was good company. I'd been working with him for the better part of a year helping out at church with our Young Peoples' meetings. I just want you to know that I had no romantic intentions with Brad."

"My God. I'm finding it hard to absorb all of this. What's playing over and over in my head is what an idiot I was forbidding you to contact me. If only I had known. If only I had known. All those wasted years because I was such a childish ass. I understand you dating Brad. Loneliness is hard to bear. It was I who cut off all communication with you. What a fool I was."

"I don't know if it's too late now, Ada, but I want you to know that I still love you with a passion."

"No, it's not too late, Rob. This is the happiest day of my life. Regardless of all that's happened, I still love you and always will."

"This is the happiest day of my life, too," Rob continued. "Thank God we've been given another chance. I'll phone you tomorrow and be down to see you and Roberta as quickly as I can, if that's alright with you."

"Any time you get here can't be soon enough for me."

"I just got word that my old boss, Michael Francis, passed away. He had been suffering from cancer for some time. You'll remember him. He used to tease you when you worked the school break at the ranch a few years past. He was like a father to me after my dad was killed. Then, asshole that I was, I started drinking. I'll be down to see you after the funeral."

"So, I'd better sign off for now, Ada. All my love to you. I'll give you a phone call tomorrow at about three pm your time if that time is good for you."

"My condolences to you over the loss of Michael. I have fond memories of him too. I'll be waiting for your call. All my love to you too."

"Good phone call?" Ruben asked.

"It's the best news I've ever had in my entire life, the very best. I can hardly believe it! I knew from Jacob's letters that Norman, Ada's new husband, was a real phony. Still, I apologized to her for acting like an ass and cutting off contact with her. Ada caught him cheating on her and got divorced a few months after their marriage. She adopted her little daughter to help ease the pain of losing me and the pain of a marriage that went nowhere. She named the little girl Roberta, after me. I still love her and she said that she still loves me."

"Ada was also remorseful for her part in all of it. She took responsibility for allowing herself to be conned into abandoning me and taking up with this Norman character. The church she attended had put a lot of pressure on her to do so. Thank God we've been able to resolve things."

"I can't thank you enough for helping me get back on the path again, Ruben. You are a Godsend."

"Just remember, Rob, you, Lynn and I all suffered from that 'Poor me,' 'Why me,' 'The universe is against me,' syndrome. Those of us who have this propensity must always be aware of our weakness and constantly work to keep ourselves on track. That means using self-discipline and with the Almighty's help, accessing the inner strength he has instilled in all of us. I'm positive you can do it, Rob."

CHAPTER 24

B Y MID-MORNING ROB was heading out to the ranch. Before he got to the building site he stopped at his dad's grave.

"Thanks for being there when I tried to kill myself, Dad. I now know you kept my finger from pulling the trigger. I just know that. I've turned over a new leaf. Never again will I touch liquor. I promise that I'll do better now so you can be proud of me again."

"So good to have you back with us again," Maud said when she greeted Rob. "The vision of my dear husband that you witnessed and his last words about you stopping drinking meant so much to all of us. There's no doubt that it's all a miracle."

"If you've licked the liquor thing you're welcome back," Carl added. "Dad always talked longingly of you swearing off liquor and returning."

"I've sworn off liquor forever," "Rob replied, "but let's not talk about me. We just lost one hell of a man. It seems just like yesterday Michael and I rode the range together in that huge saddle he had. I was only four or five then. I'll be ever grateful for him being the father-figure to me when Dad died.

As we all remember, he was there when Dad's spirit came back to comfort me."

"The funeral will be held on Wednesday," Maud said. "The boys and I decided on having Michael's funeral outdoors, here at the ranch. In the event of rain, we will move indoors to one of the large hay sheds. Although he's well into his eighties, Don Neufeld, the same minister who buried William, agreed to conduct Michael's funeral."

Before eating lunch, Paul and Carl took Rob aside.

"Our offer still stands," Paul began. "We'll take your word that your drinking days are over. We all talked about bringing you back and making you a junior partner. Dad was so looking forward to working with you again. I know Dad is resting easy now."

"Thanks," Rob replied, "I'll break my back trying to earn all of your trust back again."

After lunch, Rob followed Edith back to her place. Rob told Edith of all the miraculous things that had happened to him in the last few days.

"Yes, a miracle has happened for both you and Ada," Edith said. "Thank God Ruben was able to help you out of the doldrums. It sounds like you'll be going back to the ranch. If it would help, you're welcome to move in with me for the time being rather than pay another month's rent at your rooming house."

"Thanks for the offer. If it won't put you out too much, I'll take you up on it."

Once Edith was on her way to see Ruben, Rob phoned Ada from her place.

"You don't know how wonderful it is to hear your voice again!" Rob exclaimed.

"Hearing your voice again is wonderful for me too. Our former youth pastor is now a few hundred miles south, but last night I couldn't help but phone him to tell him of us getting back together again. When he cautioned me about rushing into another relationship again with you, I told him that it was he who had advised me to leave our healthy relationship to be with that loser Norman. He didn't have much to say after that."

"Well dear, I have to be a pallbearer at Michael's funeral on Wednesday," Rob continued. "When is your last day of school?"

"School will be out for the summer on Tuesday afternoon. I'll be finished my school end reports sometime Wednesday."

"I'll be leaving Medicine Hat on my way to see you Wednesday evening and should be arriving sometime Friday. I can't wait to see you again. We have a lot of catching up to do."

Rob filled Ada in on the problems he had with alcohol. "I've turned over a new leaf now, though. I swear I'll never touch another drop of liquor again as long as I live."

Rob told Ada of his visit with Ruben, his experience at the Sacred Rock and his new daily ritual of calling out to God to help him access his inner strength.

"I knew about your drinking from my mom. She was corresponding with your mom. I'll take your word that you won't go back to drinking again. Remember dear, I grew up with you. I know how solid you were back then. Yes, we both had set backs, but now God has given us a second chance. I too can't wait for us to be back together again."

Once Rob got off the phone with Ada, he drove back to his room, emptied out what was left of his liquor and gave his landlady his notice. As his car was small, it took him two trips to move all his belongings to Edith's place.

Early the next morning, Rob was back at the ranch and helping with anything they needed a hand with. The whole crew was glad to see him back. He advised Paul that after the funeral he'd spend a week or so down with Ada and then start working with them full-time again.

The morning of the funeral dawned clear and warm with a gentle breeze from the southwest. As it was being held outside, many of the neighbors brought their own chairs. By two pm a large crowd had gathered. When they ran out of chairs, they made do with a few blocks of wood draped with blankets.

At two-thirty the service opened with one of the local ladies singing 'Amazing Grace.' Pastor Neufeld then stood up.

"Back in 1883, I conducted a funeral a few miles from here for two workers, killed while they were working on the building of the new railroad. A partially built trestle collapsed and they fell to their deaths. William Burke, one of the other young men working on that trestle escaped serious injury by falling onto a large poplar tree. Then, several years later I was called to do the funeral service for William when he was killed by a grizzly. Now, sadly, we must say goodbye to Michael Francis, the founder of this ranch."

Once the eulogy had been read, the minister asked if there was anyone who wished to add their comments. Rob got to his feet and went to the front.

"I was only five when my dad died. Up until Dad's death, Michael was like a grandpa to me. After Dad's death, he was more like a surrogate dad to me. Many a day he took me out riding the range with him. Goodbye my kind, tough old buddy. You were one hell of a man."

"I would now like to read this poem on death that was written by an old friend of mine."

"Michael Francis fought courageously with cancer for a long time. I'll dedicate the poem to Maud, Paul, Carl and their families."

SAFE HARBOUR

I'm standing at the seashore,

A ship is set to leave.

I marvel at its grandeur,

Its full sails catch the breeze.

I watch intrigued as it ploughs the waves.

I'm so moved by its strength.

But then, it's shrinking from my sight

And as I watch, at length,

It's shrunk to just a tiny speck.

A voice cries out "Look there."

I strain, but it has slipped from view,

The sea's completely bare.

"It's gone," he says, "It's gone for good!

We'll see it never more."

"Not right," I say. "I don't agree,

There is a distant shore.

They'll welcome him as he glides to port

With arms thrown open wide.

You say he's gone, but he still lives on.

You see my friend, HE'S DIED.

Yes, death does sting, but there's far more.

His soul's alive, it's free.

It's true our hearts were breaking when

THE LORD SAID, 'COME TO ME!'

But soon we know there'll come that call.

Our ships will leave this shore.

We'll join our loved ones, Oh What Joy!

Together Evermore."

By Michael Parlee

With tears in his eyes, Rob headed back to his seat.

Michael was laid to rest in a grave next to William's. There they lay, two cowboys of the early west, their bodies at peace, their souls in the next dimension, the prevailing southwest wind ever sweeping over their graves.

CHAPTER 25

L ATE THE NEXT afternoon, Rob was on the train heading down to Tennessee, back to his beloved. As the miles rolled on, Rob kept repeated over and over again, "Thank you God for giving Ada and me another chance."

As Rob's train pulled in, Ada, Roberta, Jacob, Jed and Eva were there to meet him. When Rob stepped off the train, Ada came rushing up with Roberta in her arms. Rob would soon discover that this little lady was quite a candid sort.

"You have a hard hug," she said to Rob. "When mommy hugs me, it's soft. My name is Roberta. Mommy said I was named the same name as you have. Is your name Roberta?"

"No, my name is Rob. That's the front part of your name. You sure are a talkative young lady."

There was no stopping the young lass.

"I have a Mommy, but I don't have a daddy. Would you like to be my daddy? Mommy said that someday you might be my daddy."

Ada was most embarrassed, but Rob was really enjoying his conversation with Roberta.

"We'll have to ask Mommy about me being your daddy. If Mommy says it's okay with her, then I'd really like to be your daddy."

"Let Mommy talk now," Ada said, as she handed Roberta over to her mom.

Ada was in Rob's arms again. This time without Roberta's chattering, they had a real warm, hard, soft hug. Once the round of hugs was completed, they all headed to Jed's and Eva's place for supper.

Roberta wasn't content until she was sitting on Rob's knee. Ada was tickled pink with the closeness that was developing between Rob and Roberta. Although the twosome spilt a bit of food on the floor, both ate a good supper.

After they had eaten, Ada and Rob went for a short walk to Ada's school.

"I phoned Brad, the youth pastor yesterday," Ada said. "I told him you were coming for a visit today and I wouldn't be able to help him with Young Peoples' tonight or possibly next Friday's Young Peoples' as well. He seemed to be quite uptight. I have a feeling that he thought that on the personal end of it, that things were going good between him and me."

"Those are the breaks, I guess. There's always winners and losers. We had four years of separation, but other than that, we've been close friends since we were seven."

"After my marriage fell apart, I was in an awful dilemma. I wanted to get in touch with you, but you warned me never to contact you again. Then to top it all off, I was ashamed and upset with myself for abandoning you in favor for that jerk. Why, oh why didn't I use the brains God gave me?"

"Yes, we all make mistakes. If I'd been a man, even though the news of you and Norman broke my heart, I should have kept the lines of communication open with you."

"I wonder if we haven't lampooned ourselves enough," Ada replied. "Our separation has been hard on both of us, but now, let's open a new chapter in our lives."

"Maybe you're right. Yes, on second thought, I know you are right. It's time for us to move on."

Once back from their walk they all visited till well past midnight getting caught up on their respective lives. Roberta would spend the night at Grandpa's and Grandma's place. Finally, after they had finished visiting, Rob and Ada left for her place.

"Together at last," Ada said, walking hand in hand with Rob to her apartment. "After the divorce, I was constantly praying we'd get back together. I was almost at the point of giving up. That's why I went out with Brad a few times. I was just so desperately lonely. He was always putting pressure on me to go on more dates with him. In fact, the evening you made your first phone call, he had asked me to go to a ball game with him. Thank God, I told him I was busy with school work. Brad and the senior pastor were always after me to get more involved in the church activities, but I was a little leery of getting in too deep after the church's involvement in the Norman thing."

"I understand."

"I think we've waited long enough to be a bit friendlier," Rob said with a grin, once they were back at Ada's apartment. "You know, maybe we could take things a little farther than when we were together at the ranch? First though, here's a little something for you. I want to spend the rest of my life with you and Roberta."

Rob handed Ada a small velvet box. With trembling hands, Ada opened it.

"Oh, my God!" Ada cried out, slipping her engagement ring on. "I thought that your first phone call was the happiest day of my life, but this trumps that. I'm so looking forward to spending the rest of my life with you as your wife!"

"Two weeks ago, if someone would have told me that we'd be back together again I'd have thought them crazy," Ada continued. "We were both in misery. You were so fed up with life you tried to end it all and I was also nearing the end of my rope. Here we are back together again, so in love."

Ada took Rob by the hand and led him into the bedroom.

"Please be patient with me," Ada whispered. "My experience with Norman in bed was not at all good. It seemed to me that he thought that sex was designed to only pleasure the man. Having sex with him lasted all of twenty seconds. He told me that the youth pastor who married us told him it wasn't scriptural for a woman to become really turned on by sex."

They lay naked, discovering each other's bodies. Neither one had ever been so stimulated. After, as they lay in each other's arms, Rob whispered, "That was just so unbelievably beautiful. Was it enjoyable for you too?"

"It was unbelievably enjoyable for me too," Ada sighed.

Soon they were asleep, cuddled close to each other.

"I guess we should make some plans," Rob said in the morning over coffee. Maud and her sons Paul and Carl want to make me a junior partner in the ranch like my dad was. What do you have in mind for yourself?"

"Well, I always loved the ranch, but do you have any idea of what kind of work there could be for me up there? Is there a possibility that I could get a teaching position somewhere near the ranch?"

"Before I left, I was talking to Paul. He told me they were looking for another teacher for their small rural school. When I was born, they had the school right on the ranch, but with the country opening up with more ranches, they built a new school more central to all of them. It's only a few miles from our ranch. After talking to Paul, I took the liberty of contacting Ross Mattel, the chairman of the school board. I told him that you had two years of teacher training and were finishing your second year of teaching, here in the States. I added that you might be interested in teaching at our little rural school. The chairman said they certainly would like to talk to you."

"That sounds interesting. We'll have to look into it more. I can tell you one thing. I want to stay close to you. As we both found out, those long-distance relationships are for the birds."

Soon they were on their way to Ada's folks place, Ada driving her Model T Ford. There were many hugs and tears of joy when Ada showed off her engagement ring.

"We got a call from the youth pastor early this morning," Eva said as they were eating breakfast. "Dad answered the phone. Brad told Dad that he was very concerned with Ada getting back with a boyfriend who had a drinking problem. You know your dad; not above raising a little hell. He told Brad that you and your old boyfriend spent the night at your apartment."

"There will be prayers a plenty being raised on your behalf Ada," Jed said, shaking his head and chuckling. "If I'd known you two were engaged, I'd have broken that news to him too. About all I can add, Ada, is that there's no question that you've finally picked the right man."

Soon Roberta was sitting on Rob's knee. "Are you going to live with us?" she asked. "If you did you could even sleep with me in my bed."

"That's very kind of you Roberta, but what about Mommy? Wouldn't she be sad sleeping all by herself?"

"She might, but if she'd like, maybe she could sleep with us too."

After they had eaten breakfast, Ada asked her folks if they could use their cabin for a few days.

"No problem," Jed replied, "but shouldn't either Mom or I go along as a chaperone?" he added with a grin.

"What about Roberta?" Ada asked.

"I'm all for taking Roberta along with us," Rob interjected before anyone else could respond. "After all, she already has all the sleeping arrangements worked out."

"That's awfully kind of you," Ada responded, "but are you sure?"

"Well, we're all going to be a family soon, aren't we? Besides, I think it only proper to take the boss along."

"Mom's and Dad's cabin is by a small lake about thirty miles from here. I thought it would be fun to hang out there for a few days.

"The cabin's yours, but you'll have to get some groceries," Eva said.

"No problem," Ada replied. "Rob and I will shop before we go."

Soon they were on their way. A few miles down the road, Roberta was asleep.

"It was so kind of you to ask for Roberta to come along. You made big points with Mom and Dad. I'm so happy it doesn't bother you that she's colored."

"I couldn't care less about the color of little Roberta's skin. You love me and I'm white and I love you and Roberta and you're both black."

"Yes, you proved your mettle years ago, when you tied a licking on anyone who tried to give Jacob and me a hard time. I don't know if you knew what that meant to me, Jake and my folks."

"I don't really need to make points with anyone. The little lady already has me under her spell. I just have this feeling that things are going to work out fine between the three of us. Who knows? Down the road a bit, our family might have two with black skin, one with white skin and one or more black-white skinned ones."

"Are you saying we should have our own black-white kids?"

"Can you think of one good reason why we shouldn't?"

"You're such a marvel as I guess most northerners are. There's so much discrimination down here. I know I'll miss the folks and Jacob, but I'll be happy to get out of such a prejudiced, segregated environment. It will be especially good for Roberta."

"Maybe you should contact the schoolboard chairman I talked to," Rob said. "I always believe in striking while the iron's hot."

"As soon as we get back, I'll phone him or send him a telegram. You're right. It sounds like a good opportunity that we shouldn't miss out on. It would be so good to teach in a non-segregated school. I'd love to raise Roberta in a community where she won't be disadvantaged because of the color of her skin."

Soon they arrived at the cabin. Roberta was a little cranky when her nap was cut short, but it wasn't long before she was back to her sunny self. After they'd eaten a late dinner, they were out on the veranda in their rocking chairs. Grandpa had made Roberta her own miniature rocker. He had also built a roof over the veranda so they could be in the shade.

Ada finally got up and made them some iced tea. After they'd had their tea party, they struck off on the half mile

Michael Parlee

trail down to the lake. Rob carried their canvas chairs. It was a beautiful warm late summer afternoon with scores of birds singing from their perches in the trees along the trail. Roberta tried to mimic each singing bird that they passed. When the little hiker played out, Rob handed Ada the chairs and hoisted Roberta up on his shoulders. Soon they were sitting on the small dock, dipping their feet in the water.

They looked up to see an old black fellow, fishing rod in hand, ambling up to the dock.

"Ma'am," he said addressing Ada. "Pleasant day. Mind if I do a little fishing?"

"You're more than welcome, Sir," Rob replied. "If we're in your way we can move."

The old man nodded, an astonished look crossing his face.

"You folks from these parts?"

"No, this lady is my girlfriend. She and her little daughter live in Crossville. We're staying a few days at her folks' cabin. I'm from Alberta. That's up in Canada."

"Fine place, that Canada is. I understand they treat us blacks much better up there. At times, they treat us pretty rough down here. Yes-sir-ee, pretty rough. We was treated worse a few years back. When I was a boy, we was treated way, way worse. They lynched us black folk, back then, sometimes for doin' next to nothin'. Sad, sad days they were. Of course, the whites said they did it in God's name. I'd best stop or I gets all worked up."

"In all my life, this is the first time a white man has called me Sir," the old lad said after a long pause. "And it feels good. Yes, damn it. It feels good. What might you do up in Canada?"

"I work on a ranch. I'll be headed back there in a week or so. My girlfriend is a teacher. She and her daughter will soon be moving up to Canada to be with me."

"If I were a whole lot younger, I'd be thinking of moving up there myself. It does my old gizzard good to see folks of different color getting along. Best of luck to you all and thank you again for calling this old black guy, Sir."

With that, the old lad went out to the end of the pier and began fishing.

As soon as the old fellow was out of ear shot, Ada turned to Rob.

"You see Rob, down here while we may work alongside each other, it's quite uncommon for whites to mix on a personal level with us blacks. It's especially true in rural areas. That's why that old man had such an astonished look on his face when you addressed him as 'Sir'. Years back, before we came up to Ontario, Mom and Dad taught Jacob and me not to speak to an older white person unless they spoke to us first. That's just the way of the South. Jacob and I spent our first five years down here. I'm not the only one who wants Roberta to be raised in a different climate. Dad has always talked longingly of returning to Canada. Other than the rough time he had when that sick dame tried to blackmail him, both Mom and Dad much preferred living in Canada."

"As you'll remember, when we were youngsters you came down with us for a visit. Grandpa was still healthy then and he and Grandma were still farming. When we moved back here, Dad took over the farm for a number of years after Grandpa's heart attack. When Grandpa died, the farm was sold, we moved into town and Dad went back doing carpentry full-time. Dad and Jacob had been doing a bit of carpentry while we were still on the farm. Both Dad and Jacob liked building far more than farming anyway. Dad and Jacob now have a small construction business in town."

"Things are booming up in Alberta right now, especially in the Medicine Hat area. I'm sure there would be a business opportunity for your dad and Jacob. There's also a brick factory just out of Medicine Hat that I used to work at. Wouldn't that be a blast if all your family would move up to Alberta?"

"It would be wonderful. I always loved it in Canada."

Soon it was time to head back to the cabin for supper. They had an old ice cream making machine at the cabin and they'd brought along some ice. Soon they churned out a batch of ice cream. All the fresh air and exercise had tuckered out Roberta. After she ate her supper and had a large dish of ice cream, she was more than ready for bed. After a kiss from Mom and Rob, Ada put her in her little bed. It didn't take her long before she was in dream land.

When Roberta was sleeping, Ada went outside to be with Rob as he repeated his simple mantra thanking God for his inner strength and asking the Almighty for help in accessing that inner strength.

CHAPTER 26

O VER THE NEXT few days, the threesome walked the trails around the lake, spent time at the lakeshore or sat in their rocking chairs watching the rest of the world go by. It was a relaxing time and Ada was so grateful for the bond that was developing between Rob and his dark little friend. It had been a good week, but Saturday morning it was time to pack up and head back.

Once home, Jacob and his girlfriend, Henrietta, dropped over. While Ada and Henrietta went shopping, Rob and Jacob got caught up on their respective lives.

"Man, am I glad to see you on the scene again," Jacob said. "I mean, Ada getting hooked with that jackass Norman was an awful mistake. Dad and I tried to talk her out of marrying the jerk, but she was headstrong. The church didn't help either. Not only did this Norman creep have Ada fooled, he had both ministers and a host of other people in church fooled too. Even Mom was half-assed in his camp. She wanted Ada to get to know him a bit more before they got hooked up though."

"Yes, I guess it was a bad scene," Rob said, shaking his head. "I should not have cut off contact with Ada. That was just stupid immature thinking on my part. I mean, the summer she worked on the ranch we were talking of getting married and things couldn't have looked better. Oh well, the best way of putting it is we both screwed up. Thank God, it's all behind us now. I gather that your old man tied quite a beating on Norman when he caught him screwing some slut in Ada's bedroom."

"Yeah, he hammered the living pee right out of him. I wish I'd been there to give Norman a few good shots myself, but the old man did a good job on him."

"Ada told me about Brad," Rob said. "She said she went out with him to have company after she got divorced."

"Yeah, Brad is a decent sort. Ada told me he was good company, but she said that she had no romantic feelings toward him."

"I had a bad bout of drinking when I lost Ada, but that's all behind me now. When I get back, I'll be going back to the ranch again. They want to make me a junior partner like my old man was. I sure don't want to get pushy, but if it suits you guys, you should consider moving back to Canada. Alberta is really booming. In addition to opening up more land for ranching, they're opening up a pile of land for farming. Right now, Medicine Hat has a lot of building taking place."

"It's an idea. The folks, my girlfriend and I have been talking about the possibility of moving back to Canada. I think it would be worthwhile to take a trip up there to check things out. We're managing not too badly here with our carpentry, but there's still a lot of white folk down here who won't have anything to do with us business-wise. Dad, of course worked as a carpenter when we lived in Ontario and he said he was treated a lot better up there."

"I'll be heading back up North next week and if you like, I could do a little scouting, work-wise, for you and your dad."

"Thanks, we'd have no problem with that. With you and Ada planning on getting married, I imagine she'll be looking for work up there."

"Yes, she already has a good lead getting on as a teacher in that small school that's a few miles from the ranch."

Ada had her folks, Jacob and Henrietta over for supper. After the company had left, she and Rob were cleaning up.

"I wonder if it would be a good time to phone Ross, the schoolboard chairman," Rob said.

"That's a good idea," Ada replied. "Maybe you should try to get him on the phone."

Rob kept his fingers crossed as rural party lines could often be busy.

By the luck of the draw, the phone lines were open and Ross had just walked in the door. He was soon on the phone with Ada.

"I've had two years of teacher training from a college here in Tennessee and just finished my second year of teaching here in Crossville," Ada began. "Rob and I will be getting married soon and of course, I'll be moving up North to be with him."

"I can almost guarantee you the position here. We've been looking for another teacher. Just give me the name and phone number for your principal and possibly your school inspector."

"I should mention that I'm black. I hope that isn't a problem. My family lived in Ontario from the time I was five until I was 15, so I'm somewhat familiar with the Canadian elementary school curriculum."

"Here in Canada and especially out here in western Canada, we could care less what color your skin is. My grandmother on my dad's side was a Cree Indian. You no doubt will be teaching a few native kids. As I just said, I can just about guarantee you the job. This is frontier country and we're always hard-pressed to get teachers in the rural spots."

"Well that certainly sounds positive," Ada said once she gave Ross the information he needed and was off the phone. "I'll contact my principal and get a recommendation from him."

Roberta was a bit cranky so they decided to put her in her carrier and Rob carried her on his back. Soon the little lady was asleep.

"What about tomorrow?" Ada asked, after putting Roberta to bed. "I should go to church and tell them I'll be leaving soon. What about you? Do you want to go to church? I'd love to have you there with me and show you off, but it's entirely up to you."

"I wouldn't mind tagging along with you. I'll enjoy being shown off by my beloved."

In the growing darkness, Ada and Rob sat on the couch, holding hands and reliving the days in Ontario when they were kids, growing up. They also talked of the carefree days they spent together on the ranch. Soon it was time to turn in for a bit more love-making.

Sunday morning, Ada, her mom and Rob went to church. Roberta was a little under the weather so Jed stayed at home with her. Before the service started, the ladies in the congregation did a lot of oohing and aweing over Ada's engagement ring. Many had been privy to Ada's story of Rob fighting for her and Jacob's honour in school and were pleased to meet Ada's hero.

Ada introduced Rob to Brad and showed him her ring. She told him she'd be moving up to Alberta before school started in the fall. He congratulated her and tried to be polite, but his face told how disappointed he really was.

"I'll drop off the material I have for Young Peoples'," Ada said to Brad. "As Young Peoples' meetings are off for July and August, this will give you time to find someone else to replace me."

It was a lively service. Rob really enjoyed the singing and music, but was not overly taken with the hellfire and brimstone sermon. On the way home from church, Eva and Ada both apologized to Rob.

"We have to look the other way at times with Pastor Daniel as he gets carried away with his own rhetoric," Eva said.

To everyone's delight, Jed had cooked up some southern fried chicken with parsnips and mashed turnips for dinner. They finished off the meal with Eva's specialty, a rhubarb-strawberry pie, liberally anointed with cream.

On Monday morning, Ada drove to her school principal's house and briefed him on her application to teach in Canada.

"I just got off the phone with Ross Mattel," the principal said. "Although we'll be sad to see you leave us, I highly recommended you to him. I will be mailing him my assessment and recommendation. Once he gets my input, he said he'd be contacting you formally offering you the job. The best of luck to you in your new venture."

Later in the afternoon, Ada got a phone call from Ross Mattel. The teaching position was hers, subject to his receiving the principal's letter of recommendation. As soon as Ada got the phone call, she phoned Brad and then drove over to his place to drop off her Young Peoples' material.

Roberta wanted to stay with Rob rather than going to Grandma's house.

"We'll certainly miss you," Brad began. "I wish you the best in your new venture, but I'm concerned for you. Are you sure that Rob's drinking days are in the past?"

"Yes, I'm very sure. We all make mistakes. Mine was to marry that jerk of a Norman. The former youth pastor's and Pastor Daniel's mistake was to highly recommend Norman to me without looking into his past. Rob was so broken- hearted over my betrayal of our love that he turned to liquor as his solace. That was his mistake. Out of Rob's kindness towards me, he's suggested we wait a few months before we marry. He volunteered this as a way to prove to me that he no longer relies on liquor. You see, Brad, as we grew up, Rob was always there for Jacob and me. If anyone tried to give us a hard time because of our color, he'd come to our rescue. Rob and I were very close before Norman came along. The summer I worked on the ranch in Alberta we had talked of getting married."

"As your pastor, I should advise you that there will be a temptation for the two of you to slip into some sexual intimacy before you get married. In the Bible, that is referred to as fornication. From a Christian's perspective, I trust you'll be aware of that."

"Please Brad," Ada responded, a little agitated. "What Rob and I do in private is nobody else's business. I love him with a passion, he loves me with a passion and he and Roberta are really bonding. Besides, we are formally engaged."

"Anyway, I should run now. I hope we can still be good friends."

Ada walked over to Brad and hugged him goodbye. As she drove back to her apartment, she was deep in thought. While it was apparent to her that Brad still had strong feelings for her, she recognized that his comments on fornication were most inappropriate and done out of a desperate need to hold on to her. She realized that Rob had so much more going for him than Brad.

When she opened the door, she could hear Roberta giggling.

"Mommy, Mommy," Roberta cried out, running to her mom. "Uncle Rob is telling me silly stories again that make me laugh!"

"How did your visit go?" Rob asked, chuckling. "Roberta and I are having a great time."

"Well, so-so. It's obvious Brad still has feelings for me. When I went out with him, I told him I wasn't interested in another relationship, but he must have been hoping that things would work out between him and me. When he tried to warn me about the fornication thing, I had to politely cut him off."

"So, Roberta, what kind of silly stories was Rob telling you?" Ada asked, turning to Roberta.

"He said that fish can fly, that frogs can read and go to school and that mother elephants feed their baby elephants jelly beans. I really like his silly stories!"

"Yes, Rob is full of silly stories. I like it when he's silly too."

"What are your immediate plans?" Ada asked. "What about Roberta and me? When do you think that we should head up to Alberta?"

"Well, I should get back to the ranch fairly soon. I was thinking of heading out in a couple of days. Just the day before I left Alberta and headed down here, Grandma Mildred wired me my share of Grandpa's estate. As Grandma married a fellow who was well off, she took the money that she and Grandpa had left over from the sale of the farm and split it between Aunt Beth, Aunt Becky and me. Grandma held off a while in giving me my share as I was drinking heavily. For now, there's our old house that the three of us could stay in. It's small, but we could manage. There's enough in what I got from Grandma and the little bit of savings I have to build us a new house. Maybe we should build it this summer and move in once we're married. I would suggest that you and Roberta could come up to the ranch as soon as you get everything tied up down here."

In the evening, Rob, Roberta and Ada dropped in on her folks. Jacob and Henrietta were also visiting. Rob and Ada told them of their plans. Rob asked Jed and Jacob if they would be interested in building a new house on the ranch for Ada, Roberta and him.

"Before I came down here, I was talking to the ranch owners, Maud and her two sons Paul and Carl. They said they were planning on getting a large barn built. That might be an opportunity for you guys if you're at all interested in coming to Canada again. Once I get back, I'll check things out construction-wise. If things are looking up, I'll give you guys a holler."

"That sounds good to us," Jed replied. "We all have been talking about moving back to Canada. We're managing to keep the wolf away from the door, but as Jacob probably told you, the discrimination down here is pretty hard to cope with. A lot of white folk look the other way when it comes to hiring a black contractor. We do good work, but a fair percentage of the white people treat us as if we have the plague."

"In western Canada you won't have to deal with that problem," Rob replied. "Out West, although the odd person won't have anything to do with our natives, the vast majority of people couldn't give a rat's rump what color one's skin is."

"Before you guys dropped in, I was listening to the radio," Eva interjected. "They announced that the remnants of the hurricane that has lashed the southern coastal regions will be hitting us later this evening."

It had been very sullen all day with angry clouds coming in. By the time Ada, Rob and Roberta left for Ada's apartment, light rain was falling. An hour later, they were in the grips of some extreme weather.

"I think it's wise to stay inside out of the elements for the night," Ada said. "At times, these remnants of tropical storms can get pretty wild down here. A few years back I had a friend who went out in a strong wind storm. A tree blew over on top of him, breaking his leg."

"I'll be more than content to stay hunkered down with my two girls and keep nice and warm," Rob replied. "Maybe we can throw a few sticks of wood in the cook stove and pop us up some popcorn."

It had been a full day for Roberta and she was tuckered right out. After a small bowl of popcorn, she fell asleep on Rob's knee. After laying the sleeping beauty down in her bed, Ada came back out and sat down beside Rob.

"There's some news I forgot to tell you about," Ada said. "You remember Daniel, our senior pastor. Well, when we were out, he phoned Mom this morning. He spouted off to Mom that he didn't think it was in God's plan for me to marry someone with a drinking habit. Mom tried to explain to him that you only drank to ease the pain of losing me, but she didn't seem to get through to him. He wants to talk with me. I imagine he's heard from Brad that I plan on going with you to Alberta. No doubt he'll be lobbying for me to drop you again and stay down here. He told Mom that he wanted to meet with me in his study at the church. I talked to his secretary and we're to meet tomorrow afternoon. What I didn't tell the secretary was that I'll be accompanied by my boyfriend."

"You're a sneaky one. I suppose my role there will be for moral support?"

"Exactly, dear, exactly."

"Well I'm looking forward to our meeting. It will be interesting to see how the minister handles having me there with you."

At two pm, the next afternoon, Ada and Rob drove up to the church. To say that Pastor Daniel was taken aback when Rob walked in with Ada would be an understatement.

"Now Ada, it was my understanding that we could talk in private," Pastor Daniel began. "Young man," he continued turning to Rob. "Would it not be possible for you to excuse yourself so Ada and I can talk privately?"

"I don't think so," Rob replied, smiling. "Ada has asked me to be here with her for support. Ada and I are formally engaged, so go ahead."

"I'd appreciate it, Ada, if we could talk in private."

"As Rob just said, I asked him to be here with me for support. We will soon be getting married so you should have no trouble in talking to us as a twosome."

"Very well then, but you both must be prepared for me to be blunt."

"Go ahead," Rob countered. "Both of us will have no problem with that, just as long as your comments are well thought out and fair."

"All right," Daniel replied, opening his Bible. "Let me refer you to God's Word. The Apostle Paul admonishes us not to be unequally yoked. Now I know that Ada is a Christian. I'm very concerned that you'll be marrying a non-Christian, Ada. Add to that Rob's problems with alcohol and I'm doubly concerned."

"In regards to putting a label on who is a Christian and who isn't one; I don't think anyone should go there," Rob quietly replied. "Remember, God's Word also states, 'Judge not, lest you be judged' and that's what you've just done with me. Only God can determine if we are a Christian or not. Remember, it was you and the former youth pastor who lobbied long and hard for Ada to abandon me and marry that promiscuous jerk of a Norman. According to what Ada told me, not only did Norman claim he was a Christian, you and the youth pastor claimed he was a Christian. He certainly didn't comport himself like a Christian, though, did he? From the Bible's point of view, his works didn't live up to his words. He was trash and he got what he deserved from Jed for screwing some tramp in Ada's bed. Now, as to my past history of drinking. I fully admit that I turned to booze to deaden the pain of losing Ada. That was my weakness, but now that's all in the past. I vow that with the Almighty's help, I'll never touch another drop of the poison again as long as I live. You see, the Lewis family has known me for close to 15 years and know that I can be counted on."

Pastor Daniel was taken aback by how forthright Rob was. Before he could respond, Ada barged in.

"Rob is right. You and the former youth pastor worked hard to convince me, an impressionable young woman, to abandon a stalwart, loving, kind man and replace Rob with that unfaithful Norman. I married Norman because I was suggestable, weak and yes, stupid. Rob's downfall was, as he mentioned, turning to alcohol to lessen the pain of losing me. We both made big mistakes, but we've learned from our mistakes. I didn't know why you wanted to talk to me today, but I had my suspicions. I see now that you're trying to drive a wedge between us. You are trying to destroy the relationship that both of us had so longed for. Your effort to derail our relationship isn't going to work. I hate to be abrupt with you, Pastor Daniel. I hope you don't take it personally, but our meeting is now over."

Before the shocked pastor could respond, Ada and Rob were on their feet and heading out of the church.

"I just couldn't take Pastor Daniel's hypocrisy any longer," Ada said as they were walking to the car. "Pastor Daniel has never once acknowledged or apologized to me for his part in convincing me that I should drop you and marry that loser of a Norman. Now he wants me to abandon you again."

"Although I used to help out Brad with the youth ministry and go to church on Sundays, after the Norman episode, I was never much of a Pastor Daniel fan. After what he tried today, I'm certainly not turning away from my religious convictions, but I won't be attending any more of his services."

"I guess he thought he could sway you again as he did in the past," Rob responded. "I know it's going to be a hard assignment for us, but we should try not to be too upset by what the pastor was trying to do. Actually, he and his like are to be pitied. There are many clergy of all faiths who are good, sincere men or women of God. Unfortunately, there are some like Pastor Daniel who use their head for nothing more than something to keep their ears apart."

All afternoon, the fiasco meeting with Pastor Daniel weighed heavy on Ada. After stopping at her place for a bite to eat, they headed to her folks' place so she could vent.

"It's good to get things off your chest," Jed said after Ada finished telling about the incident with the pastor. "Maybe we shouldn't pick on old Daniel, but after he found out what an arse his nephew was, he should have bent over backwards to apologize for misleading you. We all make mistakes, but it takes a real man or a real woman to take responsibility for their screw-ups. For whatever reason, Pastor Daniel wouldn't or couldn't do that. When he preaches, from what I see and hear, he's nothing but a shouting bully. That's why I don't go to church much anymore."

"Enough about Pastor Daniel," Eva interjected. "Let's talk about something more positive. I'm just so grateful to have Rob back in our family again. The last few years have been so heavy for both him and Ada. In fact, with Jacob's sickness, they've been hard on us all. Let's hope that the sledding will be easier from here on out."

"It's so good to be back with all of you," Rob replied. "What with Jacob's remarkable cure and Ada and I getting back together, we have much to be thankful for. The future for Jacob, Ada, Roberta and me now looks a million times brighter."

CHAPTER 27

A S ROB WOULD be leaving the following afternoon, they all put their heads together, discussing the plans for Ada, Roberta and the rest of the Lewis clan. Ada and Roberta would be coming up North in a couple of weeks while Jed, Eva, Jacob and Henrietta would wait until they got an update from Rob on business opportunities in the Medicine Hat area. If things looked promising, Jed, Eva and Jacob would come up to Alberta to check things out in detail. They would then decide whether or not to make the move back to Canada.

"I've decided to drop in on Mom and Emil on my way back to Alberta," Rob said as they were eating supper. "I'll spend a day or two with them. They'll want to know that Ada and I are back together."

"While the three of you were at the lake, Myrna phoned me." Eva replied. "She found out from Edith that all was well with you two again."

The next afternoon, Ada, Roberta and all the Lewis clan were at the train station to see Rob off. As Rob was hugging Ada and Roberta goodbye, the little lady was very sad. Finally, Rob took his little friend in his arms.

"I don't want you to go, Daddy," she sobbed. "Why can't you live with us?"

"In two weeks, Mommy and you will get on a train just like this one and come to the ranch and live with Daddy. We will build a new house on the ranch for Mommy, you and me and you will have your own bedroom and your own small bed. Mommy will teach school just like she did here and when you're a little older you'll go to school and Mommy will teach you. Maybe after you and Mommy come to the ranch, we could get you a dog or a cat."

"I'd like that," Roberta replied breaking into a smile. "I would really like a puppy. I like it when they lick your face, but I don't like cats. Cats scratch and pee on the bed."

With the assurance that he'd soon see them all, Rob was up the train steps and the train pulled out.

As the miles slipped by, Rob was repeatedly thanking God that his life had turned from gloom and doom into a life of hope, love and peace. As the train clattered on into the darkness, he repeated his mantra, thanking God for the strength He had placed within him and asking for help in accessing that strength.

Myrna, young Emil, Myrna's mother Maria and Mildred were at the station to greet Rob. It was a day of renewal for them all. Later in the afternoon, Emil, Ed and Ken joined the group. Rob wove the story of the painful period of his life up until Ruben helped him back to a positive mindset. All were happy that Rob and Ada had resolved their differences and were back together.

"You'll never know how many hours I've spent praying for you and Ada," Myrna said. "Emil and I felt so helpless that we couldn't get you to change your outlook on life. Thank God for Ruben. Thank God it all worked out in the end. Your dad would be so proud of you for beating the liquor thing."

"Both Ada and I made some stupid moves," Rob continued. "I guess that's what life's all about. It's about learning from one's mistakes."

"Out of curiosity, Mom, did you ever hear what happened to Morris? I always promised myself I'd look him up some day and work him over for physically abusing you."

Without responding, Myrna got up, went to the cupboard, came back with a letter and handed it to Rob.

"A year or two back, I got this letter from Morris addressed to both of us. It was about at the time you were fired from the ranch. You were in so much emotional turmoil, I thought I'd better wait until you were in a better frame of mind before I let you read it."

Dear Myrna and Rob:

This letter is a long time coming. Years ago, when I was released from prison, I was a very angry man. I managed to exist for a few years. Finally, with the help of a psychologist, I got back teaching again. It's taken me a long time, but by continuing to see the psychologist, I finally got my thinking straight. I apologize to both of you for the physical and emotional pain I've caused you. I realize now that my upbringing warped me right out of shape. I'm hoping now to turn over a new leaf. Someday if the two of you would agree to it, I wouldn't mind meeting with both of you to try to make amends. Please contact me if you can.

Yours truly, Morris

"I immediately wrote him a reply. I told him I was happy he got his thinking straight. I mentioned that you were out in Alberta. I said I'd contact you and see if the three of us could get together. A month or so after I sent Morris the letter, I got this note attached to his eulogy."

My name is Debbie Morrow. Morris was a good friend of mine. As you'll see in the attached eulogy, Morris recently passed away. He was teaching school on an Indian reservation. A couple of years ago he told me that he had been suffering from angina. For reasons only he knew, he chose not to get medical help. Last month when he didn't show up for school, they checked his room and found him dead. The doctor presumed that he had died in his sleep. The autopsy showed he had a massive heart attack.

"When I compared the date on his letter and the date of his death on his eulogy, I discovered that he passed away some time after I mailed my letter to him. I hope he got my letter before he passed on."

"Sometimes we're given a second chance, sometimes we're not," Myrna continued, shaking her head. "At least it's good that he got his thinking straight before he passed on. As you'll recall, Rob, when he was with us, he was a very mixed up, angry man."

"You got that right," Rob responded. "It's strange, but for years, I was planning on working the snot out of him for abusing you. About all a person can say now is that we're sorry for him; sorry how rigid thinking and anger ruled his life for so many years and how he spent all that time in his own self-made prison."

After a long pause, Rob added. "I can relate to poor Morris, because if I'm honest, for a number of years, with my addiction to liquor, I too was in my own self-made prison."

The next afternoon, everyone was at the train station to see Rob off.

"Ada and I will be getting married later this fall and you're all invited to our wedding."

"Edith and Ruben will also be getting married in a few months," Mildred added. "If you could have a double wedding, we'd only have to take one trip out to Alberta to get to both weddings."

"It's a thought," Rob replied. "I'll have to talk to Ada, Edith and Ruben and see what they think. We should be able to come up with some arrangement that will satisfy all of us."

As the miles slipped by on his long trip back to the ranch, Rob had plenty of time to ponder all that had happened in the last month or two. As he relived his failed attempt to end his life, he whispered. "Thank you, God, Dad and Ada for being there to save me."

When Rob arrived at Medicine Hat, Edith and Ruben were there to greet him. As they were eating supper, Rob filled them in on his adventures in Tennessee with the Lewis' and visiting his family in Ontario.

"Things are clicking into place," Rob added. "In another week or so Ada and Roberta will be moving up North to be with me. Come September, Ada will be teaching in the new school they've built just a few miles from the ranch. If the local business opportunities look good, the Lewis family may also be coming up here too."

"As I mentioned before, Ruben, I can never thank you enough for your help in getting me back on track. Thank God I survived my time in the wilderness."

"You, Lynn and I owe so much to young Barb, and old, blind, crippled Nell," Ruben replied. "All this happened because of their compassion. They overlooked their own infirmities to reach out to others in need. We also have to include dear Edith in this compassionate group," Ruben continued, reaching for his beloved's hand. "She was always there for you and then reached out to give a lift to this old, blind disabled guy. You and I owe her so much."

"You got that right," Rob replied, turning to Edith. "You sat with me for countless hours and days trying to help me out of the doldrums."

In the morning, Rob picked up his car, loaded up as much of his belongings he had room for and headed out to the ranch. It was a warm summer day with a soft breeze blowing. There was that familiar chinook arch to the southwest. The scenery never looked better to Rob. As the miles slipped by, he kept repeating, "Thank you, God Creator, for a new beginning."

Rob was given a royal welcome when he pulled in to the ranch. Soon he was back in the saddle, both figuratively and literally. Every night he went to bed tired, but so grateful for a second chance.

One evening, at Paul's and Carl's request, Rob met with them. They made Rob an offer to become an active partner.

"I know it was Michael's wish for me to become a junior partner and I appreciate your offer more than you'll ever know. However, I think it would only be fair to Maud and both of you to have a few months for me to prove myself. I swear I'll never touch the poison again, but still, I was a binge drinker. No, I have to be honest. I was an alcoholic for several years. I'd feel more comfortable if you would allow me to first prove myself. Let's talk again about partnership in another couple of months. I've also told Ada that we should wait till fall to get married. This is to prove to her that I'm off the sauce for good."

"I appreciate your honesty as I'm sure Paul does," Carl replied.

"Indeed, I do," Paul added. "We're both confident that you've licked the booze thing, but if it would put your mind at ease, we'll talk about our partnership offer a bit later."

Rob couldn't have been happier. He was back on his beloved windswept prairie, doing what he loved to do best. He would go to bed content and wake up in the morning looking forward to what the day would bring. Each evening after supper he'd go to his dad's grave and repeat his mantra.

Ten days after arriving back at the ranch, Rob was on his way to Medicine Hat to pick up Ada and Roberta, his two beloved girls. When the girls stepped off the train, Roberta let out a cry of glee when she saw Rob. After a round of hugs, Rob loaded the few things Ada and Roberta had brought into a small trailer that he pulled behind his car and they were on their way.

"Where did all the trees go?" Roberta asked as they drove along.

"The trees hardly ever grow here on the prairies," Rob replied. "That's the way God made it. It's mostly just grass. That's what the cows eat. Back at the ranch we have some trees that are part of the ranch. Someday we will ride on horseback up into the hills. There are lots of trees there."

Soon they were at the ranch cookhouse. For supper, Sue had roasted a half-dozen prairie chickens that the hands had shot. Dessert was strawberries with sugar and cream.

For the next few days, Rob booked off his regular work to help Ada set up the old house. They made several trips to town for supplies. Once their little home was in order, Ada was busy getting herself acquainted with the Alberta school curriculum for the grades she would be teaching and Rob returned to his work with the cattle.

Up until school started, Ada stayed at home and was able to look after Roberta while she prepared for the upcoming school year. She would be teaching with Wilma at the new school located some four miles from the ranch. Joy, Wilma's 18-year old daughter, was living at home and agreed to look after Roberta once Ada started teaching.

Roberta soon found some ranch kids to play with. One day, Brenda, a seven-year old girl, took her for a walk to show her some of the livestock.

"Brenda took me to see the cows today," Roberta said as they were eating supper. "Brenda said that the cows were called harfors. The cows were all red and white. We watched one cow trying to jump on the back of another cow. Brenda said that one of the boy cows was playing leap frog with a girl cow. He didn't jump over the girl cow though, he just stood behind her with his front feet up on her back. It looked like he was just resting."

"Yes," Rob replied with a grin. "The cows are called Herefords. Probably you're right, Roberta. I've seen that before too. Sometimes when the boy cows are tired, they put their feet up on the girl cows to rest."

"Oh, dear mercy," Ada interjected, rolling her eyes and shaking her head.

One evening, Rob, Ada and Roberta drove in to Edith's place to see Ruben and Edith and talk over their respective wedding plans.

"I'll be retiring from the Old Folks Home on the 15th of September," Edith said. "We were thinking of having our wedding in the last week in the month. Maud wants us to have the wedding at the ranch. Ruben and I will be going back to Ontario for our honeymoon. We'll only be gone for a week or so because in early October, the Old Folks Home is having a retirement party for me and another employee who will also be retiring."

"I talked to my folks and Henrietta before I left," Ada said. "For them, the most convenient time to come up would be the middle of October. The middle of October would be better for me too. September will be pretty busy for me what with starting in a new teaching position. Mid-October will work out well for our wedding. You and Ruben will be back from your honeymoon. Maud also wants our wedding to be at the ranch."

"I talked to Mom and Grandma Mildred about the weddings when I visited them a few weeks back," Rob added. "They definitely want to attend both weddings, but didn't want to make two trips out West. Grandma Mildred and Ken mentioned that they would like to go to the mountains and then on to the West Coast. If they were to attend your wedding first, they could go to the coast and be back in time for our wedding."

Edith and Ruben set their wedding date for the last week in September, while Ada and Rob set theirs for mid-October. When Rob contacted his mom and Grandma, they were happy with the two dates. Mildred and Ken would take the train West to the coast after Edith's and Ruben's wedding, returning in time for Ada's and Rob's wedding. Myrna would stay with Rob and Ada so she could take in both weddings. Since Emil's mom was very ill, Emil felt obliged to stay with her rather than coming out West. Son Emil Jr. was recovering from a tonsillectomy so Myrna thought it wise for him to stay with the babysitter and his dad. Ed and Maria were unable to come for the two weddings. They sent wedding gifts for Ruben and Edith and Ada and Rob with Mildred and Ken.

A few days before Edith's and Ruben's wedding, the entourage from Ontario arrived. Mildred and Ken stayed with Edith.

Ada was embarrassed to the point of being speechless when Mildred and Ken arrived one evening for supper. Brenda, Roberta's friend who had taken her to see the cattle, had been giving her little friend some rudimentary lessons on pregnancy. The lessons were quite heavy on the rudimentary side of things and a little light on the factual side of things. Brenda's mom was expecting.

Roberta had just turned five.

"Are you going to have a baby?" Roberta boldly asked Grandma Mildred when they first met. "Your stomach looks a little big."

Mildred had recently put on a fair amount of weight. Before an embarrassed Ada could respond, Mildred came to her rescue.

"No, I'm just a little overweight, Roberta. That's why my stomach is a bit bigger than it should be. You see only young ladies can have babies. Young girls like yourself and old ladies like me can't have babies. That's just how God planned it. When I was younger, I had three children, William, who was your Grandpa, Aunt Beth and Aunt Becky."

"Daddy told me that a bad bear killed his daddy a long time ago. I don't like bears."

Mildred and Ken spent a delightful evening with Rob, Ada and Roberta. They were impressed with Rob's choice for a mate and enthralled with little forthright Roberta.

Mommy asked Roberta if she would like to be flower girl for the upcoming weddings. Roberta was gleeful. She was so looking forward to being part of the wedding party.

CHAPTER 28

S OMETIME BACK, EDITH and Rob had dropped in on retired Pastor Neufeld and asked him if he would conduct the two weddings. Don cheerfully accepted the assignment.

"I'm happy for the change of venue," Don began at the start of Edith's and Ruben's wedding. "My last three services here were funerals. It does our hearts good to see older folk finding love and happiness in their later years."

Edith and Ruben had Mildred and Ken standing up for them. They held the wedding in Maud's large living room.

Ada spent many hours coaching Roberta on the duties she was to perform as a flower girl. The young damsel loved her frilly dress and never grew tired of twirling around in it in front of the mirror. When it came time for her to walk down the makeshift aisle and spread flower petals, the young lass was more interested in making twirls with her dress than spreading petals, but to her credit, she did lay down a few petals. Maud and Myrna spruced up and decorated the cookhouse for the reception.

"Until Edith and I met, I had pretty well given up on ever finding a mate," Ruben said as he began his groom's speech. "What with being disfigured, crippled and going blind, I'd reconciled myself to being a bachelor for the rest of my life.

Dear Edith loved me despite all my infirmities. Thank God we've found each other, even though late in our lives."

After the reception, Edith and Ruben drove into Medicine Hat to catch the train to Ontario for their honeymoon.

The first week in October, Jed, Eva, Jacob and Henrietta were on the train heading up to Alberta to attend Ada's and Rob's wedding.

When Jed, Jacob and Eva sat down with Paul, Carl and Rob, the Lewis' were in for a pleasant surprise. Paul and Carl offered them financial backing if they wanted to start a construction business in Alberta. In addition, Paul and Carl offered Jed and Jacob the job of building their barn. Rob had already offered them the job of building Ada's and his house.

While Maud, Ada, Eva and Henrietta were preparing for the wedding, Rob drove Jed and Jacob around looking for other building opportunities.

Convinced that the work opportunities in the Medicine Hat area were bright, after some deliberation, the Lewis' accepted Paul's and Carl's offer of financial backing and decided they would move to Medicine Hat shortly after the wedding.

Rob had contacted his old workmate, Linton, about the turn around in his life. Linton was elated that he had licked his need for booze. Rob told him he was getting married and invited him and his wife, June, to the wedding. A couple of days before the wedding, Linton and June arrived. Rob and Jed picked them up at the train station. As the introductions were being made, Linton had a puzzled look on his face when he was introduced to Jed.

"You wouldn't have been a boxer in the States a few years back?"

"Yes, I was," Jed replied, "I was the Light-Heavy-Weight Champ for the northeastern states some twenty years back."

"Do you ever remember fighting a native fellow by the name of George Lavallee?"

"I sure do. George was quite a scrapper, good boxer too. He stayed with me for six rounds. I only fought another two or three fights after fighting him before I hung up the gloves. Back in those days there wasn't much money in boxing and I decided to make my living doing something else."

"Your fight with George was in Chicago, right?"

"It was indeed."

"Well I was at ringside in George's corner. George was my uncle."

"Well I'll be damned!" Jed responded. "Small world isn't it? What's George doing now?"

"He's gone. He just drank his self to death. The little he made from boxing he drank up. Sad, but that's the story of a lot of us. As I told Rob, some time back, June and I drank pretty heavy until she nearly died from tying into some over-proof rum and getting alcohol poisoning. It's been over ten years since we touched a drop."

"Good for you and your wife! There are so many stories of booze ruining people's lives."

"Well, the wife and I done really good since we stopped drinking. We bought a small farm and house down south in Washington."

"I'm so happy for you, Rob, that you licked the drinking habit," Linton added turning to Rob. "Booze never got anyone nowhere. I quit working for the old Biggs outfit about six months after you quit. The boys told me that you quit because of that asshole Adam. I couldn't get along with that arse either. After I quit, my aunt lent us enough to finish paying for our farm. June and I will have her loan paid off by next year."

There was plenty of room at the ranch so Linton and June were billeted there.

A few days before Ada's and Rob's wedding, Ruben and Edith had returned from their honeymoon. Mildred and Ken had also returned from their trip to the coast. Edith joined forces with Maud, Mildred, Myrna, Eva and June in the ongoing wedding preparations. Ada helped as much as her school work allowed.

Ada's and Rob's wedding was held on Saturday afternoon. Ada wanted the wedding to be held outside, weather permitting. Their wedding day dawned clear and warm for mid-October. By 2 pm, some 100 guests were out on the lawn, sitting on chairs or bales.

Jacob was Rob's Best Man; Henrietta, Ada's Maid of Honour.

As Pastor Neufeld was up in years, he had his days when he felt none too robust. He began the wedding ceremony by leaning heavily on the improvised pulpit. Before he got into the exchanging of vows, he had to excuse himself and sit down for a spell to regain his strength.

This time, Roberta did better in performing her duties as flower girl and only made one twirl with her frilly dress as she spread the flower petals. The reception was held in a large empty hayshed at the ranch. They had borrowed chairs and tables from the local hall to accommodate the guests.

"My beloved Ada, her twin brother, Jacob, and I met back in Ontario when we were seven," Rob began in his groom's speech. "For the first few years, Ada sort of played the tomboy with Jake and me. As our hormones began kicking in, our relationship slowly changed to the girlfriend-boyfriend thing. Yes, we had a few curves thrown at us, but by God's grace, our love prevailed and we're together again. I'm so looking forward to spending the rest of my life with Ada and our daughter Roberta."

As Ada was teaching, they decided that they would take their honeymoon at the Christmas break and head down to Tennessee.

The weekend after their wedding, Ada took Friday off. She, Rob and Roberta took the train to Banff for a mini-honeymoon. It was the first time Ada and Roberta had seen the mountains. Roberta was mesmerised by the scenery. She called the mountains, 'big, big hills.'

Shortly after the wedding, Myrna, Mildred and Ken were heading back to Ontario, while Jed, Eva, Jacob and Henrietta were on their way back to Tennessee to get ready for their big move back to Alberta.

Once all the wedding guests had left, Rob, Ada, Paul and Carl drew up a partnership agreement. With some of Rob's inheritance money, he bought a few cows from Carl's and Paul's cattle herd. It was a similar plan to what Michael had made with William years past. Until Rob's herd built up, he would still work for the Paul and Carl for wages.

Back in Tennessee, the Lewis' were hard at it tying up loose ends, getting ready for their big move.

By the first of November, the Lewis family and Henrietta arrived at Michael's and Maud's ranch. They temporarily lived at the ranch and began building Rob's and Ada's house. It was an open fall and by mid-December, they had the outside work on the house pretty well finished. They would be working on the inside of the dwelling throughout the rest of the winter.

Ada, Roberta and Rob were looking forward to their Tennessee holiday at Christmas.

Five days before they were to leave, calamity struck. After school one day, a neighbor lady and her young daughter paid Ada and Roberta a visit. The lady had what appeared to be a bad cold and was not all that circumspect in covering her coughs. A few days later, Roberta was under the weather with a headache, a stiff neck and a high fever. By the next afternoon, when Ada got home from school, Roberta's temperature was up to 104 degrees F.

Realizing the seriousness of Roberta's illness, Ada and Rob bundled her up and headed to the hospital in Medicine Hat. Just before they got to the hospital, Roberta had a seizure.

Once in the hospital, an older nurse assessed Roberta's condition and her symptoms. Roberta's speech was now affected and when she spoke, it appeared that she was delirious. Roberta's temperature was a shade under 106 F.

"The doctor is out making a house call a few miles out of town and won't be back for a couple of hours," Nurse Cummings said. "I hate to make a diagnosis without him here, but from the little girl's symptoms and hearing about your neighbor with a cough, I'm suspicious that she might have meningitis. If it's Bacterial Meningitis that can be very serious, especially with the fever getting high."

When the nurse took Roberta's temperature again, it was 106.5. There was a look of grave concern on the nurse's face.

"Isn't there anything that can be done?" Ada asked in desperation.

"We'll try to cool her down with ice packs. If it's viral meningitis there's not quite as much of a concern. Bacterial Meningitis is the dangerous one. If the doctor suspects that it's Bacterial Meningitis, they do a spinal tap to see what type of antibiotic to use. The only problem is we are not as yet equipped to do the procedure here. Only Calgary can do the spinal tap. All we can do is wait for the doctor. I just got him on the phone. He should be here in less than an hour."

Once the nurse had placed ice packs around Roberta, she left to attend to her other patients. Roberta's temperature was 106.8 F the next time the nurse took her temperature.

"It's worrisome that the ice packs don't seem to be lowering the little girl's temperature, Nurse Cummings said. If there is any change in her condition give me a call. I'll be out on the ward."

Ada and Rob tried repeatedly to get a response from their little girl, but she would not respond.

"Dear Lord, save our baby," Ada chanted over and over again. Rob prayed silently.

The nurse had just returned to check on Roberta. "I have just made contact again with the doctor." she said. "Doctor Gaimey will be here in 15 minutes or so."

The nurse left and had only been gone a few minutes when something very strange happened. Ada had just readjusted the ice pack on Roberta's forehead when the little girl started stirring and then sat up.

"I'm so cold, Mommy. Can you get me a blanket?"

Ada felt Roberta's forehead. Miraculously, it was now cool! Ada went running for the nurse. In a jiffy, the two returned with a couple of blankets. Rob had already removed the ice packs and draped his jacket around Roberta. The nurse had Roberta lay down again and covered her. She had just finished taking Roberta's temperature when the doctor came rushing in.

"It's unbelievable!" Nurse Cummings exclaimed. "The little girl was burning up with fever. When she arrived, her temperature was just a shade under 106. The second reading a half an hour later was 106.5. Fifteen minutes ago, it was 106.8. Unbelievably, now it's 99.6. If I hadn't taken all three readings myself, I wouldn't believe the change."

"She had a high fever, a horrible headache, and a sore neck at home," Ada added. "She was quite delirious and had a seizure on our way to the hospital."

Before the doctor could reply, to the amazement of all present, Roberta opened her eyes and sat up again.

"I must have been sleeping, 'cause I had a dream that Grandpa William came to see me. I was very hot and he touched my head and I got cold."

"Are you sure it was your Grandpa?" the doctor asked, trying to humor the young patient.

"Yes, I'm sure. He looked the same as he did in the picture we have at home."

"That would be my folks' wedding picture," Rob added.

After Doctor Gaimey checked his little patient over, Nurse Cummings again took her temperature. It was now normal.

"This is hard to comprehend," the Doctor said, shaking his head. "In my forty years as a doctor, I've never seen the like of it. The little girl's temperature dropped eight degrees in less than hour. I'm not into the paranormal thing, but I'd have to classify this as a miracle."

"Although everything seems normal with Roberta, I think we should keep her here in hospital for three or four more hours just to be on the safe side. After that, if everything is still normal, she can be discharged. Because you folks live a fair distance out of town, I think it would be wise to spend the night in town. I'd like to check Roberta over again in the morning."

"We can manage that," Rob responded. "My aunt and uncle live here in town. We can spend the night with them and check in again with you in the morning." When Rob phoned Edith, she said they'd be delighted to put the threesome up for the night.

"Was I abopted, Mommy?" Roberta asked as they were driving to Edith and Ruben's place. "When Grandpa was talking to me, he said I was special cause my first mommy and daddy died and you abopted me. He said you and Daddy got me so I could have a real Mommy and Daddy again and then he said that Mommy pretty soon would have a baby boy. I asked him if I was abopted if the baby would be my brother. Grandpa said he would."

"That's called adopted, Roberta and yes, Grandpa was right, I did adopt you."

"My God," Ada continued, turning to Rob. "How on earth would she know all of this unless her grandpa told her? No one here even knows that she was adopted and other than family, those back in Tennessee didn't know any of the particulars of how I got Roberta or the fact that her birth Mom and Dad died tragically. You see, the last foster home Roberta was at was out-of-state. To top it off, tell me how she'd know that I'm pregnant? I'm not positive yet, but my period is three weeks late. I have an appointment with the doctor when we get back from our honeymoon."

"What happened to my first Mommy and Daddy?" Roberta asked.

"I wasn't going to tell you about their deaths until you were older, Roberta. I had you a year before I found out. I learned from your first mommy's and daddy's doctor that they ate some poison mushrooms that killed them. Remember Mommy telling you not to eat wild mushrooms when we were out by the lake? A neighbor lady was looking after you while your mommy and daddy were out picking mushrooms. Anyway, before they picked you up, they ate the mushrooms and became very sick. Your mommy and daddy were taken to the hospital, but died. You were just a wee baby then."

Soon they were at Edith's and Ruben's place. They both were overjoyed that all had turned out well with Roberta.

"There isn't the slightest doubt in my mind that you were visited by your Grandpa," Edith said to Roberta after the young lass told of her remarkable experience. "I don't know if your mommy or daddy ever told you this, but your grandpa's spirit visited me too, right after he died. His spirit came in through the closed door, smiled at me and went out through the wall. Then a few weeks later his spirit visited your daddy by the cross where he died."

"Yes, Mommy told me about that."

While the four adults were discussing the miracle that had just taken place, Roberta was busying herself playing with some toys that Great Aunty had.

The next morning, they checked in at the hospital. Doctor Gaimey gave Roberta a clean bill of health and advised them to stay in close contact if her symptoms returned. Soon the three were heading back to the ranch. Ada and Rob were grateful to the Almighty that their little girl had made a miraculous recovery.

CHAPTER 29

A FEW DAYS LATER, Ada, Roberta and Rob were on the train heading to Tennessee for their honeymoon-Christmas holiday. At first Ada had been hesitant whether or not they should take Roberta along, but seeing that she had been given a clean bill of health, she and Rob finally decided that it was only right to have their miracle girl with them. Dr. Gaimey advised them that it would be safe.

They all had a pleasant holiday. They visited Ada's and Roberta's numerous relatives and friends.

On the evening of the twenty-fourth, they went to the church Christmas Eve service. Although Brad was a bit uptight when they met, Roberta certainly wasn't. Brad had always been friendly with Roberta and when they met, he asked her how she was doing. She proceeded to tell him about her illness and miraculous recovery. Before her mom could intervene, she blurted out, "Grandpa told me that Mommy was going to have a baby. He said that the baby will be a boy, so I'll have a brother." All Roberta's embarrassed mommy could do was try to change the subject matter being discussed.

Soon, the three were on the train heading back to Alberta.

Ada had brought along a bundle of kid's books to entertain Roberta on their long trip to Tennessee and back. Now, on their return trip, after being read many stories, the young lass had reached the saturation point and was becoming restless. The books were set aside.

Ada was catching a few winks of sleep so Rob took over trying to entertain Roberta. It wasn't long though before she was losing interest in her dad's silly stories.

"Maybe by the time we get home, Brenda's mommy will have her baby," Roberta said, interrupting one of Rob's tall tales.

With Brenda's mom in the late stages of pregnancy and now confident that she would soon have a brother, Roberta was fixated on babies.

"Brenda told me a lot of things about babies," Roberta said to her dad. "She said her mommy told her that how the baby gets into the mommy's stomach and how it gets out is too yucky to talk about. Brenda said when the baby gets tired of being in the mommy's stomach, it just pops out."

"Does someone catch the baby?" Rob asked.

"Oh Daddy," Roberta replied shaking her head. "Don't be silly. There are always ladies there to help out. And then you know what? The baby is very thirsty so it lies on the mommy's chest and starts to suck milk out of the mommy's breast, sort of like calves do. Brenda said that mommies have to put diapers on their babies because babies poop and pee a lot."

"My, my, Roberta. You sure know a lot about babies."

"Well, Brenda said we should know about babies cause when we get older, we'll have our own babies."

Once they returned, they were back to the regular routine with Roberta's health remaining robust. Grandpa had been right. When Ada visited her doctor, shortly after returning, she found out that she was pregnant. Her expected date of delivery would be sometime in mid-summer. Roberta was very tuned in to her mom's pregnancy and never tired of running errands for the expecting lady. By early spring the new house was finished. Roberta was elated that she had her own bedroom and her own new bed. Both Ada and Rob were also happy with their new abode.

Roberta was a very excited little girl when Mommy and Daddy gave her a border collie puppy. They named her little pup Thumnes. Everywhere that Roberta went, Thumnes was sure to follow.

The local neighbors had a housewarming party for Ada, Rob and Roberta. When it was time for lunch, the junior lady insisted on helping her mom hand out the goodies to the guests.

Once Rob's, Ada's and Roberta's house was completed, Jed and Jacob started building the barn. The erection of the barn was going well. When there was any heavy bull work that Jed and Jacob couldn't handle on their own, the ranch hands, often with a team of horses, would come to their aid.

Henrietta, like Ada, was a teacher and was now teaching in Medicine Hat. She commuted to the ranch on weekends. Once the barn was finished, Jed and Jacob were planning on building their own house in Medicine Hat.

"I was thinking about Grandpa's visit to me when I was sick," Roberta said to her mom and dad one day in early spring. "I forgot about it till just now, but Grandpa said some time we should go to the cabin and the cross. I didn't know what he meant."

"That would be the cabin back in the bush," Rob replied. "You'll remember the cross and the cabin back in the bush, Ada."

"Yes, I'll always remember the cross and the cabin," Ada replied wistfully. "You, Jacob and I stopped at the cross and the cabin the first time Jacob and I came out West with you. Then you and I stopped there the summer I worked at the ranch."

Rob and Ada decided that they should go out to the cabin sometime in mid-May. They phoned Edith and invited Ruben and her to accompany them.

"You know dear, talking about going to the cabin brings back some bad memories for me," Rob said. "I don't know if I ever told you about my gun going missing on the day I tried to do that thing to myself."

"No, you never did," Ada replied, shaking her head.

"I'll have to word this carefully for the young lady's sake. As you'll recall, the day I tried to do my thing, my trigger finger wouldn't work. Well, anyway, when I saw that vision of you, my mind was so blown, I just jumped in the car and took off. After driving for a couple of miles, I remembered that I'd put the 44, case and sack on the block. I turned around and headed back. When I got there, the sack, case and 44 were gone. I searched high and low for them, but they had just disappeared. I never have found the 44, the case or the sack. One of those mysteries we'll never solve, I guess."

"Yes, that certainly is weird," Ada replied.

On a Saturday, near the end of May, Edith and Ruben arrived in the late morning. They decided to have a picnic after visiting the cabin. Soon Ada and Edith were preparing the picnic lunch. Roberta was right in the midst of the preparations, getting in the way the odd time, but helping as much as she could. Both of the older ladies thanked her for her contribution. Soon the group was on their way.

"I think we should visit the cabin first," Rob said, "We could have our picnic beside the cabin. There's a nice open spot there. On our way back, we could stop at the cross. I just wonder what this is all about."

"I wonder if William wants to communicate with us," Edith replied.

Rob unlocked the padlock, opened the cabin door and they all filed into the cabin. "My God!" Rob called out.

"Do you smell what I smell, Edith? It's hard to believe and I don't know how this could be, but I'd swear it reeks in here of my dad's 'Anglers Dream' pipe tobacco smoke."

"You're right, Rob," Edith said. "Without question, it smells like your dad's old pipe tobacco."

"Now here's the eerie part," Rob added. "For the last year, Paul and Carl have kept the cabin locked. When I picked up the key, Paul told me that no one has been in the cabin since last summer."

"After supper, Rob's dad would take out his pipe and light up," Edith added. "It definitely smells like the tobacco he used to smoke."

"There' s something supernatural happening here," Ruben added. "I can feel it in my bones."

Soon they were out beside the cabin having their picnic.

"How did that smell get into the cabin?" Roberta asked. "Did Grandpa bring it?"

"We don't know," Edith said. "Spirits can go through walls or a closed door."

Once they had finished the picnic, Rob locked the cabin door and they drove out to the cross.

"What's this?" Ada called out, walking over to the cross. "It looks like there's an old sack sitting on the block."

Rob rushed over to where Ada was standing.

"OH, MY GOD!" Rob cried out as he reached into the sack. "It's the old gun case."

He carefully pulled out the gun case and opened it. "The old 44 Colt looks as polished as the day I attempted to use it." He picked the 44 up reverently and ran his hand over it. "It's Dad's old 44 Colt. Now doesn't this ever blow one's mind!"

"As I told you, the 44, the case and the sack disappeared that infamous day. Some time back, I came out here and spent two hours or more searching for them. I had no luck. We have no idea how long the 44 and case have been here, but I'd have to say they haven't been here that long as neither look like they've been affected by the weather."

"There is something miraculous going on here," Ruben added. "Could it be that your dad removed that 44 out of harms way while you were driving back to the cross that day for fear you'd be tempted to use it again? Quite possibly his spirit recently returned the 44 along with the tobacco smell. We will never know how it all happened, but it definitely looks like Divine intervention."

"Look," Roberta said, pointing to the sky. "That big black bird just came and now it's going around and around."

They all glanced up. There was a big raven, a few hundred feet in the air, slowly circling them and the cross.

"That's the mysterious raven again," Rob said quietly, still glancing skyward.

"Years ago, Dad had a raven so tame it would eat out of his hand. Then when Michael and I were visited by Dad's spirit, Michael saw a raven circling above this cross. And remember Mom's story of the raven landing beside her here on the cross and croaking at her?"

"Like Ruben just said, something divine is going on here," Rob added solemnly, shaking his head.

"We know you're here with us, Dad," Rob continued, looking upward.

No sooner were the words out of Rob's mouth than the raven stopped it's circling and winged its way back into the forest.

"Thank you, Dad for coming to us again," Rob whispered.

"Thank You, Thank You, Thank You."

ABOUT THE AUTHOR

MICHAEL PARLEE WAS born and raised in the Peace River Country of northwestern Alberta. He took up writing some twenty years ago when complications from a work-related injury forced him into early retirement. Tanya, his first adult book was published in 2007, followed by Son of Sister Maria in 2011 and We Must Forgive to Live in 2013. He has also written two children's stories: Grandpa's Magic Beard, published in 2015 and Jaycob's Magic Spaceship, published in 2016. All of these books have been published by AuthorHouse. Michael and his wife Pauline are currently co-authoring their family biography, The Parlee-Hudz Chronicles. Michael and Pauline live in Bowden Alberta. E-mail address is mpparlee@shaw.ca

ABOUT THE COVER ARTIST

JUANITA PARLEE IS Michael's and Pauline's daughter. She lives in Montreal, Quebec. She taught art to kids in a summer arts program in Grande Prairie a number of years ago. In 2016, Juanita illustrated her father's children's story, Jaycob's Magic Spaceship. She has done a masterful job of the cover of The Sacred Gem Within.

CPSIA information can be obtained
at www.ICGtesting.com
Printed in the USA
LVHW042010100419
613726LV00001B/17